Galatians

Timely, lucid, and reliable, this is an excellent commentary for preachers, Bible study leaders and others. David McWilliams admirably succeeds in his aim for *brevitas* and *claritas*, the two qualities in commentators that Calvin most commended. He distils a great deal of scholarship into uncluttered and readable prose. Paul's message in Galatians has rarely been so urgently needed as today, when justification only by faith is under attack from many sides. McWilliams explains it with judicious care.

Dr. Robert Letham,
Senior Tutor in Systematic and Historical Theology,
Wales Evangelical School of Theology, Wales, UK

Pastor-Theologian David McWilliams has produced a preacher's commentary on Paul's epistle to the Galatians, that momentous announcement of the good news of righteousness and freedom in Christ alone, by grace alone, through faith alone. Dr. McWilliams addresses interpretive issues with clarity and cogent discernment, and he engages recent misperceptions of Paul's central concern—which is not merely sociological or ecclesiastical, but soteriological (How may guilty sinners be reconciled to their holy Creator?)—all the while keeping in view the aim of preaching this good news of sovereign grace. The author's fresh translation of Galatians enables readers to experience the fervor of the apostle's passionate alarm for his spiritual children in Galatia as they flirted with eternal ruin, and the comment that supports the translation demonstrates that the issues addressed in Galatians are not matters for aloof theological conversation, but matters of life and death. I highly recommend this resource to my fellow-preachers of the good news of God's Son.

Dr. Dennis E. Johnson,
Professor of Practical Theology, Westminster Seminary California,
Escondido, California, USA

Galatians

A Mentor Commentary

David B. McWilliams

⅏ENTOR

Copyright © David B. McWilliams 2009

ISBN 978-1-84550-452-6

10 9 8 7 6 5 4 3 2 1

Published in 2009
in the
Mentor Imprint
by
Christian Focus Publications,
Geanies House, Fearn, Tain,
Ross-shire, IV20 1TW, Great Britain

www.christianfocus.com

Cover design by Daniel van Straaten

Printed and bound in Great Britain by the MPG Books Group

Contents

Abbreviations

Journal, Lexical and Encyclopedic Abbreviations

BDAG	A Greek-English Lexicon of the New Testament
BJRL	Bulletin of The John Rylands Library
EQ	Evangelical Quarterly
IDB	Interpreter's Dictionary of The Bible
ISBE	International Standard Bible Encyclopedia
JBL	Journal of Biblical Literature
JETS	Journal of The Evangelical Theological Society
JSNT	Journal For The Study of The New Testament
JTS	Journal of Theological Studies
NT	Novum Testamentum
NTS	New Testament Studies
OCD	Oxford Classical Dictionary
SJT	Scottish Journal of Theology
TDNT	Theological Dictionary of The New Testament
WTJ	Westminster Theological Journal

Version Abbreviations

AV	Authorized (King James) Version
ESV	English Standard Version
Goodspeed	The New Testament An American Translation
Moffatt	The Holy Bible A New Translation
NEB	The New English Bible
NIV	New International Version
NRSV	New Revised Standard Version
Phillips	The New Testament in Modern English
REB	The Revised English Bible New Testament
TEV	Today's English Version of The New Testament

To my beloved wife Vicky,
faithful companion in life and ministry
and
To our dear son, Evan, for whom we are
thankful to God

Preface

He doesn't know it, but this exposition was written with Paul Joiner in mind. Paul is campus minister for the Presbyterian Church in America's *Reformed University Fellowship* at the University of South Florida. As I contemplated preparing this exposition of Galatians I kept Paul in mind for two reasons. Firstly, is there any book that more needs expounding to college students than Paul's epistle to the Galatians? Surely, as Pastor Joiner evangelizes and disciples students this crisp, clear letter on grace is the one thing needful! Secondly, contemplating Paul Joiner's ministry helped to keep the exposition on track. I asked myself: "If I were a campus minister with limited time and my large group meeting on Wednesday night is working through Galatians, what kind of exposition would I want to pull off my shelf?" And my answer was: "An exposition that is true, scholarly, and sound, thoroughly researched but that cuts out the extraneous, having the quality of *brevitas*." This has been my goal and I must leave to the reader to determine whether I have been successful. Nonetheless, I have reason to hope that keeping this one minister and his work in mind has helped me to produce an exposition of Galatians that will benefit many ministers in their work of preaching the gospel. Preaching is my concern and even though I hope that Christians in a variety of callings may benefit from what they read here, my longing is to help preachers to understand Galatians and to preach it!

I wrote the exposition with the intent that it be read straight through. May I recommend that if you are about to prepare sermons or a class on Galatians that you read through the exposition over a short period of time and then go back to it as you prepare sermons or classes.

Before moving on to this masterly epistle of Paul to the Galatians please allow me to record my thanks to those who have encouraged this work: Sinclair Ferguson, who suggested it, and Moisés Silva, who read early drafts, Malcolm Maclean (editor for Christian Focus), and Richard Gaffin, Robert Letham, Dennis Johnson and Dustyn Eudaly, who have read the manuscript in various stages. I am deeply appreciative of their time and energy. I must also thank my former student at Westminster Seminary, Rev Glen Clary, who has not only read drafts of the manuscript but has "field tested" portions of it in his sermon preparation for his series on Galatians.

May our Triune God, who has in grace given to us His inerrant Word, be pleased to bless this exposition to the glory of His matchless name!

David B. McWilliams, Ph.D.
The Minister's Study

Introduction

When Paul's epistle to the Galatians is read with intelligence and faith, there burns within the heart a flame of fire. Who can miss the passion for the gospel of grace that pours from Paul's pastoral heart or fail to catch his inspired love for the church of Christ? The modern reader should take note that there is "a clear and present danger that the devil may take away from us the pure doctrine of faith and may substitute for it the doctrines of works and of human traditions". Therefore, believers should not doubt that "this doctrine can never be discussed and taught enough!" (Luther, *Galatians,* Preface).[1] That is justification enough for another exposition of this monumental epistle of Paul, the apostle to the Gentiles.

Luther was certainly right to warn the church. Even though what follows is essentially a positive exposition of Galatians, I have kept in mind the various mischaracterizations of Paul's

---

[1] I have minimized bibliographical footnotes in this exposition by placing basic bibliographic data within parentheses in the flow of the text except for single references or in cases in which it seems that clarity demands a bibliographical footnote. The Bibliography at the end of the exposition makes it easy to identify authors and works thus cited. An author cited in parentheses with no page number means that the quotation can be found in the text of that author's commentary which deals with the verse or passage I am explaining.

epistle that have become dominant recently in some circles. These new ideas profess that Paul is not concerned with the impossibility of good works and human merit for acceptance with God but rather is concerned principally with the condition on which Gentiles become members of God's people. The exposition you are about to read maintains that a correct understanding of Paul demands that we see that his primary concern is with the eternal salvation of sinners and that membership among God's people and ecclesiastical harmony are the fruit rather than the root of Paul's doctrine. The words of J. Gresham Machen written in another context are applicable here: "Paul was not devoted to the doctrine of justification by faith because of the Gentile mission; he was devoted to the Gentile mission because of the doctrine of justification by faith."[2] Everywhere in every way Paul's concern is with the gospel; he is concerned with the personal salvation of sinners.

Who Were the False Teachers?
Who were Paul's opponents in Galatia, commonly called the Judaizers? No one has successfully set aside the traditional view that Paul's opponents were Jews, zealous for the law and eager to persuade Gentile Christians to accept circumcision. Whether these Jews were connected directly with factions of the Jerusalem church or arising from some other venue is not easy to determine.

Even though it is not easy to ascertain who precisely the Judaizers were, the main lines of their thought are not difficult to discern. After Paul founded the largely Gentile churches of Galatia, false teachers entered espousing that obedience to the Law of Moses was an essential part of the gospel (1:7; 4:17; 5:10). This false gospel (1:6-7) of law-keeping implies that the false teachers were themselves Jews. Indeed, they attempted to compel the Galatian believers to be circumcised (5:2ff.; 6:12) and to observe special Jewish feast days (4:10). The false teachers did not overtly deny cardinal Christian

---

[2] J. Gresham Machen, *The Origin of Paul's Religion*, 278, 279.

truth, but by teaching that justification was by law (5:4; 4:21) they denied the gospel of free grace and substituted a false for the true gospel (1:6-7). This was an overt denial of the freedom purchased for believers by Christ (5:1), and it was essentially the issue later responded to by the church at the Jerusalem Council in Acts 15:1: "Some men came down from Judea to Antioch and were teaching the brothers: 'Unless you are circumcised, according to the custom taught by Moses, you cannot be saved.'"(NIV).

It seems clear that the false teachers even claimed that Paul preached the same message that they did (5:11). In view of this serious defection from the truth of the gospel and the potential threat that the gospel of justification by grace alone might altogether be abandoned, Paul wrote the epistle to the Galatians with flaming heart and clarity of mind, calling upon the believers in these churches not to be deceived!

The Theology of Galatians

What theological reflection does Paul apply to the Galatians who were tempted to desert the gospel of grace? We will leave the exposition to uncover the details to that question. Here I mention only two essential factors of the theology of Paul in Galatians which are indispensable in interpreting its meaning.

The first element is Paul's *eschatological viewpoint.* For Paul, the coming of Christ into the world has brought about a radical newness that is at the heart of God's revelation in Christ. Christ's coming in "the fullness of time" (4:4) to deliver us "from the present evil age" (1:4) by his death and resurrection (1:1) thrusts into prominence Paul's eschatological viewpoint that is often on the surface of his letter[3] (Yet even when it is not on the surface, it is determinative of Paul's overall viewpoint). Paul's "two-age construct", whereby he stresses that Christ's resurrection determines the point at which the new age has overcome decisively the hold of the old aeon over sinners, is everywhere present in Galatians and informs Paul's approach

---

[3] See 1:1, 4, 12, 16; 2:2, 16, 19-20; 3:2-5, 8-16, 19–4:7; 4:25-27; 5:1-14, 16-26; 6:13-17.

to the law and his reading of the Old Testament. Galatians reveals Paul to be the greatest redemptive-historical theologian of the church.

The second most important factor for interpreting Galatians, inseparably related to his eschatological framework, is Paul's teaching concerning *justification by faith*. How may a sinner be declared right with God? By what means may a sinner be accepted by God? Righteousness had largely been identified in the Jewish mind with law- keeping. "God's justice was committed to requite men strictly according to their deeds....Judaism had no hesitation about recognizing the merit of good works, or in exhorting men to acquire it and to accumulate a store of merit laid up for the hereafter."[4]

Paul, on the other hand, recognized that the demand to keep the law as a means for acceptance with God required total and complete law-keeping (3:10) and that the atonement would be nonsense if one could be saved by law-keeping (2:21). Imperfect law-keeping could never make a sinner acceptable with God. Rather, sinners are accepted by means of faith in Christ alone (2:16; 3:6-25). As T. R. Glover has said, the cross "solved the problem of God's righteousness and man's sin" since, as Paul discovered, God provided through that means "a moral and spiritual more-than-equivalent for the Judgment".[5]

Paul's theology, then, is applied to the works-righteousness of the Judaizers. For, as Calvin observed, "it is no light evil to quench the brightness of the Gospel, lay a snare for consciences and remove the distinction between the old and new covenants. He (Paul) saw that these errors were also related to an ungodly and destructive opinion on the deserving of righteousness. And this is why he fights so earnestly." (Calvin, *Galatians*, 4)

Destination and Date
Although it is possible to benefit from commentaries on Galatians vastly differing on introductory matters, the questions surrounding the destination and date of the epistle are far

---

[4] George Eldon Ladd, *A Theology of the New Testament*, 441. This quotation is from G. F. Moore, *Judaism*.

[5] T. R. Glover, *Paul of Tarsus*, 87, 88.

from unimportant. While an expositor of the epistle must be humble in view of the plethora of viewpoints held by notable scholars, no commentator or preacher should avoid the hard questions he faces relating to destination and date as he works through the book. Even though the focus of this exposition is on the theology of Paul and understanding the text for proclamation, it is necessary to set out some of the main lines of introductory issues associated with Galatians.

There are three perspectives on the destination and date of Galatians worthy of attention. They are the familiar North and South Galatian theories and the attendant conclusions regarding the dating of Galatians attached to each, with some variation on the latter. One central question is whether Paul wrote Galatians prior to or after the Council of Jerusalem related by Luke in Acts 15 (c. A.D. 49) The North Galatian theory is associated with a late date and the South Galatian theory is generally associated with an early date. However, the South Galatian theory does not necessitate an early date for the epistle and this possibility opens up a third perspective.

Galatia in Paul's day could be applied to two regions in modern-day Turkey. First, Galatia referred to the territory which was associated with Celtic groups who migrated from Gaul, forming a region extending in the north to Pontus and Bithynia, bounded on the southwest by Phrygia and to the east by Cappadocia. This territory, inhabited by Celtic tribes who were defeated by Attalus I, the king of Pergamum, were associated with the cities of Ancyra, Tavium and Pessinus. But the Roman conquest of this expansive region resulted in 25 B.C. in the creation of a separate province, including the cities of Iconium, Lystra and Derbe in the southern Lycaonian region visited by Paul on his first missionary journey (Acts 14). The inhabitants of this area were not Celts and were designated "Galatians" because they lived within the borders of the Roman Province, Galatia. Since there are two possible meanings of "Galatia", this presents an interpretive problem for the exegete.

From the available data it is clear that Paul did not visit the northern region on his first missionary journey. However,

Paul did travel "throughout the region of Phrygia and Galatia, having been kept by the Holy Spirit from preaching the word in the province of Asia" (Acts 16:6) during his second missionary journey, following the Jerusalem Council of Acts 15. This is a possible reference to the North Galatian area where Paul may have planted new churches. It is therefore admittedly possible that Paul established churches in North Galatia which were in need of a letter helping them to understand the nature of the gospel and its implications. This view corresponds to the North Galatian theory of the destination of the epistle and its date following the Jerusalem Council.

This North Galatian viewpoint has had a number of supporters, the most famous being the justly revered J. B. Lightfoot. Moreover, the North Galatian theory is still the prevailing one among interpreters in Europe. On this view "the region of Phrygia and Galatia" (Acts 16:6; 18:23) must mean "Phrygia and the Galatian region", pointing to Galatia as distinguishable from Phrygia, and indicating a North Galatian destination for the letter. However, it is more probable that Acts intends the "Phrygio-Galatic region", pointing to Paul's travels upon leaving Lystra and Iconium (Acts 16:2).

It was Sir William Ramsay who most effectively cast doubt on this North Galatian theory and argued for a South Galatian destination of the epistle. He argued that Paul wrote his epistle to Christians in the region extending to Pisidia, Lycaonia and some other locations in the South, the area visited by Paul on his first missionary journey.

Many interpreters, following Ramsay, have also thought that the South Galatian destination cleared up a knotty problem of interpretation, namely, why Paul did not refer to the Jerusalem Council of Acts 15 in his epistle. The reason, Ramsay thought, was quite simple: Paul did not mention the Jerusalem Council because the epistle was written to the South Galatian group of churches founded on his first missionary journey, and the biographical data in the epistle bearing upon the date preceded the Council.[6] Therefore rather than identifying

---

[6] It should be noted that Ramsay held initially to a South Galatian destination for the epistle and to a date following the Council of Jerusalem

the visit to Jerusalem in Galatians 2 with the visit in Acts 15 as Lightfoot had done, even though there was no express reference to the Council's decree, some interpreters think that Galatians 2 can be identified with the earlier "famine visit" to Jerusalem (Acts 11:27-30).

The main elements of Ramsay's arguments may be read in his *St. Paul The Traveller and The Roman Citizen, The Church in The Roman Empire* and *Historical Commentary on the Galatians*, including his concern that Acts is silent on the establishment of North Galatian churches whereas Luke stresses Paul's relationship to the South Galatians. It was to Ramsay's credit that he took seriously the historical reliability of Acts and its importance in interpreting Paul's writings.

The North Galatian theory, therefore, ascribes a date to Galatians following the Jerusalem Council whereas the South Galatian theory, often though not always, assumes a date prior to the Jerusalem Council. There is however another option. It is also possible to adopt the South Galatian *destination* of the epistle while holding to a *date* following the Jerusalem Council. Some holding this view are impressed with the arguments in favor of the South Galatian destination along with Ramsay and against Lightfoot, but are influenced by Lightfoot's arguments for the identification of Galatians 2 and Acts 15 against Ramsay.

Those who agree with Ramsay that Galatians 2 and Acts 15 must not be identified point out that in Galatians 2 Paul is said to have gone up to Jerusalem by revelation whereas in Acts 15 the church at Antioch sent Paul. Titus is mentioned in Galatians 2 but not in Acts 15. John is included in the leadership of the Jerusalem church in Galatians 2 but is not mentioned in Acts 15. Moreover, Paul's meeting with the church leadership in Galatians 2 was private, but the Council of Acts 15 was public. Therefore, some conclude, Galatians 2 makes no mention of the Jerusalem Council and the best explanation of that is simply that the Council had not yet taken place. Others, however, conclude differently.

(Acts 15), but in his mature thought held to a date prior to the Council. See *The Teaching of Paul In Terms of The Present Day,* 372-403.

Silva, who lists the apparent discrepancies, concludes that "the first four items on the list...may be regarded as natural under the circumstances: they represent just the kinds of discrepancies that we expect from reliable but independent witnesses."[7] For example, Paul's travel to Jerusalem "by revelation" need not contradict the commission of the church in Antioch. But what is to be made of Paul's silence concerning the Jerusalem Council in Galatians 2? Isn't it odd that Paul would fail to mention something as monumentally important as the Council's decrees if Galatians had been written after the Council?

Silva assumes that Paul's silence is due to the fact that the Galatians were already aware of the Jerusalem Council's decrees and that "by pointing out that the Jerusalem apostles did extend to him and Barnabas the 'right hand of fellowship,' perhaps he accomplishes by indirect means the same purpose that would have been served by an explicit mention of the decrees" (134).

Rather than making much of the silence of Paul regarding the Jerusalem decrees Silva thinks that it makes more sense methodologically to dwell, with Lightfoot, on the similarities of Galatians 2 and Acts 15. Lightfoot points out that the *geography* is the same: "In both narratives the communications take place between Jerusalem and Antioch." The *time* is the same. "St. Paul places the event 15 or 16 years after his conversion: St. Luke's narrative implies that they took place in about the year 51." The *persons* are the same. "Paul and Barnabas appear as the representatives of the Gentile Churches, Cephas and James as the leaders of the Circumcision. The agitators are similarly described in the two accounts." In addition, the *subject of dispute* is the same. Moreover, the *result* is the same: "the exemption of the Gentiles from the enactments of the law, and the recognition of the Apostolic commission of Paul and Barnabas by the leaders of the Jewish Church." Lightfoot concludes that "a combination of circumstances so striking is not likely to have occurred twice within a few years."[8]

---

[7] Silva, *Interpreting Galatians*, 133.
[8] J. B. Lightfoot, *The Epistle of St. Paul to the Galatians*, 127-28.

Lightfoot's argument is indeed persuasive but not conclusive. In particular, some have argued, since the Council's decrees would have been relevant to Paul's argument against the Judaizers, it is still difficult, on this theory, to think that Paul would fail to make overt reference to the Council and its decisions. Most importantly, Luke mentions three visits of Paul to Jerusalem (in Acts 9, 11 and 15), and in Galatians Paul's biographical points are hinged upon two visits to Jerusalem. It is best to view the "famine visit" of Acts 11:30 as corresponding to Paul and Barnabas' private interview with the pillars in Galatians 2. On this view, Galatians 2:1 may be taken quite literally as Paul's second visit to Jerusalem, and this therefore removes the difficulty of the omission of the decrees of Acts 15 from Galatians. Following the suggestions of Donald Guthrie and F. F. Bruce, this view allows a reconstruction of the data permitting the epistle to be dated prior to the Council, perhaps even as Paul traveled there. In any case, Galatians would be viewed on this reconstruction as the earliest of Paul's epistles.[9]

The viewpoint taken in this exposition is the South Galatian theory and a date for Galatians prior to the Council of Jerusalem. There is no evidence that Paul ever visited or established churches in North Galatia. But no one contests that Paul established churches in South Galatia. Moreover, Paul came to the South Galatian region initially to recover from illness (Gal. 4:13). It would not have been likely that this could refer to the hinterland of North Galatia. Also, when Paul speaks of geographical regions he uses Roman Provincial designations. Therefore in 1:1 the "churches in Galatia" must mean the South Galatian Province. In addition, Barnabas is mentioned three times in Galatians 2, indicating familiarity with the readers. Since Barnabas was Paul's traveling companion on the first missionary journey, Barnabas was well known to the churches of South Galatia. Also consider, taking the relationship between Acts and Galatians seriously argues for the South Galatian viewpoint. Paul's biography mentions two visits to Jerusalem which would correspond to the visits of Acts 9:26 and 11:27-30 prior to the Council of Acts 15.

---

[9] See Donald Guthrie, *New Testament Introduction*, 461-63

The date of composition maintained in this exposition is prior to the Council of Acts 15. Commentators will differ on the weight that should be given to the absence of any reference to the Council in Galatians, but to my mind this weighs heavily in favor of an early date. There seems to be no reference to the Council at all in Galatians. Galatians 2 is a private rather than a public meeting as was held in Acts 15. In short, we agree with Bruce who notes that, as we are told in Acts 15:1, Judean visitors came to Syrian Antioch teaching the necessity of circumcision for salvation and it is probable that "others who wished to press the same line visited the recently formed daughter-churches of Antioch, not only in Syria and Cilicia, as the apostolic letter indicates (Acts 15:23), but also in South Galatia." Bruce concludes that if this is the case Paul wrote his letter as soon as he received news of the Galatian trouble "on the eve of the Jerusalem meeting described in Acts 15:6ff. This...would yield the most satisfactory correlation of the data of Galatians and Acts and the most satisfactory dating of Galatians. It must be conceded that, if this is so, Galatians is the earliest among the extant letters of Paul" (Bruce, 55).

Paul's Argument
Paul begins his defense of the gospel against the Judaizers by insisting that the gospel he preached was not from men but from God alone. His gospel was a matter of revelation (1:11-12) and was completely independent of the apostles in Jerusalem (1:13–2:21). Paul did not consult with the apostles after his Damascus road conversion (1:13-17). Moreover, when he did go to Jerusalem he saw Peter briefly (1:18-24), and when he later discussed his gospel and ministry with the apostles they expressed their approbation and unity (2:1-10).

Paul records his rebuke of Peter at Antioch when he was not consistent with the gospel (2:11-12), demonstrating once again the divine, revelatory nature of the gospel preached by Paul. Peter's withdrawal from table fellowship with the Gentiles was a contradiction of justification by faith (2:15-21).

Paul expounds justification from 3:1 to 4:31. He begins by arguing that the eschatological Spirit was received, not by works of the law, but by faith (3:1-5) and stresses the history of Abraham (3:6-14) in order to demonstrate that justification is not by law but by faith. Indeed, the law that came after the covenant that God made with Abraham in no way nullifies the promise (3:15-18).

Since sinners are not justified by the law Paul must answer the question of the purpose of the law (3:19–4:6). The law played an indispensable role in redemptive history by showing the inadequacy of works to save sinners and by anticipating the Redeemer. The law, rather than providing an avenue of escape, is a prison from which there is no escape by human means. Its purpose was "that the promise of faith in Jesus Christ might be given to those who believe". Thus freedom has been purchased for the sons of God (3:26–4:7).

The Gentile Galatians had also been enslaved to "the basic elements of the world", and should they succumb to the Judaizers' false gospel, they would once again submit to slavery (4:10-11), which would erase their joy in Christ (4:15). In 4:21-31 Paul again references the Abrahamic narrative against the Judaizers by directing their attention to the story of Isaac and Ishmael. The two sons represent a fundamental contrast shaping the whole of redemptive history.

In the final portion of Galatians (the ethical portion of the epistle), Paul enlarges upon the theme of Christian liberty. The preaching of the law as a means of justification is enslaving and would remove the scandal of the cross (5:1-11). Christian liberty is demonstrated, however, not in antinomianism but in living by the Spirit (5:16-26). Liberty is manifested in loving and caring relationships in the church (6:1-10).

Paul concludes by exposing the false motives of the Judaizers (6:12-13) and by expressing, in an unforgettable way, his own, cross-centred motives (6:14-15). The conclusion is no formality. Critical themes from Galatians are brought together at the end. Taking the pen from his amanuensis he writes with "large letters" a final barrage against the false teachers and puts forward the cross and grace of God as the one method of salvation and of Christian living.

With that brief overview secure in our minds, let us now turn to the exposition of Paul's epistle to the Galatians.

Not According to Man

*The Liberating Message
of Paul's Epistle to the Galatians*

1.
Not According To Man
(1:1-5)

Translation
Paul, an apostle, not by human sources, nor by human appointment, but by Jesus Christ and God the Father who raised Him from the dead, and all the brothers with me, to the churches of Galatia. Grace to you and peace from God our Father and Lord Jesus Christ, who gave Himself for our sins so that He might deliver us out of the present evil age according to the will of our God and Father, to whom be glory forever and ever. Amen.

Summary
Although Paul defends his apostolic authority in this passage, his main concern is not apostolic authority but the defense of his gospel against Judaizing detractors. Paul defends his gospel and apostolic authority, which were received from God alone and not from mere man. His calling to apostleship demonstrates God's method of grace. Even his greeting of peace supports his contention for the gospel of grace alone that is being contested by the Judaizers. Right from the start Paul defines his grace-driven message of atonement and eschatological deliverance. Contemplating the work of Christ Paul breaks into doxology.

Comment

Paul speaks of his person and calling with the same deliber-
ateness with which a soldier might give his name, rank and
serial number and with the authority akin to an ambassador
just come from the court of his king with an urgent message.
The introduction resonates with urgency. It was customary in
Paul's world to specify the writer and those to whom a letter
was addressed.[1] However, Paul's approach to his hearers is
terse, nervous and tense. That Paul found it necessary to assert his apostleship in this way is due to the antagonism of
his opponents. A glance at the opening of Paul's other epistles
demonstrates, by contrast, that here he feels that he must affirm, assert, and even force the issue of apostolic authority.
His call to apostleship demonstrates God's method of grace;
we should never forget that defense of apostleship is secondary to Paul's pre-eminent concern – the nature of the gospel
itself![2]

**Paul, an apostle, not by human sources, nor by human
appointment, but by Jesus Christ and God the Father who
raised Him from the dead.** The highly strung atmosphere
calls forth the double negative *ouk ap anthrōpōn oude
di anthrōpou*. Paul, by means of this double negative and
accompanying prepositions, defines his apostleship with
careful nuance. Paul's apostleship is not traceable to human
origin, but also to no mere human medium.[3] It was through

---

[1] For an assessment of Paul's use of ancient epistolary form, see Jerome
Murphy-O'Connor (1995), *Paul the Letter-Writer,* The Liturgical Press.

[2] Lategan points out (417) that the term *apostle* and derivatives occur in
Galatians only four times whereas *euangelion* (gospel) and its derivatives
occur fourteen times. "This is reason enough to try a different approach and
to analyse the argument from a reader's point of view…"

[3] Lategan further notes: "One of the most important results of a
pragmatic analysis is making the exegete aware of the tension between
God and man which dominates the first two chapters…Galatians 1 and 2
reveal a fundamental opposition between God and man which forms the
presupposition of Paul's whole argument. In the very first verse of the
letter, this contrast which occurs throughout the letter, is announced in a
double chiastic form: ἀνθρώπων … ἀνθρώπου / Ἰησοῦ Χριστοῦ … θεοῦ. An
actual analysis confirms the importance of this contrast, which creates an
element of tension right through these chapters and which is only relieved

no mere man that Paul, the apostle, was divinely called, **but by (through) Jesus Christ and God the Father** which, incidentally, speaks worlds about Paul's view of the person of Christ. It is natural for Paul to distinguish Christ from mere men and to associate Him inseparably, in a single breath, with God the Father. Everywhere Paul assumes the Deity of Christ.

The medium (corresponding to the second of the two negatives *oude di anthrōpou*) through which Paul was called to be an apostle was Jesus Christ who cannot be severed from the Father **who raised Him from the dead.**[4] Paul's purpose for adding these words is not only to trace the salvation of sinners to the Father's design in Christ but also specifically to affirm his own apostleship as one who had himself seen the risen Lord. The former cannot be excluded, however. We cannot read on in the epistle's quick movement toward the main theme without realizing that Paul immediately begins an attack on every attempt to detract from the gospel of grace. The eschatological event of the resurrection is God's breaking by grace into our human situation and need, exclusive of human merit. The resurrection of Jesus provides the source

---

in 2:20." On 4:21 he adds: "It is significant that the formal reference to Paul's position as apostle in the prescript is immediately qualified by the double contrast between man and Christ/God.... His apostleship and the way he received it is an illustration of the unusual and unexpected way God works – in accordance with the οὐ κατὰ ἄνθρωπον nature of the gospel itself." On the three co-ordinate prepositional phrases modifying the verbal adjective apostolos ("a person who has been sent"), see Martyn who thinks that 1 Corinthians 1:9 "tips the balance in favor" of rendering both instances of *dia* ("by") meaning "originating actor." "In the whole of this verse Paul is concerned not with misunderstandings as to who may have mediated his sending, but rather with misconceptions as to who sent him."

[4] Betz points to other Pauline parallels to this "resurrection formula": Romans 4:24; 8:11; 10:9; 1 Corinthians 6:14; 15:15; 2 Corinthians 4:14; 1 Thessalonians 1:10. See also Silva, 170, 171, who remarks: "Scholars who point out that Galatians makes no emphasis on Christ's resurrection fail to note that aside from Romans this is the only letter in which at the very beginning Paul calls attention to that event." He adds: "By highlighting this truth already in the greeting, Paul effectively lays down his most basic assumption, namely, that the transition from slavery to freedom has been made possible through an eschatological event."

and context for Paul's entire theology and ministry. Ramsay notes: "Paul's whole theory of life had been founded on the belief that Jesus was dead; but when he recognized that Jesus was living, the theory crumbled into the dust. If He was not dead, He was not an imposter." He adds: "The power which Paul's Gospel had over the Galatians lay in its origin out of his own experience. He was the living proof that it was true. It had given him his new life. What it did for him it could do for all." Indeed, "it remade the universe for him; it recreated his life and soul and thought and energy; the simple fact that he stood and spoke before them was the unanswerable proof that his message was true" (Ramsay, *Historical Commentary*, 333, 334).

By adding **and all the brothers with me, to the churches of Galatia** (Derbe, Lystra, Iconium, Pisidian Antioch), the apostle indicates that he is not alone in his concern for the straying believers to whom he writes. By **all the brothers** Paul probably intends co-laborers in the gospel at Antioch. Paul's closest associates support the letter written by him to the Galatians, with its stern warning and pastoral pleading. Though Paul writes the letter, those he names also speak authoritatively and with deep concern to the Galatian churches. Antioch would be considered the mother church of the Galatian churches who, through the Holy Spirit's leading, had chosen Barnabas and Saul for the evangelistic work which led to the Galatians' conversion. Ramsay points out in his *Historical Commentary* that since Antioch shares in the sending of the letter it must have been publicly read or in some manner approved by the church, perhaps through its representatives. Moreover, this origin explains why Antioch, so inseparably associated with Galatian evangelization, is not explicitly mentioned as the mother church in the body of the epistle. On the surface it seems that Paul speaks only of his own work and when he does mention Antioch it is by way of criticism of their one time defection from consistency with the gospel. "But when all Antiochian Christians are associated with the Apostle as issuing this authoritative letter, we feel that the Church of Antioch is placed in the honourable position which she had earned" (Ramsay, 244).

Paul then gives the greeting, **Grace to you and peace from God our Father and Lord Jesus Christ.** The order **grace** followed by **peace** arises from the essence of the gospel itself. **Grace** precedes and becomes the foundational principle for **peace.** By **grace** Paul means the blessings that come to us through the atonement. Greek letters characteristically incorporated the term *charein* ("to rejoice") for which Paul substitutes *charis* ("grace"). **Peace,** the common Jewish greeting, is added to **grace,** but with heightened meaning and greater depth. Since Jesus purchased our peace by satisfying God's wrath (Rom. 3:21-31), the peace of God should permeate our lives (Rom. 5:1). "When things 'go wrong,' as is now happening among the Galatian congregations, Paul does not first of all reach for a word of exhortation. He simply takes the congregations back to their birth. He takes them back, that is, to God's graceful election. Brought back to that point, the churches can see once again that not a single thing which human beings can do could possibly serve as the fountainhead of their redemption. God, the gracious one, and he alone, shows himself to be the new creator in Jesus Christ, the one whose grace is more powerful than is evil" (Martyn). This is a powerful truth and at the same time brimming with pastoral instruction. The minister of Word and Sacrament whose life blood is the gospel will help his flock look to grace in times of need, whatever the circumstances may be.

Both subjective peace and eschatological renewal are founded upon the objective accomplishment of atonement. Paul's concept of the church calls from his robust heart a greeting that transfigures the peace greeting of his day by the salvation event of Christ. The gospel transforms convention. "For Paul the ultimate source of grace is always God. In consequence, grace cannot be a mere benign regard, as the translation 'favor' might suggest, but a positive display of power better rendered by 'benefaction'."[5] In one sense the entire epistle is an unfolding of the salutation!

Grace and **peace** stream **from God our Father and Lord Jesus Christ,** indissolubly united as in verse 1. It is according

---

[5] Betz, 54.

to the plan of God the Father and the entrance of Christ into the world that redemption has been achieved. In verse one the Fatherhood of God speaks of a relation existing in the nature of God between the Father and His Son. Here **God our Father** anticipates Paul's later emphasis on adoption (cf. 3:21–4:6). Hence, the relation existing between the Father and the Son is crucial for the adoptive relation between the Father and the believer. **Lord** is the title applied to the Savior as risen, ascended, regnant and coming again (see especially Phil. 2:9-11). Paul did not preach himself but Jesus as Lord (2 Cor. 4:5). That Jesus is Lord means that He is YHWH, the Creator and Redeemer, Jehovah, the covenant God who revealed Himself to Moses in Exodus 3. It means that Jesus was worshipped and acclaimed as God. In Philippians 2:9-11 Paul transfers Isaiah 45:23, a passage that insists that God has no rivals, directly to Jesus. In the same way, Jesus has no rivals. Before Him every knee will bow! The *ontological* (His essential nature) and *economical* (His achievement) recognition of Jesus' Lordship stand side by side. That is, who Christ *is* and what He *accomplished* are inseparable. Note Romans 14:9: Christ died and rose again to establish His lordship over the dead and the living.[6]

The **Lord Jesus Christ** is the Redeemer **who gave Himself for our sins so that He might deliver us out of the present evil age.** Christ is the Redeemer who delivers us by voluntary sacrifice. The participle *tou dontos* indicates the freedom of Christ's sacrifice, the voluntary, deliberate and intentional nature of the atonement (cf. 2:20; 1 Tim. 2:6; Titus 2:14). Christ **gave** His life **for our sins.** *huper tōn hamartiōn hēmōn* is the language of substitution.[7] Through His self-deliverance to the cross Christ **delivered us.** *hopōs exelētai hēmas* is redemptive language. Behind it lies Paul's deep concern over salvation, which presupposes the wrath of God against sin.

---

[6] On Christ as Lord, see especially C. F. D. Moule (1977), *The Origin of Christology,* Cambridge University Press, 35-46.

[7] Meyer, 12: "...*in respect of our sins* (Rom. viii. 3), *on account of them,* namely, *in order to atone for them.* See Rom. iii. 23 ff.; Gal. iii. 12 ff." Meyer stresses that in essentials *peri* is not different than *huper*, "and the idea of satisfaction is implied, not in the signification of the preposition, but in the whole nature of the case."

Apart from Christ's redemptive work there is no salvation, no deliverance from sin. The cross of Christ needs no legalistic augmentation!

The historical cross is an eschatological event. Christ freely sacrificed Himself **so that He might deliver us out of the present evil age.** As in Jewish thought, the New Testament, and Paul in particular, know of two ages, two contrasting aeons, distinct and discernible.[8] The present age, the age ushered in by the arrival of the Messiah, is distinguishable from the age to come. Paul, however, grasped that Christ's achievement transfigured the two-age scheme. Paul understood that the new age had found its inauguration in the death and resurrection of Jesus and that His redemptive work found its meaning, composition and texture within this eschatological frame of reference. This age, or world order, from which the believer is delivered in Christ's redemption is pointedly **the present evil age,** the world order characterized by sin and its attendant consequences, disorder and death.[9] The *hopōs* of verse 4 indicates that Paul's "age" perspective is an unfolding of the redeeming work of Christ. Implicit in Paul's proclamation of deliverance *from* this age is deliverance *to* the age to come. The coming age is implicit. Believers have already been delivered to the coming age, the new eschatological order (2 Cor. 5:17; Gal. 6:15). If in Judaism the crucial matter is still future, for the Christian what is vital is the achievement of Christ in the past. The cross and resurrection together form the context of proclamation in the present and determine the Christian's orientation toward the future since the achievement of Christ is the turning point of the ages. In Christ, the coming age is the overwhelming present reality that defines the Christian's present privileges and obligations. Since the resurrection of Christ inaugurated the age to come, the two aeons, then, are contemporaneous and overlapping. The new age is now concurrent with the present age. "Heaven, so to speak, has received time and history into itself, no less than time has

---

[8] See Geerhardus Vos, *The Pauline Eschatology,* 1-41.

[9] Cf. Romans 12:2; 1 Corinthians 1:20; 2:6, 8; 2 Corinthians 4:4; Ephesians 1:21; 1 Timothy 6:17; 2 Timothy 4:10; Titus 2:12.

received unchangeableness and eternity into itself."[10] This two-age construct, moreover, has implications for Christian existence.

Christians might think of the two-age construct in terms of musical harmony. You find yourself in a room and a cacophonous band begins to play loudly and erratically. Then, from another room, you hear for the first time a Bach motet, at full volume; in beautiful, entrancing harmony the sounds invade the room in which you are living. As the music of Bach wafts into the room, the cacophony also continues. Immediately, under the spellbinding attraction of the motet, you make your way toward the harmonious music. "That is my home! That is where my heart is! That is where I long to live," you say to yourself. "That will be my destination! Harmony has invaded my life; the beauty for which I long answers to the purpose of my existence." Even though you as a Christian still live in the midst of discord as you journey toward the room from which harmony, beauteous concord, emanates, you have come to disown the cacophony of this world as you journey steadily onward toward the next, your real home. Like a Bach motet intruding into cacophony, in Christ the beauty and harmony of eternity have entered into time.

The apostle's emphasis upon deliverance from the present evil age through the cross contradicts the teaching of the Judaizers.[11] To negate and challenge their perspective meant for Paul stressing the redemptive accomplishment of Christ. Galatians can be understood only if we appreciate that Paul is confronting a view that reinterprets, denigrates and denies nothing less than the gospel (1:7; 2:14)!

Paul adds that this deliverance accomplished by Christ is **according to the will of our God and Father.** Paul's emphatic teaching about God reminds us that the fundamental error of the Judaizers, which is also true of all serious deviation from truth, originates in a wrong doctrine of God! It is the Father

---

[10] Vos, *The Pauline Eschatology,* 40.

[11] This concept of deliverance by Christ's atonement within the redemptive-historical, eschatological framework is the controlling motif of the epistle. Cf. 2:19-20; 3:23-26; 4:1-9; 5:1, 2; 6:14.

who has purposed the redemption of His people and designed their deliverance from this evil age of corruption to the age that is to come. The redemption achieved by Christ sacrificed on the cross was **according to the will** of God. Paul's gospel is radical. Redemption was no accident but was purposed in the divine good pleasure. The atonement of Christ and the deliverance purchased by Him, therefore, is thoroughly adequate, altogether sufficient to accomplish its purpose. The cross needs no supplement. At this point Paul's passionate soul bursts into a surge of worship.

Grace to you and peace from God our Father and Lord Jesus Christ, who gave Himself for our sins so that He might deliver us out of the present evil age according to the will of our God and Father, to whom be glory forever and ever. Amen. Paul cannot contain his gratitude, and will not restrain his praise for deliverance through Christ, a deliverance willed by the Father. To Him Paul ascribes splendor and the weight of majesty![12] Martyn says helpfully that Paul brings the Galatians climactically into God's presence "by inviting them to utter the word 'Amen!'" and he is robbing the Galatians "of the lethal luxury of considering themselves observers. With him, they stand in God's presence. Fundamentally, then, they are dealing with God, not merely with Paul." Paul, then, presents his word as God's Word to the churches.

---

[12] Kittel, *TDNT*, II. 237: glory "denotes 'divine and heavenly radiance,' the 'loftiness and majesty' of God, and even the 'being of God' and His world."

2.
No Other Gospel
(1:6-10)

Translation

I am amazed that you are so quickly deserting from the One who called you in the grace of Christ to a different gospel, which is really not another. But there are some who are throwing you into confusion and wishing to pervert the gospel of Christ. But even if we or an angel out of heaven preaches to you other than that which we preached to you, let him be accursed. As I have said before, so now I repeat, if anyone preaches to you a gospel besides the one you received, let him be accursed.

Well then, am I seeking men's approval or God's? Or, am I seeking to please men? If I were still seeking to please men, I would not be Christ's slave.

Summary

Paul, bypassing thanksgiving and prayer, is amazed at the Galatians' defection from the gospel of grace. He accuses the Judaizers of wishing to cause confusion and turn the Galatians from the truth. Paul is nothing less than pugilistic. He pronounces an imprecation on all who would preach any other "gospel" than the true gospel. Paul responds to accusations against his character and ministry as totally contrary to his strictures. He seeks to please only the Lord as Christ's bond-slave.

Comment

The abbreviated epistolary form is explained by Paul's passionate, pastoral heart. He is apprehensive over the defection of Galatian converts from the gospel and, therefore, passes by the expected thanksgiving and prayer.[1] The apostle is utterly astonished at the Galatian defection from the truth of the gospel. **I am amazed that you are so quickly deserting from the One who called you in the grace of Christ to a different gospel, which is really not another.** In the place of commendation is astonishment. That is, at the place in his epistles where normally Paul, after the pattern of a Hellenistic epistle, would include an expression of affection or thanksgiving he places here an expression of astonishment. The bewildered apostle can hardly believe the *volte-face* of the Galatians who have **so quickly deserted** the truth after their conversion. Duncan endorses Moffatt's translation **shifting like this, deserting,** maintaining that the dual sense is imbedded in the compound verb *metatithesthe.*

This entails deliberate desertion **from the One who called you in the grace of Christ.**[2] By **the One who called you** Paul does not refer to himself, as if to emphasize disappointment that the Galatians have not been faithful to him as an apostle. Rather, Paul refers to the call of the gospel to which the Galatians have not been faithful. Stress on the call of grace contrasts with the works-righteousness of Paul's opponents. Further, Paul's amazement is heightened by the exchange of grace for works of the Law. The Galatians were actually

---

[1] Meyer, "He probably wrote without delay, immediately on receiving the accounts which arrived as to the falling away of his readers, while his mind was still in that state of agitated feeling which prevented him from using his customary preface of thanksgiving and conciliation, …the very foundation and substance of his gospel threatened to fall to pieces."

[2] Ridderbos, 47, observes: "So much can be inferred from the term *called,* the technical term for the divine activity with the gospel (cf. Rom. 8:30; 9:12, 24; 1 Cor. 1:9 and others). This at the same time implies something about the nature of this calling. As divine calling it is full of power and effect (cf. Rom. 11:29), never a single, innocent invitation, carrying an obligation with it. All the same, it does not realize itself outside the pale of human responsibility, but places precisely those who pay no attention to this calling in a highly culpable position."

embracing the new doctrine of the Judaizers as superior to and in the place of Paul's teaching. Moreover, it is probable that the Judaizers had convinced the Galatians that Paul himself had embraced a perspective different from the one he had preached to them (5:11). See 1:8.

In deserting Christ the Galatians abandoned the true gospel embracing **a different gospel, which is not really another.** This is intended to demonstrate that there can only be one gospel and that the "gospel" preached by Paul's opponents is not it! The two "gospels"cannot stand alongside one another. There is only one gospel and to choose for the Judaizers' philosophy is to choose against the Christ that Paul preached and to choose for a perversion of the gospel. Paul's decisive presentation of the nature of the issue should not be missed. He leaves no room for indecision. Moreover, the nature of the issue of debate is at the very heart of the nature of the gospel itself. The matter before them is that of the foundation of salvation. Paul stresses this as he continues.

But there are some who are throwing you into confusion and wishing to pervert the gospel of Christ. Those who perverted the gospel, Paul insists, are *hoi tarassontes humas*, **those who are throwing you into confusion**, which must be the case when the sufficiency of Christ is called into question.[3] The gospel is God's remedy for sin, His provision for restoration to a relationship with Himself that sinners need and must have if we are to fulfill our chief end. Outside of the sphere of the gospel confusion reigns. Paul, however, does not see the preaching of the Judaizers as simply a well-intended mistake, a slight misstep or inaccuracy. The Judaizers have chosen intentionally to pervert the gospel and are **wishing to pervert the gospel of Christ** (*kai thelontes metastrepsai to euangelion tou Christou*). The Judaizers were not simply

---

[3] Martyn's view of *hoi tarassontes humas* is worthy of consideration. In view of early Christian use of the word *tarassō* (Luke 1:12; 24:37-38; with Acts 15:24 and 15:1) he concludes that Paul is not merely saying that the false teachers are "confusing" the Galatians, but "that they are frightening the Galatians out of their wits, intimidating them with the threat of damnation if they do not follow the path prescribed in the Teacher's message!"

misguided about some applications of the gospel. As serious as some misapplications may be, such misapplications are not Paul's principal concerns. Paul's dominant concern is that the Judaizers have willfully perverted the gospel and desired to draw others into their fundamental and fatal error.

The Judaizers denied the very gospel itself; hence the severity and uncompromising nature of Paul's language. **But even if we or an angel out of heaven preaches to you other than that which we preached to you, let him be accursed.** The apostle nails the issue by means of hypothetical argument[4] (**even if we or an angel,** *alla kai ean hēmeis ē angelos*). Even if an angel came down from the presence of God and preached to you a message that is different from that preached by Paul, that is, even if an angel preaches to you the message preached by the Judaizers, that message would not be true, must not be accepted, and the messenger would be deserving of God's curse and infinite displeasure – **let him be accursed.**

Anathema originally meant something offered to deity but came to mean something given over to God's wrath and curse. This is the overwhelming sense of the word in the New Testament. Paul is not referring to excommunication but to damnation.[5] "For Paul," observes Behm, "the word denotes the object of a curse". Behm rightly cites 1 Corinthians 12:3: *Therefore I tell you that no one who is speaking by the Spirit of God says "Jesus be cursed"* (*anathema Iēsous*). "It would be

---

[4] *alla kai ean* with a subjunctive "eventual condition" (Zerwick paragraph 320).

[5] *TDNT*, I. 354: "We can hardly think of an act of Church discipline, since the apostle uses the phrase = [*apo tou Christou*] (R.9:3) and also considers that an angel from heaven (Gl. 1:8) or even Jesus Himself (I C. 12:3) might be accursed. That he would willingly see himself separated from Christ and given up to divine judgment (*huper tōn adelphōn mou tōn sunenōn mou kata sarka*] (R.9:3) is a supreme expression of the readiness of Paul for redemptive self-sacrifice for the people which excludes itself from the divine revelation of salvation (Exod. 32:32)." See also Lightfoot: Anathema "seems never to signify 'excommunicated,' a sense which is not found till much later than the Christian era." For a contrary opinion see Betz: "The whole act of the curse has strong legal overtones and amounts to a ban or excommunication – in fact Galatians 1:8-9 is the first instance of Christian excommunication."

a self-contradiction for the Christian pneumatic to curse
Jesus, i.e., to deliver Him up to destruction by God." After
citing 1 C[orinthians] 16:22 and G[alatians] 1:8 he turns to
R[omans] 9:3: *anathema einai autos egō apo tou Christou,*
I could wish myself accursed from Christ and expelled from
fellowship with him. "That he would willingly see himself
separated from Christ and given up to divine judgment…is
a supreme expression of the readiness of Paul for redemptive
self-sacrifice for the people which excludes itself from the
divine revelation of salvation (Exod. 32:32)" (*TDNT*, I. 354).
For Paul, *anathema* refers to the infinitely just curse of the
infinitely just God.

The apostle insists that anyone who alters or modifies the
truth of the gospel deserves damnation. Legalistic attachments
to the gospel so alter its character as to make it no gospel at
all. Those who add such requirements to Jesus' work deserve
God's curse. Nor is the apostle content to make one statement,
strong as it is. To press the point Paul adds another: **As I have
said before, so now I repeat, if anyone preaches to you a
gospel besides the one you received, let him be accursed.**
Paul referencing the occasion on which he first preached the
gospel to the Galatians now reiterates his imprecation with this
difference: before he conjured up the hypothetical possibility
of angelic deception. Now he speaks in more realistic terms
– **if anyone preaches.…** One need not reach far to understand
those of whom he speaks. However, note that the apostle
includes himself in the imprecation if he should depart from
the gospel. Paul's authority is derived from the Christ of the
gospel and is not autonomous.

In view of recent debates concerning Paul and his gospel
it is instructive to contemplate Paul's severe statements demonstrating his unqualified commitment to the gospel of grace.
The whole tenor of his discussion thus far and to follow, and
especially the severity of his imprecation, preclude the possibility that Paul is referring only to the question of ecclesiology or something less than eternal salvation. The gospel is at
stake, a gospel defined by atonement and eschatological deliverance and, as shall be demonstrated, by the justification

of the sinner. Paul must warn the Galatian believers against
the Judaizing perversion of the gospel. He cannot be silent or
soft. Too much, indeed everything, is at stake! As his readers
approach the precipice, Paul's language screams "Beware!" It
is possible that **so now I repeat** refers not to the previous imprecation but to a warning given in person, perhaps during
his second visit (Acts 14:21ff.)

Paul asks two rhetorical questions in response to accusations against his character and ministry. **Well then, am
I seeking men's approval or God's? Or, am I seeking to
please men?**[6] Evidently, the Judaizing faction accused Paul of
conducting his ministry to gain converts by pleasing men.[7]
Perhaps they offered his gospel of free grace as evidence of
a desire to win adherents, even at the cost of compromising
a Judaizing "gospel". After all, a gospel without law attainment, the Judaizers might argue, could only be preached for
the purpose of pleasing men. Perhaps other circumstances
similar to Paul's later circumcision of Timothy (Acts 16) were
used as an attempt to demonstrate that Paul preached different messages depending on the occasion.[8] In view of Paul's

---

[6] We take *peithō* to mean "gain approval", but the possibility that it retains
its usual meaning "persuade" must be recognized. "On this understanding
Paul's rhetorical question is directed against the charge that he was trying to
persuade God to accept Gentile converts on less stringent terms than those
laid down by the law, 'persuading God' being thus materially identified with
'pleasing men'" (Fung). Cf. Bultmann, *TDNT*, 6: 2, 3. The *ē* is disjunctive
underscoring the God/man contrast. See Lategan, 422: "The real contrast
...lies in 10c, which is the direct opposite of being Christ's slave."

[7] I am indebted to Dennis Johnson for pointing out to me in personal
correspondence the incident recorded in Josephus, *Antiquities*, 20.2
describing an occurrence in Adiabene where a Jewish merchant/missionary
attempts to dissuade the Gentile king from receiving circumcision fearing
backlash from the pagan populace. Professor Johnson cites this as an
interesting example of compromise for the sake of winning converts in his
work *The Message of Acts in the History of Redemption*, 126.

[8] There is nothing in Paul's circumcision of Timothy that contradicts
his position regarding circumcision in Galatians. Paul was always willing
to bend as far as possible for the sake of the gospel when principle was
not at stake. But when principle was at stake and the nature of the gospel
was at issue, Paul was unyielding. It is easy to see, however, how Paul's
attitude as seen in Acts 16:3 could be misrepresented by his opponents. The

strictures and uncompromising language, however, he can make good on his claim that he is no man-pleaser. Therefore, he answers, **if I were still seeking to please men, I would not be Christ's slave.** Paul is not out to please men, but is Christ's *doulos*, His bondservant, and His willing slave.[9] Paul is not autonomous, nor may he determine the content of Christ's gospel. The slave is answerable to his master, is devoted to his service. The gospel so frees Paul that he does not constantly look over his shoulder to determine what others think of him or his message. In this way he avoided the trap into which the church often falls, desiring to become popular, to win men at the expense of faithfulness to the gospel message, rather than to be faithful, true and loyal to the message of grace. Calvin rightly reminds us that "those who determine to serve Christ faithfully must boldly despise the favor of men".

---

issue in Galatia regarding circumcision was completely different from the circumcision of Timothy (see Gal. 5:2ff.; 6:13).

[9] Betz: " 'Man-pleasing' and being Christ's 'slave' do not go together. See Ephesians 6:6; 1 Corinthians 7:22-23; Colossians 3:25."

3.
The Revelation of the Gospel (1:11-24)

Translation

For I make known to you, brothers, that the gospel that was preached by me is not contrived by man. For I neither received it from man, nor was taught it, but it came by revelation of Jesus Christ.

You heard about my way of life when living among the Jews, how I persecuted the church of God off the scale and tried my hardest to annihilate it, all the while progressing in Judaism beyond many contemporaries among my people, being more zealous for my ancestral traditions than they. But when God, who separated me from my mother's womb and called me through His grace, was pleased to reveal His Son in me for the purpose of preaching Him among the Gentiles, I did not immediately consult with any man, nor did I go up to Jerusalem to those who were apostles before me, but went away to Arabia, and went back to Damascus.

Then after three years I went again to Jerusalem to visit Cephas, and remained with him fifteen days; but I did not see other apostles, but only James the Lord's brother. I swear to God I am not lying about the things I am writing to you. Next I went into the regions of Syria-Cilicia. But I was unknown by sight to the churches of Judea that are in Christ; only they were hearing that "the one who once persecuted us now preaches the faith he once attempted to annihilate." And they continually praised God because of me.

Summary
Paul emphasizes the divine origin of his gospel and the freedom of grace. He begins to unfold his personal history in order to defend the gospel's gracious nature. Paul's gospel came by revelation and not through human sources; his past as a faithful Pharisee and zealous persecutor of the church and his subsequent change demonstrate the remarkable character of grace and that works of the law for acceptance with God are valueless. The gratuitous disposition of the gospel is traceable to God's sovereign election and call. God worked wondrously in Paul's life both in his conversion and in his call to apostleship! Having received God's call Paul did not visit the apostles in Jerusalem but ministered in the regions surrounding Damascus. Paul relates these facts to underscore the independence of his gospel from human origin. It was not until three years after his conversion that Paul visited Cephas and James, and then only briefly. He afterward went into the regions of Syria-Cilicia and was unknown by sight to the believers of Judea. Paul is keen to demonstrate that his gospel needed no man's approval and, further, no legalistic supplement. Paul concludes this segment of his argument by reflecting on how the Jewish believers responded to news of his conversion and preaching by glorifying God with praise!

Comment
The apostle addresses the Galatians formally and gravely (as indicated by *gnōridzō*; cf. 1 Cor. 12:3; 15:1, 2; 2 Cor. 8:1): **For I make known to you, brothers, that the gospel that was preached by me is not contrived by man.** Undoubtedly, they should have known that Paul's gospel was not of human origin, and therefore may not be tampered with or altered to suit the designs of any party. The divine origin of the gospel corresponds to Paul's insistence on the downward movement of grace. In view of that grace he still calls them

brothers! Nonetheless, Paul finds it necessary to remind them of fundamentals as if they have not heard these things before. Not only was Paul's apostolic call not of human origin (1:1), but the gospel itself was not devised by man. This is the apostle's main concern, the nature of the gospel itself, which is his pre-eminent interest from the beginning, even from the first verse of the epistle.

For I neither received it from man, nor was taught it, but it came by revelation of Jesus Christ. Speaking now of his own past the apostle begins to unfold his personal history in relation to the gospel in order to defend the gospel's gracious character. Duncan is surely right to see in the two clauses – **neither received it from man, nor was taught it** – the stages of Paul's life before and after his conversion, of which he speaks in verses 13ff. Paul's "apprehension of the gospel is not to be explained by reference to his early environment and religious education". Moreover, "his understanding of the gospel did not come to him through sitting at the feet of teachers who explained to him its essential truths" (Duncan).[1] The gospel did not come to Paul by human means at all **but it came by revelation of Jesus Christ**. The genitive *Iēsou Christou* is best viewed as an objective rather than a subjective genitive.[2] God revealed Jesus Christ to Paul. As Silva points out, "Paul elsewhere seems to view God the Father as the source of revelation". Moreover, "an objective genitive in Galatians 1:12 would hardly mean a downplaying of Paul's focus on the divine origin of the gospel. In fact, the very lack of symmetry

---

[1] Machen explains the emphatic "I" (*egō*) as due to "the simple contrast between the gospel that Paul preached and Paul himself in his connection with that gospel. "The gospel that I have preached," says Paul, "is not according to man; for, what is more, I the preacher of that gospel, did not receive it from man. It might have been a divine gospel and yet have been handed over to me by a purely human agent. But as a matter of fact that was not the case. Not only was the gospel that I was to preach divine, but I received it in a divine manner – namely by direct revelation from Jesus Christ."

[2] Exegetes differ on this matter. For example, Lightfoot says it means "from Christ" while Bruce says: "That *Iēsou Christou* here is an objective genitive is rendered most probable by the wording of vv. 15f: God was pleased to *reveal his Son* (*apokalupsai ton huion autou*) in me."

entailed in that interpretation could be understood as a way of highlighting Paul's claim." Silva paraphrases Paul's thought in this way: "This message did not come from man but rather [from God, who gave it to me in the most remarkable way:] by revealing Christ himself" (Silva, 68). This conclusion seems to coincide best with Paul's following argument. **By revelation** is the equivalent of **not by human sources, nor by human appointment** (v. 1). For Paul, everything is determined by the appearance of the resurrected Christ on the Damascus road. Prior to that he had known something about Christ and His church and had persecuted the church with rigor. However, he did not receive the gospel until God revealed Christ to Paul on the Damascus road. Here, as in the opening verses, Paul insists that he is uniquely qualified by his call to apostleship to be heard above the din of the false teachers who deny the true character of the gospel. Paul has the right by virtue of his calling to pass on the *kerygma* to the churches of Galatia. Once again, however, it is essential to realize that Paul's main concern is not the defense of his apostleship. Paul's apostleship is subservient to the indispensable question of the nature of the gospel itself!

Paul now turns to his life prior to and soon after his call to Christ and to apostleship. His insistence on the divine, gracious intervention into his life and the supernatural revelation of the gospel is further emphasized by reference to his life, which had been known to his readers, prior to his Damascus road conversion. **You heard about my way of life when living among the Jews, how I persecuted the church of God off the scale and tried my hardest to annihilate it, all the while progressing in Judaism beyond many contemporaries among my people, being more zealous for my ancestral traditions than they**. Paul's ethical conduct[3] among the Jews was antithetical to and hostile toward the gospel. Paul reminds the Galatians that he **persecuted the church[4] of**

---

[3] *anastrophē* indicates ethical conduct.

[4] "By calling it *the church of God,* the apostle makes the frightfulness of his former activity the more manifest. At the same time, the phrase communicates the idea that the believers in Christ are the continuation of Israel as the people chosen of God. Indirectly this implies that the criterion for belonging to the people of God lies in faith and nothing else" (Ridderbos).

God off the scale and tried hardest to annihilate it. Paul's hatred of the gospel and of the church was so deep that with all of his heart he persecuted it. His persecuting activity was *kath huperbolēn,* excessive, extraordinary and fierce; hence we have translated **off the scale.**[5] Martyn suggests that Paul viewed himself in conscious succession to pious and zealous Israelites such as Phinehas, Elijah and Mattathias.[6]

As Paul persecuted the church he was progressing (*proekopton*) in his Pharisaic zeal and commitment, surpassing even other zealots in commitment to the *halacha,* the codified traditions of his fathers. The succession of verbs in the imperfect that tumble across the page indicate a process of destruction begun but not completed by Paul.[7] Paul vehemently tried to destroy and annihilate the church, and progressed in his ancestral traditions![8]

---

[5] REB translates, "how savagely I persecuted the church of God and tried to destroy it" NRSV: "I was violently persecuting the church of God and was trying to destroy it." Machen comments: "the very point of the passage in Galatians, where he alludes to his persecuting activity, is the suddenness of his conversion. Far from gradually coming nearer to Christ he was in the very midst of his zeal for the Law when Christ called him. The purpose of the passage is to show that his gospel came to him without human intermediation.... When he laid the Church waste he thought he was doing God service. In the very midst of his mad persecuting activity, he says, apart from any teaching from men – apart, we may certainly infer, from any favorable impressions formed in his mind – the Lord appeared to him and gave him his gospel" (*The Origin of Paul's Religion,* 61-62).

[6] Martyn adds: "The Galatians will not have failed to see that the picture Paul paints of himself prior to his call by God is similar to the picture the Teachers are now presenting of themselves" and that "nomistic devotion led him to persecute *God's* church, something the Teachers are doing in their own way at the present time."

[7] Though Silva, 68ff. argues that the distinction between the aorist and imperfect in the indicative mood is very small, on pages 70-71 he says: "Scholars have noticed, however, that Greek writers sometimes use the imperfect (which represents activity as in progress rather than as complete) to indicate an attempted action that was not brought to conclusion." He adds: "Paul was not merely intent on destroying the church – he had actually begun the process of destruction (action in progress) but was prevented from completing it. In short, the function of the imperfect here is quite normal: action in progress but not complete."

[8] 1:13: *Ekousate gar tēn emēn anastrophēn pote en tō Ioudaismō hoti kath uperbolēn ediōkon tēn ekklēsian tou theou kai eporthoun autēn.*

As we read these moving, emotional words that testify to the sovereign grace of God, we see clearly that Paul not only describes the circumstances in which the gospel was revealed to him, but that he is glorying in the gospel, announcing the triumph of grace in such a way that the contrast with the Judaizers is utterly stark. Not only did the gospel come to him by revelation, but also one must stand amazed that the Lord has revealed his gospel to *Paul*! Paul was ever amazed and could never get over the grace that God had shown to him, the sinner. Who Paul was and his zealous persecution of the church made his call to apostleship also all the more remarkable.[9] Pauline autobiography in this passage exists to demonstrate the nature of the gospel that Paul came to love and preach. All things were now, for Paul, viewed through the brilliant light of the revelation of God's grace in Christ crucified and risen from the dead. Moreover, "the sacrifice of Christ had exposed the utter valuelessness of the Law-service for obtaining righteousness for Jew and Gentile alike" (Verseput, 51).

It is to this purpose that Paul stresses the sovereignty of grace and his independence from the Jerusalem leadership in the verses that follow. **But when God, who separated me from my mother's womb and called me through His grace, was pleased to reveal His Son in me for the purpose of preaching Him among the Gentiles, I did not immediately consult with any man, nor did I go up to Jerusalem to those who were apostles before me, but went away to Arabia, and went back to Damascus**. It is not so much the independence

---

1:14: *kai proekopton en tō Ioudaismō uper pollou sunēlikiōta en tō genei mou perissoteōs zēlōtē huparchōn ton patrikōn mou paradoseōn.*

[9] Paul is, therefore, concerned in this passage first of all with the revelation of the gospel apart from human intermediary. "As a persecutor of the Christians and a Pharisaic zealot, he could not but be the less fitted for human instruction in the gospel, which must, on the contrary, have come to him in that superhuman mode" (Meyer). However, Paul is also concerned to glory in the grace that the Judaizers denied. "But those who read his words must also have been prompted to ask themselves the question: if for so ardent a Jew as Paul the gospel involved a radical breach with his religious traditions, how can it be that for us who are Gentiles by birth the gospel is incomplete unless we add to it the tenets of Judaism?" (Duncan).

of his apostleship as the freedom and utterly gratuitous nature of the gospel that is the point of these verses. Grace alone is behind the strong contrast: **but when**! These words break the life of Paul in two; before Christ and after Christ's gracious apprehension of his heart. This break corresponds to the two ages, the present evil age to which he belonged before Christ and the age to come, overlapping this present age, due to Christ's resurrection that now determines his life.

In sovereign freedom God showed His divine grace to this man who had once been bound by Pharisaic tradition. By saying **but when God was pleased to reveal His Son in me**, Paul accentuates the absolute sovereignty and good pleasure of God in Paul's salvation. This is the significance of the combination of the terms **was pleased to reveal**.[10] The expression **in me** emphasizes the personal nature of God's revelation of His Son to Paul.[11] The revelation of **His Son in me** must indicate that Paul had insight into the person of Jesus. Paul, by means of God's revelation of His Son to him, came to understand who Jesus was and what He came to do.

Are the words, **who separated me from my mother's womb and called me through His grace,** to be connected with Paul's gracious conversion or with the words, **for the purpose of preaching Him among the Gentiles**? Even though the assumption of a connection in Paul's mind of these

---

[10] "There is a sovereign ring about εὐδόκησεν in Galatians 1:15, the apostle being set in a dependence on God which makes him independent of men" (Schrenk, *TDNT*, 2. 741).

[11] Duncan distances himself from Lightfoot here, thinking it to be beyond question that Paul is concerned with the revelation of the gospel to his own soul. He writes: "But the context of the passage, together with Paul's use of the word 'reveal' puts it beyond doubt that the apostle is here concerned to tell of a revelation which God made to his own soul. By using the phrase 'His Son' in this connection Paul implies that God had opened his eyes to see Jesus in His true character – He was not a mere teacher; neither, despite His crucifixion, was He an accused blasphemer; rather He was one whom God acknowledged as His Son (cf. Rom. 1:4)." Ridderbos, on the other hand, is among those who do not think that too much emphasis should be placed upon the subjective nature of the encounter and prefers to translate *to me* or simply *me* rather than *in me* (citing Bl.-Debr., para. 220; *TWNT*, III. p. 535).

thoughts with Jeremiah 1:5[12] is probably correct, the question might be pedantic. These things are inseparable in Paul's mind. **Called me through His grace** "refers here not only to the effectual call to salvation… but also to assignment unto plenary apostleship" (Hendriksen). In other words, God's call of Paul to salvation and to apostolic office is likely implied. After all, isn't the thrust of these words that Paul is aware that the sovereign purpose of God has worked magnificently in his life both in conversion and in his call to apostleship? Both in his calling to Christ and to apostleship, Paul was *chosen* in sovereign and free grace without any merit to call grace forth! This remains true of all who are called to Christ and to his service.

Paul's call to faith in Christ and to apostleship **for the purpose of preaching Him among the Gentiles** was willed by God and not by Paul. The sovereignty of grace in Paul's call to Christ and to apostolic ministry is emphasized by **who separated me from my mother's womb**, meaning God's determination in his own counsels before Paul's birth.[13] Students of Paul have observed frequently that in using the term "separated" (*ho aphorisas*) he may have been contrasting his life of Pharisaism (the root word of which means "separated") and the perspective of the Judaizers with God's gracious separation of Paul to God's service. Yet it is important to see, as Martyn points out, that what stands opposite to the tradition of the fathers is God's Son. "What is at stake in the Galatian crises is the Galatians' bond to Christ

---

[12] Some, such as Bruce, also think that Paul has other prophetic references in mind. Bruce cites Isaiah 49:1-6, adding: "It is not by chance that in Acts 13:47 these last words (*that my salvation may reach the ends of the earth*) are quoted by Paul and Barnabas in the synagogue of Pisidian Antioch as their authority for taking the gospel to the Gentiles. In Paul's view, it was for others to take up the Servant's mission to Israel, but he knew himself called to fulfil that part of the Servant's vocation which involved the spreading of God's saving light among the Gentiles, near and far…"

[13] See Betz, p. 70, note 136, and Bruce, p. 92: "Before ever he was born, Paul means, God had his eye on him and set him apart for his apostolic ministry." Bruce cites Judges 13:5; Psalms 22 [LXX 21]: 10; 58 [LXX 57]:3; 71 [LXX 70]:6. Martyn: "Paul is saying that God's elective grace is God's act of new creation. It has no basis in the human side of the picture. Having not yet

himself (5:4). Thus, Paul does not say that his mission began with the preaching of a wiser path of life, a better route to happiness, and so on. He does not even say that his task was to preach a non-Law gospel in contrast to the Law. God called him to preach Christ, the good news being Christ's advent into the world (3:22–4:7)."

On the heels of this powerful affirmation of sovereign grace Paul insists **I did not immediately consult with any man, nor did I go up to Jerusalem to those who were apostles before me, but went away to Arabia, and went back to Damascus.** After Paul's conversion one might have expected that a visit to the apostles would be his first order of business. However, Paul did not go up to Jerusalem nor did he visit those who were apostles before him. Though a part of the church, of which **Jerusalem** is largely a metonym (Martyn), Paul did not derive either his commission or his understanding of the gospel from the apostles. Rather, he **went away to Arabia, and went back to Damascus. Arabia** must mean the regions surrounding Damascus, the kingdom of the Nabateans.[14]

Seyoon Kim has shown that Paul's visit to Arabia should be viewed as an almost immediate apprehension of the application of Isaiah 42 to his call to serve Christ as an apostle. In Isaiah 42:11 the Servant [Ebed] is called to bear light and salvation to the Gentiles and leads the inhabitants of Kedar and Sela to sing the Lord's praises. Kedar and Sela would, for Paul, have referred to Arabia, the Nabatean kingdom. "Thus, Paul's first missionary attempt in 'Arabia' immediately after his apostolic commission (Gal. 1:15-17) seems to indicate that he indeed interpreted his call to an apostleship to the

---

been born, Paul could have done nothing to merit or warrant God's calling of him (cf. Rom. 9:11)." Martyn also rightly observes, "Paul transforms the category of biography into a theological witness focused on *God's* activity in the gospel" – a theme that would be helpful in the modern church approach to giving one's "testimony".

[14] *ISBE*, p. 221: "King Aretas, elsewhere identified as an Arabian (cf. Josephus *Ant.* xiv.1.4), is mentioned in 2 Corinthians 11:32, and we are reasonably certain that he is to be identified with Aretas IV, king of the Nabateans, whose kingdom extended E and S of Damascus, with its capital at Petra."

Gentiles on the Damascus road in the light of Isaiah 42." Kim adds significantly: "if Paul went to Arabia 'immediately,' his interpretation of his call in the light of Isaiah 42 must have been equally immediate! This immediacy militates against the view that he began to interpret his Damascus experience years later or that Galatians 1:15-17 represents only a later interpretation of it for an apologetic, rhetorical, or paradigmatic purpose at the time of writing Galatians" (Kim, 104).

Kim has provided fascinating insights into Galatians 1:15-17. He concludes that Isaiah 42 was a primary Old Testament text by which Paul interpreted God's revelation and call to him on the Damascus road. He is impressed with how most of Galatians 1:15-17 alludes to Isaiah 42. Comparison of Isaiah 42 with this passage in Paul, he thinks, illumines Paul's gospel of God's righteousness, his Gentile apostleship, his understanding of God's plan of salvation, his mission to Arabia and, especially, his endowment of the Holy Spirit helping to explain the overwhelming importance of the Holy Spirit in Paul's thought and ministry. Of special importance is Kim's insistence that Paul had almost immediate insight into his call and mission and that Christ's revelation on the Damascus road brought with it a call to fulfill "the Ebed role of Jesus Christ, or rather the risen Christ Jesus carried on fulfilling the Ebed's role through Paul" (Kim, 127). In this way Kim strengthens his thesis that "Paul's gospel is basically an unfolding of the revelation of Jesus Christ on the Damascus road" (Kim, 5). This thesis is not new to Kim; it is found in such writers as Ramsay and Bruce. But Kim has expanded and explained the thesis admirably. All of this also serves to demonstrate how artificial it is to sever Paul's gospel from his call to apostleship since, for Paul, the one was demanded by the other.

In order to underscore the independence of his gospel from human origin Paul lays the facts squarely before the Galatians. He continues by adding: **Then after three years I went again to Jerusalem to visit Cephas, and remained with him fifteen days; but I did not see other apostles, but only James the Lord's brother.** This refers to Paul's first visit to Jerusalem and his stay for fifteen days. **After three years** does not mean "three years after" but, as Ramsay points out, counting from A.D. 31 **after three years** would be A.D. 33, "the third year after"; but "three years after" in our way of expression would mean A.D. 34. "This rule of interpretation is regular in ancient times; the day or year which forms the starting point is reckoned in the sum" (*Historical Commentary,* 274). Paul's purpose in visiting Cephas, and then only three years after his conversion,[15] was to make Cephas' acquaintance (*historasai*). Paul visited with Cephas only fifteen days. Further, Paul **did not see other apostles,but only James[16] the Lord's brother.** In attestation to these facts Paul adds a solemn oath: **I swear to God I am not lying about the things I am writing to you.**[17]

Paul then rounds out the recital of his itinerary, stating **next I went into the regions of Syria-Cilicia.** Ramsay points out that Paul always speaks with Roman divisions of the empire in mind, that is, he speaks of the Provinces "in accordance both with his station as a Roman citizen and with his invariable and oft-announced principle of accepting and obeying the existing government." Therefore, Paul speaks of Achaia,

---

[15] Although Paul could possibly mean three years after returning to Damascus, the context seems to favor dating in relation to his conversion (v. 15).

[16] It is unlikely that Paul is referring to James as an apostle. Machen writes: "As a matter of fact, however, the Greek phrase meaning 'except' is sometimes used to introduce an exception to something that is more general than that which has actually been mentioned.... So in our passage, Paul's mention of his meeting with James, even if James was not an 'apostle,' was in the nature of an exception to the assertion, 'Another of the apostles I did not see'" (77,78). However, as Machen also recognizes, the language may include James as an apostle. This is not an easy matter to determine. For arguments pro and con, see Bruce, 77, 78. Our immediate concern is the theology of Paul.

[17] Bruce, 79: "It has been observed that in Roman legal procedure the proffering of oaths in court was generally discouraged, unless it was absolutely necessary; here Paul takes the voluntary oath (*iusiurandum voluntarium*) as 'a forceful and even dramatic means to emphasize both the seriousness of the issue and his own truthfulness.' It is with good reason that Paul took his own statements so seriously, for the very truth of the gospel as he understood it was at stake in the veracity of the narrative. The vehemence of his language also implies, probably, that a different account, which misrepresented the nature and purpose of his visits to Jerusalem, was current among the Galatian churches, and that he was eager to counter this with his statement of the facts."

Asia, Macedonia, Galatia, Illyricum – the Roman names for Provinces rather than the Greek names of countries. "The Roman citizen and conqueror Paul, who was looking forward to the Christianisation of the Roman Empire, …counted his progress by Provinces." So here when Paul speaks of Syria and Cilicia "he designates it by the double name, like *Provincia Bithynia et Pontus*", the common article embracing the two parts of the one Province. Verse 21 indicates, then, that Paul "spent the following period of his life in various parts of the Province Syria-Cilicia; and it confirms the principle of interpretation laid down by Zahn that 'Paul never designates any part of the Roman Empire by any other name than that of the Province to which it belonged; and he never uses any of the old names of countries, except in so far as these had become names of Provinces'." (*Historical Commentary*, 277–78).

Paul's purpose for referencing these geographical regions was simply that these regions were not Jerusalem! Paul's gospel was not dependent upon the apostles or believers of Jerusalem. Paul further adds **But I was unknown by sight to the churches of Judea that are in Christ, only they were hearing that "the one who once persecuted us now preaches the faith he once attempted to annihilate**." Paul had not attended the meetings and worship services of the churches of Judea. Paul was not dependent upon them for his gospel or for his ministry of the gospel of grace. The churches are geographically located in Judea but more importantly in the new realm of God's renewing grace. They are the churches that are **in Christ.** Union with Christ forms their new identity. These churches ascribed praise to God upon hearing of Paul's preaching the gospel he once was intent on destroying.

Why was Paul anxious to relate these facts about his travels? It is usually assumed that Paul rehearses his itinerary in order to deny that he learned his gospel from the apostles and so defend his apostolic authority. But if Paul's *main* point has been that his gospel is not according to man, then we are led to another conclusion. The argument in this section stems from his insistence on the work of sovereign, free grace in 1:15.

"The remainder of chapter 1 emerges, accordingly, as a resolute insistence upon the independence of Paul's ministry from the Jewish Christian community of Palestine, not in the sense of a cryptic denial of human instruction, but as a logical consequence of the divine initiative" (Verseput, 40-41). Paul is not first concerned with defending his authority against detractors but is keen to demonstrate the sovereignty of grace in his life. The theme of grace is the definitive point of his entire letter in contrast to his Judaizing opponents. Verseput rightly notes: "As one chosen by God Paul did not consider it necessary to join himself either to the Jerusalem apostles or to the churches of Judea, but departed straightway into Gentile territory, thus confirming the fundamental independence of the Gentile mission from any genetic tie to Jewish Christianity" (Verseput, 41).

While Verseput may somewhat overstate his case – after all Paul does see a genetic tie between the Gentile mission and Jewish Christianity (Rom. 9–11; Eph. 2:11ff.) – yet his fundamental concern is correct. Paul is keen to show that his gospel is not according to man and that his call to mission is determined by the sovereignty of grace. In that sense his ministry is independent of the Palestinian Jewish community and leadership and, indeed, from any man. This is why Paul did not consult with anyone. He did not need man's approval for a gospel supernaturally imparted by grace. Nor was it necessary for Paul to go up to Jerusalem to consult with the apostles. After three years Paul did go to Jerusalem, "but his point is to confirm that he did not become one of them; he remained independent, and his Gentile mission a separate work of God" (Verseput, 42).

The sovereignty of grace and its relation to the Gentile mission also helps us to understand Paul's statement: **But I was unknown by sight to the churches of Judea that are in Christ, only they were hearing that "the one who once persecuted us now preaches the faith he once attempted to annihilate"**. We think that Verseput is right in insisting that Paul's point is to show independence from the Christian community of the circumcision. "By asserting his independence from the Jerusalem apostles and the Jewish mission in general, Paul is affirming the independence of Gentile salvation from the Torah covenant, boldly pulling the rug out from under the feet of his judaizing opponents" (Verseput, 43). If Paul's mission to the Gentiles stood in need of instruction, confirmation, and approval of the leaders of Jewish Christianity, then there might be some handle for his opponents to argue that the gospel needed supplementing by Jewish legalistic codes and rituals. But if Paul's gospel and mission were received by revelation and stood independently of such leadership, then it becomes obvious that the gospel is fully gracious and in no need of supplement of any kind.

The fact that he was unknown to the believers of Judea is but another way to highlight the God/man contrast. Paul's gospel is not according to man! He received it from the Lord. The gospel was in no need of Jewish supplementation. This theme must be seen in continuity with verses 11-12: **For I make known to you, brothers, that the gospel that was preached by me is not contrived by man. For I neither received it from man, nor was taught it, but it came by revelation of Jesus Christ**. God saves both Jew and Gentile by grace!

Paul concludes this segment of his argument for salvation by grace by reflecting upon how the Jewish believers of Judea responded to the news of his conversion. They heard that Jesus Christ saved the one who had attempted to wipe them out **and they continually praised God because of me**.[18] The imperfect *edoxazon* can be over read to mean a continual stream of praise. But though the grammar does not necessarily indicate it, we cannot doubt that Jewish Christians who learned of Paul's conversion were amazed at the grace of God!

Who had Paul been? A Jew earnestly practicing his faith with no love for Christ or Christians, with no predisposition to become a Christian, a hyper-persecutor of the church of Jesus Christ, who thought he was serving God. The works-righteousness system produces moralists who must defend

---

[18] Zerwick, 119, "As is well known, the NT uses *en* with almost Semitic frequency instead of the instrumental dative, e.g. Revelation 6:8…This is perhaps the reason why *en* is occasionally used for other causes than the instrumental one, and may be rendered 'because of'."

their sense of superiority. The "righteousness" of the moralist is "secure" when it persecutes the messengers of free grace. Paul was so zealous in this that he continually progressed in destroying Christians, in the Jewish way of life, and by advancing in ancestral traditions. Paul was superlative in works of the law (Phil. 3:4-6).

Albert Schweitzer, the well-known philosopher, physician and humanitarian, at the age of 21 decided he would spend nine years studying medicine, music and theology, and then devote his life to humanitarian service. He established a hospital in French Equatorial Africa, which he expanded to include a leper colony. His view of Christ was anything but Paul's! When Karl Barth met Schweitzer he "told him in a friendly way that his views were a 'fine specimen of righteousness by works'."[19] Barth was right. We can do the works of a Mother Teresa but it will not make us right with God. The conversion that Paul so desperately needed, and that all moralists need, was a conversion from one view of righteousness to another! More than that, Paul's shift was from one understanding of his source of righteousness, that which is from law-keeping to total reliance upon the merit of Christ. When the Jewish Christians of Judea saw that Paul had moved from egocentricity to Christocentricity, that he had been called by grace, that God had called and commissioned him to preach the gospel, that he was transformed from opposing Christ to depending upon Christ, they could not help continually praising God. His preaching and life showed a changed relationship with God. And those of us who have come to know Him can only say: Praise Him! Praise Him!

---

[19] Quoted by Eberhard Busch (1976), *Karl Barth, His life from letters and autobiographical texts*, Fortress Press, 183. Approval of Barth's observation does not imply endorsement of Barthian theology.

4.
The Gospel for Jew and Gentile (2:1-10)

Translation

Then after fourteen years I went up again to Jerusalem with Barnabas, and also brought along Titus. I went up according to revelation and presented to them the gospel that I preach among the Gentiles. I did this privately to those who have a reputation, lest I run or had run in vain. But not even Titus, who was with me, even though he was a Greek, was compelled to be circumcised. Because of those infiltrators, false brothers who slipped in to ambush our liberty that we have in Christ Jesus, so that they might enslave us, we did not give in to them even for a moment so that the truth of the gospel might remain with you. And from those held in high regard – whatever they were matters not to me; God does not show favoritism – those held in high regard added nothing to me. On the contrary, when they saw that the gospel had been entrusted to me for the uncircumcised just as the gospel had been entrusted to Peter for the circumcised (for He who enabled Peter to work effectively as an apostle to the circumcised also enabled me to work effectively as an apostle to the Gentiles), and knowing the grace which was given to me, James and Cephas and John, who were held in high regard as pillars, gave to me and Barnabas the right hand of partnership in order that we might serve the Gentiles and they the circumcised. Only they

encouraged us to remember the poor, and I was already eager
to do this very thing.

Summary
Having shown that his gospel was "not according to man"
and that his Gentile mission was independent of the Jewish
Christian community, Paul now demonstrates that the
Jerusalem leadership preached and approved the same
gospel. The significance of his second Jerusalem visit was the
demonstration of the independence of his gospel and ministry
from Jerusalem leadership. Paul stresses the revelatory
catalyst behind his visit during which he presented to the
Jerusalem leaders the gospel he preached among the Gentiles.
Paul presented his gospel "lest I run or had run in vain",
meaning that his labor for the gospel to the Gentiles would be
endangered if the false teachers were approved. That Titus,
a Gentile believer who accompanied Paul on this visit, was
not compelled to be circumcised by the Jewish Christian
leadership in Jerusalem confirmed the agreement between
Paul, the apostles and other leaders there. Paul describes the
"false brothers"and their enslaving purpose to which he did
not yield for a moment for the sake of the gospel. Verses 6-10
form a complex argument demonstrating that Paul had the
support of the Jerusalem leaders. They "added nothing" to
Paul's gospel but recognized that they and Paul ministered
the same gospel in different ethnic spheres. Giving to Paul and
Barnabas the "right hand of koinōnia [partnership]" sealed
their fellowship. The one request of the Jerusalem leaders was
that Paul "remember the poor", a practice to which Paul was
already committed.

Comment
Before proceeding, it seems wise to draw together the data
regarding the Jerusalem visits of Paul so that we may keep
in mind the purpose of his biographical account. **I went up
to Jerusalem** in 1:18 and **I went up again to Jerusalem** in 2:1
indicate successive Jerusalem visits and there is nothing to
suggest an omitted visit. The biographical data is important
to show that on neither visit did Paul receive his authority

from the apostles. Moreover, "Paul is not giving a complete history of what occurred on his visits, but simply tells enough to correct false impressions or statements" (Ramsay, *Historical Commentary*, 282).

Paul visited Cephas on his first visit (1:18-20) but he did not go to Jerusalem seeking to be authorized in apostolic ministry by him. His visit was only for a brief fifteen days and, besides Peter, Paul saw only James. For whatever reason, perhaps as Ramsay suggests because other apostles were away on various duties, he saw these two respected leaders only. Paul's solemn oath (1:20) probably indicates that the Judaizing party had given a different account of the matter.

The second visit now before us in 2:1-10, as Ramsay suggests, may be difficult for us to comprehend in some ways but would have been perfectly plain to the Galatians since Paul is recalling what they knew. Lightfoot and others relate this passage to Acts 15. The facts are these: fourteen years after Paul's conversion he communicated with the apostles in Jerusalem, discussing with them the gospel he preached to the Gentiles, and that they approved his gospel. "This communication was an event of the utmost importance. We must lay the utmost stress on it, as Paul evidently did. It is the essential proof of the vital harmony that existed among the four great Christian leaders" (Ramsay, *Historical Commentary*, 287). The unity and concord between Paul and the leaders of the church in Jerusalem permeates the passage. On this visit Paul and Barnabas, already known to them, went up as official messengers and Titus was brought as an assistant. Paul went up to Jerusalem due to a revelation from God. Therefore he did not make the journey for the purpose of securing recognition of his authority from the leaders of Jerusalem. Paul laid before the leaders his gospel and this fact "had an important bearing on the misrepresentations of the Judaisers: he did not lay his Gospel officially before the assembly of the Apostles, but privately before the Three" (*Historical Commentary*, 295).

Paul's entire concern in relating these details is to demonstrate that his gospel was not from men but from God and needed no official authorization from the Jerusalem leaders.

This was certainly not, it seems clear, the Council of Jerusalem. Ramsay is correct to note: "It would be absurd, and
worse than absurd, that Paul should assure the Galatians
that he consulted the Three privately, if he also laid it before
them in public in their official assembly. We must understand
Paul to imply that he made no public consultation on this
subject" (Ramsay, 295). Of course, Ramsay at this time held
to a late date for Galatians but his comments are applicable
to an early date that assumes the Council had not yet taken
place. Ramsay adds that Paul's consultation with the apostles
was not as authoritative guides but as friends. He consulted
them to avoid future misunderstanding and for the purpose
of unity in the service of Christ. The question of Titus, an
uncircumcised Gentile, was not raised; his Christian freedom
was recognized by all. Paul's concern for the Jerusalem poor
is underscored.

This private interview with the "pillars", it seems clear,
took place during the "famine visit" of Acts 11:30. Paul had
gone up in response to a revelation – as we find in Acts 11,
which describes how a prophet from Jerusalem called Agabus
had come down to Antioch and foretold a widespread famine
by the Holy Spirit. In response to this prophecy the disciples
at Antioch determined to send relief to the brothers in Judea.
Moreover, Acts 11:30 tells us that the church in Antioch sent
this relief through Barnabas and Saul.

The whole purpose of Paul's biography is demonstrated by
1:11, that his gospel was not according to man. Each of the
three parts of the biographical data makes this plain. First, his
character before being arrested by the grace of Jesus Christ
emphasizes this. Then the data telling how little opportunity
he had of coming into contact with the apostles – only one
short visit with Peter – further drives home the independence
of his gospel. Moreover, the "effect of the contrast between
fifteen days in Jerusalem and fourteen years in Syria-Cilicia is
great; and it must have been greater to the Galatians, because
they had been listening to descriptions of Paul's indebtedness
to the older Apostles, his frequent consultation of them, and
so on" (Ramsay, 302).

The purpose of the biography is to show that Paul had not received his gospel from the apostles at Jerusalem or from any man. It was not necessary for Paul to reference the Jerusalem Council since his purpose was to demonstrate that up to the time of his second Jerusalem visit he had received nothing of his gospel from men. As with Acts, so here: when Paul had preached the gospel to the Galatians he had only, since his conversion, visited Jerusalem twice. Acts relates the visits with its own purposes in mind (9:26-30; 11:27-30), while Paul relates the visits with different purposes in view – to demonstrate that the gospel he preached was not according to man. One other important piece of biographical data will be considered in 2:11ff., which details Paul's rebuking of Peter in Antioch.

We now move on to a more detailed look at the text. Paul has shown that the gospel is **not according to man** (1:11) by pointing to his thrilling call by grace and complete change from a despiser of the gospel to apostle and missionary to the Gentiles. He has also demonstrated that the gospel is **not according to man** by rehearsing his visit to Jerusalem three years after his conversion and by reciting his itinerary far from the leaders and Jewish-Christians there. Paul's gospel was not derived from man and his preaching of that gospel of free grace did not depend upon any human leadership, even the leadership in Jerusalem.

Paul is making two interrelated points about the gospel he preached. *Firstly*, he demonstrates "the nature of the gospel as contrary to human expectations, not based on human effort" (Lategan, 426). As the letter unfolds Paul will continue to show that human effort contributes nothing to justification. For example, he will preach grace over against Abraham's attempt to fulfill the promise through human effort – that is, through Hagar's surrogate pregnancy (4:21-31). *Secondly*, Paul shows that the Gentile mission was completely independent of the Jewish Christian community. This fact is important so that the Galatians could see that his preaching of free grace apart from works of the law needed no supplementation and that both Jew and Gentile were saved by grace alone. Both of these points are related to the very nature of the gospel itself. Any concern for his apostolic authority seems to be subservient to these two themes.[1]

Given the rebellious and confused nature of the human heart which continues to express itself in involved systems of truth suppression and works-righteousness, and given the various revisions of Paul's theology which throughout history have minimized the freeness of grace in his gospel, the two themes that form one strong fiber presented by Paul for the defense of the gospel must continue to inform and determine our own understanding of that gospel. The Pharisaical sect that influenced the Galatians long ago is not far removed from strivings of our own hearts apart from grace. "Since they had abstracted the law from the Gospel, they could not but regard religion in terms of merit..." (Berkouwer, *Sanctification*, 119). To be more precise, denials of grace rarely appear on the surface to be denials of grace! The grace of God is twisted through attempts to mingle grace and works in varying measures. Through Paul's controversy with the Galatians, the Lord reveals that sinners are saved by grace alone apart from works of the law; however the spirit that tries to blend the two may manifest itself in new settings.

The section 2:1-10 refers to Paul's second visit to Jerusalem. Here Paul shows that the very Jerusalem leaders to whom he

---

[1] Concern over Paul's apostleship is subservient to the defense of the gospel itself. Cousar, 16: "The opponents in Galatia have either deliberately set out to undermine the authority of Paul's message by declaring his apostleship an inferior one, or, more likely, they have implied as much by the manner and content of their own preaching." Denigration of Paul's apostleship was more than likely by implication. See also the suggestive comments of David M. Hay, "Paul's Indifference To Authority," *JBL* 88 (1969): 44: "Yet the truth takes precedence over apostleship. While Paul may often have felt he could not defend his gospel without meeting attacks on his office, he nowhere makes the latter a primary argument for the former. This is borne out by the development of thought in Galatians 2:15-21, which does not end with anything like 'I have now proven the legitimacy of my apostleship; hence my message is valid.' On the contrary, Paul proceeds in the ensuing chapters to mount a variety of arguments for his gospel, with hardly another reference to apostleship. Indeed, it seems that Paul's concluding argument for his apostleship in Galatians 1-2 is the truth of his message."

was not indebted for his gospel preached and approved the same gospel as Paul's! The adverb **then** (*epeita*) of 2:1 connects the narration with the preceding discussion and the themes found there. Paul now explains the significance of his second Jerusalem visit. **Then after fourteen years I went up again to Jerusalem with Barnabas, and also brought along Titus.** Whether **after fourteen years** means fourteen years after Paul's conversion or fourteen years after his ministry in the regions of Syria and Cilicia (which is more likely) "either way, by this time Paul had had a significant missionary career, so there was no question of his receiving his essential message on this visit" (Morris).[2] In his description of his visit to Jerusalem Paul's focus is on the independence of his gospel and ministry from the Jerusalem leadership. Paul did not come alone to Jerusalem but came **with Barnabas, and also brought along Titus.**

Paul adds significantly **I went up according to revelation** in order to stress the ongoing theme that his gospel and call to minister that gospel to the Gentiles were not according to man. His instructions were received by revelatory means and man did not prompt his movements. For whatever reasons, after all these years of ministry to the Gentiles, Paul's gospel of grace with no supplements had become controversial. So he went to Jerusalem leaders by revelation **and presented to them the gospel that he preached among the Gentiles**. **According to revelation** underscores that Paul did not present his gospel to the Jerusalem leadership out of any lack of confidence. The entire preceding context in which Paul expresses his assurance that he had received his gospel by divine revelation should rule out of court any suggestion that Paul doubted his gospel. Duncan points out that Paul "submitted" his gospel; he was not consulting the Jerusalem leaders by seeking their approval, but **presented to them the gospel that I preach among the Gentiles**.

This meeting, some think, was perhaps heated and controversial. Betz points to Paul's use of official political

---

[2] Ridderbos: "It is self-evident that the *terminus a quo* is not again (as in 1:18) to be reckoned from the date of Paul's conversion, but from the visit to Jerusalem."

language in this context and concludes that "the matter at stake was to force the church authorities in Jerusalem to give *post factum* approval to the Pauline gospel in the face of heated opposition, and thereby help to defeat the anti-Pauline forces in Asia Minor. Such an objective requires considerable leverage. Thus Paul did not go as a humble petitioner, but as a tough negotiator who forced the Jerusalem authorities to make a decision which one can imagine they made only with great reluctance."

Betz seems to push rhetorical analysis too far, or perhaps in the wrong direction. His comments sound like a hold-over from the old theories of F. C. Baur. The text does not indicate disagreement between Paul and the Jerusalem leadership. The target of Paul's concerns is not Peter, James and John but the Judaizers. Paul had the rare critical ability to see where a falsehood would lead and the courage to challenge any view that would compromise in the least the gratuitous nature of the gospel. The church of Christ stands in need of Christians with such penetrating insight now – Christians who will courageously challenge without compromise every deviation from the proclamation of grace.

Paul presented his gospel **privately to those who have a reputation, lest I run or had run in vain. Those who have a reputation** is not the language of irony. Paul apparently alludes to the manner in which the Judaizers in Galatia groundlessly appealed to the Jerusalem leadership in support of their deviations.[3]

What does Paul mean by **lest I run or had run in vain**? To think that Paul had some doubts about his gospel would be contrary to all that Paul has thus far written. Surely Paul means that his labor for the spread of the gospel among the

---

[3] Duncan: "It is merely that his opponents had grandiloquently made use of the phrase 'the authorities' in reference to the leaders at Jerusalem..."

Hendriksen is also to the point: "Since the term 'those of repute' occurs not only once but, in one form or another, no less than four times (2:2, 6a, 6b, 9), it is safe to assume that the apostle is here quoting the phraseology of the opponents. He is, however, not trying to belittle the men of prominence in the church at Jerusalem. He does not use the term 'those of repute' to heap scorn upon them or to ridicule them. True, the language he uses here implies

Gentiles would be in danger if even a hint of approbation were given to the false teachers.[4]

Paul next affirms that the Jerusalem leadership did not require Titus to be circumcised. **But not even Titus, who was with me, even though he was a Greek, was compelled to be circumcised. But** connects the thought with Paul's concern not to **run in vain.** Indeed, Titus is evidence that his ministry among the Gentiles was successful and that he had not **run in vain** (Betz). Titus was an uncircumcised Gentile believer in Christ. It is reasonable to think that Paul brought Titus to Jerusalem as a testimony to God's grace to the Gentiles through his ministry. Even though Titus' presence obviously caused a stir, prompting certain Jewish Christians to insist upon his circumcision for full membership in the church, the Jerusalem leadership agreed with Paul. As Paul puts it **but not even Titus, who was with me, even**

---

a degree of resentment, but the latter is not directed at James, Cephas, and John, but at the legalists who have made it a habit to exalt these three at the expense of Paul...."

Ramsay, *Historical Commentary*, 301, argues that the word simply means "the recognized or accepted leaders" having no depreciatory sense attached to it.

[4] Eadie: "Should the church, in defiance of his arguments, experience, and appeals, insist on compliance with circumcision as essential to admission to the church, then on this point which signalized his preaching as the apostle of the Gentiles, his labour would be so far in vain, and the Gentile churches would be in danger of losing their precious freedom."

Duncan also notes: "His (Paul's) concern was not that his gospel to the Gentiles should conform to the requirements of the Jerusalem authorities, but that they should understand and agree with him in his interpretation of the gospel."

Martyn sees it this way: "The danger of a rift in the one church is fully as horrifying to him as he writes to the Galatians as it can possibly have been to the Antioch church and to himself at the time of the meeting. If the Jerusalem leaders had uttered those terrible words, Paul would surely have stood firmly by 'the truth of the gospel,' as he will show in the next episode (2:11-14). But he would have been shaken to his roots, for that development would have destroyed his assumption that the one 'truth of the gospel' is in fact bringing into being one church of God made up of former Jews and former Gentiles (3:28; 6:15). If the Jerusalem church had failed to perceive that grand picture, the result would have been that his work was not bearing fruit *as a branch of the one vine.* That is the danger he considers in the words 'lest...I was running or had run in vain'."

though he was a Greek, was compelled to be circumcised, that is, by the official Jerusalem leadership.

The exultant conclusion to be drawn from this incident is that there is nothing to be added to the gospel of free grace, no supplement needed, for a sinner to be accepted by God or for full membership in the church. Acts 15:1 ("Unless you are circumcised according to the custom of Moses you cannot be saved") indicates that the Judaizers' requirement of circumcision was not simply a matter of conformity to ritual but a matter of salvation itself! It is for that reason that circumcision in this context is for Paul a matter of life and death. Acts 15:1 is a brief summary of the entire matter faced by Paul in the Galatian controversy.[5] At issue was **the truth of the gospel** (2:5). Even though, after the Jerusalem Council in particular, the Judaizers may not have presented the issue of law-keeping in terms of "salvation," Paul understands that the requirements they wished to place upon Gentile Christians insidiously demand such a conclusion. The Judaizers promoted a works-righteousness world-view entailing fundamentally a denial of the freedom purchased by Christ.

Paul uses anacoluthon, a grammatical break in the sequence of his thought to describe the surreptitious nature of his opponents. He describes them as **infiltrators, false brothers who slipped in to ambush our liberty that we have in Christ Jesus, so that they might enslave us.** By **infiltrators** (*tous pareisaktous*[6]) Paul probably indicates a motive of

---

[5] Some have argued that Paul had Titus circumcised so that he might not function as an outsider in the Jerusalem environment, that this was the ground for the charge that Paul was a man-pleaser (Gal. 1:10) and that he still preached circumcision (Gal. 5:11). In Galatians 2:3 Paul would then mean that, even though Titus was circumcised, it was not under compulsion. This sounds plausible but seems very unlikely in a context in which Paul is insisting that he did not yield to attempts to bring spiritual slavery through a supplement to the gospel of grace! The context surely demands that Paul opposed the attempt to force circumcision upon his Gentile convert, that he indeed was not circumcised, and that the Jerusalem leadership agreed with his grace-driven opposition to the attempt.

[6] Robertson: "Late verbal adjective *pareisaktos* from the double compound verb *pareisagō*, found in papyri in the sense of brought in by the side or on the sly as here."

stealth, though he might simply mean that they did not rightly belong to the body of professing believers. Furthermore, they were **false brothers** (*pseudadelphous*), meaning "sham Christians" (REB). Their perversion of the gospel of grace and desire to entrap others in their works-righteousness world-view disqualifies them from being regarded as true brothers. The aim of **those infiltrators, false brothers who slipped in** was **to ambush[7] our liberty that we have in Christ Jesus, so that they might enslave us.** No matter how the Judaizers viewed themselves, Paul sees clearly that adherence to their viewpoint would lead to a sacrifice of the gospel of freedom leading to enslavement.[8] Freedom is the grand theme of the epistle. The truth of the gospel sets sinners free!

The sentence is undoubtedly unfinished due to Paul's excitement over the destructiveness of the Judaizing viewpoint. Paul returns to the matter of the desire of his opponents, that Titus should be circumcised, by insisting **we did not give in to them even for a moment so that the truth of the gospel might remain with you.** Paul was the most pliable of men when the gospel itself was not at issue (1 Cor. 9:19-23; Acts 16:3; 21:17-26). However, when **the truth of the gospel** was at risk Paul was adamantine! Paul did not yield **even for a moment** so that the unsullied gospel of grace might be proclaimed to sinners such as the Galatians (**so that the truth of the gospel**

---

[7] The aorist infinitive *kataskopēsai* has been variously translated *to spy out* (Moffatt, RSV, ESV), *to spy on* (Phillips, REB, NRSV, NIV), *to find out about* (TEV). Since the word can mean in some contexts "to spy out" or "lie in wait for" (*BDAG*), combining the thought of these possible meanings with the sense of stealth indicated in the previous terminology, I have thought that translating the verb *to ambush* best captures Paul's meaning.

[8] Ridderbos: "What stands between the law and the believers, in respect not merely of the results of transgressing the law and the possibility of fulfilling it, but in respect also of establishing the content of the law, is: Christ. It is in that comprehensive sense that the believers in Christ Jesus can be said to be free (of the law). And it was this inalienable possession of the church which the false brethren tried to take away from it, by trying to bring it once more under the dominion of the law. The thing the apostle is here describing was in general the effort of the Judaistic zealots in the church, but it was particularly the effort of those whom Paul had come to know as his opponents in Jerusalem."

might remain with you). Had Paul given ground the damage done to the proclamation of free grace might have been irrevocable. And now, the Galatians themselves are in danger of accommodating a false gospel that will shackle them in the bonds of law-keeping as a means of righteousness. There was, then, far more to the Judaizing scheme of circumcising Titus than met the eye. Had Paul yielded to their demands he would have sacrificed the gospel of free grace.

Verses 6-10 that follow are incredibly complex. Betz observes that these verses appear to be "one convoluted sentence". He also rightly notes that it is not carelessly composed. Indeed the "enormous care" that Paul put into the composition of these words can only be because they are at the core of his argument.[9] Paul's concern is to show that he did not derive his gospel from the Jerusalem leadership and that they supported his ministry and preaching the gospel to the Gentiles without supplement. **And from those held in high regard – whatever they were matters not to me; God does not show favoritism – those held in high regard added nothing to me**. By referencing the Jerusalem leadership as **those held in high regard** Paul did not intend disrespect. He acknowledges that they are eminent men whose authority should be esteemed. However, *respecting the gospel* he can say **whatever they were matters not to me; God does not show favoritism**, that is, his gospel and ministry were not subject to their judgment. By **God does not show favoritism**, literally, "God does not receive the face of man" (see Deut. 10:17), Paul means that, in any case, no matter how they were hallowed, the rank of the apostles could not determine the matter of the gospel's content.[10]

---

[9] Betz: "If this is the case, then there must be a relationship between the events at Jerusalem and the present crisis in Galatia. Then the present agitators and their theological position must in some way be related to the authorities in Jerusalem. This relationship probably existed not only in Paul's mind, but in the minds of the agitators and the Galatians as well." Betz sees a relation between this passage and the "men from James" in 2:11-14.

[10] See David M. Hay, "Paul's Indifference To Authority," *JBL* 88 (1969): 36-44. On page 41 he writes: "Paul's indifference to the Jerusalem chiefs is grounded on God's... It has already been argued that 6b bears on the issue

Though Paul's gospel and ministry were not subject to the
Jerusalem apostles, as a matter of fact they agreed with Paul
that **those held in high regard added nothing to me.** The
apostles made no attempt to require Paul to accommodate his
gospel to the Judaizing element nor did they pressure him to
supplement his gospel in any way. Whatever the demands of
his Galatian opponents they could claim no assistance from
the Jerusalem leadership.

Paul adds **on the contrary** (*tounantion*), that is, rather
than supporting the Judaizing position, the apostles in
Jerusalem sustained, encouraged and confirmed Paul's view.
**On the contrary, when they saw that the gospel had been
entrusted to me for the uncircumcised just as the gospel
had been entrusted to Peter for the circumcised** – note
Paul's wording, **the gospel,** the same gospel, the gospel upon
which they were agreed! – this is Paul's point, to demonstrate
that he and the Jerusalem apostles were involved in the
same gospel ministry, only with a different ethnic focus.
The gospel had been **entrusted** to Paul to be preached to
the **uncircumcised** and the gospel had been entrusted to
Peter **for the circumcised**, but the gospel preached by both
was one and the same. Paul adds parenthetically, **for He
who enabled Peter to work effectively as an apostle to
the circumcised also enabled me to work effectively as
an apostle to the Gentiles**, in order to indicate the Lord's
efficient work through them both for the same gospel. Paul
then concludes his lengthy sentence by stressing the unity
of the apostles around the gospel of grace: **and knowing the
grace which was given to me, James and Cephas and John,
who were held in high regard as pillars, gave to me and
Barnabas the right hand of partnership in order that we
might serve the Gentiles and they the circumcised.** Even
in his use of the aorist passive participle regarding **the grace
which was given to me** (*dotheisan*) Paul underscores his
insistence on the sovereignty and freedom of grace.

---

of deciding the content of the gospel. If 6c is meant to bolster that clause, it
is best understood as meaning that God is indifferent to human distinctions
(even apostleship) when a question of his truth is at stake."

Grace is the issue faced in Galatia. The church must understand this! What the Judaizers were attempting was no small matter, but was a subversion of the very gospel by which sinners are saved. Paul stresses the agreement of the apostles on the gospel. James, Cephas and John, Paul and Barnabas shook hands on it. There was no difference in the gospel to be proclaimed, only a different target group to whom Paul and the others were focused in taking that same gospel. The Jerusalem *leaders* **gave to me and Barnabas the right hand**[11] **of partnership**[12] **in order that we might serve the Gentiles and they the circumcised.** The Jerusalem leaders, far from giving ammunition to the Judaizing arsenal, approve of Paul's gospel and support his ministry. Those who were of special eminence in the Jerusalem leadership, **who were held in high regard as pillars**, agreed with Paul. **Pillars** was probably a term applied to the Jerusalem leaders by the Judaizers who falsely claimed their support. "How Paul's soul must have exulted as he told this tale! What a travesty of the truth was all the talk of the Judaizers about the 'subjection' enforced on him by the Jerusalem 'authorities'! Here was no 'subjection', but 'fellowship' in the work of the gospel; no enforcement of a superior authority, but mutual recognition by each party of the other's God-appointed sphere of service" (Duncan).[13]

---

[11] Morris: "'To give the right hand' was apparently a widespread way of indicating friendship in the ancient world." He references Josephus, *Antiquities,* XVIII. 328.

[12] I was initially inclined to retain the original term *koinōnia* in the English translation for these reasons. Firstly, it is a term that has come into the vocabularly of modern Christians who understand that the term is richer than the one word "fellowship" can indicate. Secondly, for Paul the term has a religious content. See Hauck, *TDNT,* III, 804 who notes that Paul uses the term *koinōnia* "for the religious fellowship (participation) of the believer in Christ and Christian blessings, and for the mutual fellowship of believers." The *koinōnia* of the believer presuppose *koinōnia* with Christ and partaking of the Spirit. In the end, I have opted for the less awkward "partnership", but those expounding the text will want to bring out the fullness of meaning found in the word's usage in Paul.

[13] In view of the agreement on the gospel between Paul and the Jerusalem leaders, Duncan (53, 54) is right to call to task Burton who claimed that "even in content there was an important and far reaching difference

Paul concludes with a final result of his Jerusalem conference. **Only they encouraged us to remember the poor, and I was already eager to do this very thing.** This qualification does not detract from Paul's argument. Rather, Paul insists that no conditions were placed upon the exercise of his ministry at all. The one request of the Jerusalem leaders was that he **remember the poor.** Paul was not asked in any way by the Jerusalem leaders to modify his message. As for the one request that the poor be remembered, Paul was already **eager to do this very thing.** In fact, the very reason for the "famine visit" (Acts 11:30) was concern for the poor. The aorist *espoudasa* (eager to do) may indicate that Paul was already actively engaged in collections for the poor. At any rate, the collection for the Jerusalem poor became a hallmark of Paul's ministry (Rom. 15:25 ff; 1 Cor. 16:1 ff; 2 Cor. 8 and 9).[14]

---

between the gospel that Paul preached and that which Peter preached, the difference, in fact, between a legalistic and a non-legalistic gospel" (Burton, *Commentary*, 92). This is a serious misconstruction of the situation. It is true that circumcision was not to be enjoined on Paul's Gentile Christians, as it was to be on Peter's Jewish ones: but in the latter case it was not Peter who enjoined it, and it was not enjoined *as part of the gospel....* Thus there were not two different *gospels,* the one for the Jew and the other for the Gentile. There was a difference of soil into which the seed was cast, but the seed itself was the same; and in each case the same God was at work (v. 8).

[14] Ridderbos: "The request for collections implies particularly difficult circumstances at Jerusalem (cf. 2 Cor. 8:14). In Acts 11:29 ff. the occasion for a collection was the serious famine under Claudius. Whether the consequences of that had not yet been overcome cannot be determined. It is likely, though, that by this means the thought, expressed by Paul in Romans 15:27, namely, that the Gentile churches had a certain material obligation to the church at Jerusalem, to be given in gratitude for the spiritual gift that it had given them, had found permanent lodging also with the leaders at Jerusalem, who accordingly came out in a plea for their poor." It is interesting to note that the delegation accompanying Paul to Jerusalem in Acts 20:4 included representatives from Berea, Thessalonica, Derbe and Lystra and the Roman Province of Asia but no one from North Galatia. This would be curious if Paul had indeed founded churches in North Galatia, but if he did not it is what one would expect.

5.
Justified Through Faith in Jesus Christ
(2:11-21)

Translation

But when Cephas came into Antioch, I opposed him to his face, because he was clearly at fault. For before certain persons came from James he would eat regularly with the Gentiles. But after they came he began withdrawing and separating himself, fearing those of the circumcision party. And the rest of the Jews joined with him in his pretense; so that even Barnabas was actually led astray with them by their hypocrisy. But when I saw that they were not consistent with the truth of the gospel, I said to Cephas before them all: "If you being a Jew live like a Gentile and not like a Jew, how can you require the Gentiles to live as Jews?"

We are by birth Jews and not Gentile sinners,[1] knowing that a man is not justified by works of law but through faith in Jesus Christ, and we have believed in Jesus Christ, in order that we might be justified by faith in Christ and not by works of law, because by works of law no flesh shall be justified. But if while seeking to be justified in Christ we were found to be sinners, then is Christ a servant of sin? Absolutely not! For if I build again the things I destroyed, I prove myself a

---

[1] We are retaining Paul's thought which is not smooth, possibly parenthetical. A smooth translation might read: "Though we are by birth Jews and not Gentile sinners, [we know] that a man is not justified by works of law but through faith in Jesus Christ. And we have believed in Jesus Christ..."

transgressor. For I through the law died to law so that I might live for God. I have been crucified with Christ; it is no longer I who live, but Christ lives in me, and the life I now live in the flesh, I live in faith of the Son of God who loved me and gave Himself for me. I do not nullify the grace of God. For if righteousness is through law, then Christ died for nothing.

Summary

In order to demonstrate the gracious character of the gospel Paul rehearses Peter's compromise in Antioch. Paul opposed Peter because he withdrew from table fellowship with Gentile Christians under pressure from "certain men (who) came from James". Peter's withdrawal was a reversal of his former practice and contrary to his convictions. Peter's actions influenced others to join in his hypocritical act. Paul resisted Peter whose actions even swayed Barnabas, because "they were not consistent with the truth of the gospel". Peter, though a Jewish believer, had felt free to follow Gentile practices but now was requiring Gentiles to follow Jewish customs, the very law from which Peter had been freed! This was contrary to the doctrine of justification by faith in Christ apart from works of law. Since Peter and the Jewish believers had themselves been declared righteous apart from works, how could they place works of law between themselves and fellow believers in Christ? Paul anticipates an objection, namely, that he preached antinomianism. He insists that Christ is not "a servant of sin". But the accusation of antinomianism did not dampen his preaching against works of law as a means of justification. He explains that if one, having trusted in Christ for justification, attempts to "build again" on the basis of works, the gospel would be overturned and the believer would be submitting himself once again to the law's condemnation. Paul insists that he "died to law" because "through law" Christ bore its just demands. Co-crucifixion with Christ, however, means life for him, a new life by faith in the Son of God who "loved" Paul and "gave Himself" for him. Paul would have nothing to do with invalidating justification by re-asserting works of law. If sinners contribute one stitch to their own righteousness, then "Christ died for nothing"!

Comment
In order to demonstrate that the gospel was not according to man Paul next rehearses Peter's compromise of that gospel in Antioch. There is much that we do not know about the incident. We do not know why Peter went there, nor precisely when. We do not know whether those associated with James were his emissaries, or if they made use of James' name in a ploy to buttress the Judaizing viewpoint. What must be stressed is that from the beginning Paul saw Peter's actions as contrary to the gospel. Moreover, as Ramsay has noted, in this passage is found the whole truth of Galatians in embryo (*Historical Commentary*, 306). **The truth of the gospel** (v. 14) was at issue! Any attempt to understand Galatians 2:11-21 without remembering that **the truth of the gospel** is Paul's central concern will skew the meaning of Paul's confrontation of Peter and of the explanation of the gospel that follows.

N. T. Wright, for example, finds the starting point for interpreting this passage in the question, "What does it mean to be a member of God's people?" He interprets Paul's very first direct reference to justification (v.16) to mean "*the way in which God's people have been redefined.*" **Righteousness** (v. 21), therefore, according to Wright, means "*one's status as a member of God's people.* It means "covenant status" or "covenant membership". Paul is denying that this covenant status is defined by Torah – which it would still be if Peter and the others had their way. He is denying that Christians should separate for meals, with the Jews at one table and the uncircumcised Gentiles at the other. The doctrine of justification by faith was born into the world as the key doctrine underlying the *unity* of God's renewed people." Wright thinks "justification" in Paul is "not a statement about how someone becomes a Christian" but is "a statement about *who belongs to the people of God, and how you can tell that in the present.*" Accordingly, the point about "works of Torah … is not about the works some might think you have to perform in order to *become* a member of God's people, but the works you have to perform to *demonstrate that you are* a member

of God's people."[2] Wright's misunderstanding of Paul fails
to comprehend that his entire concern up to this point has
been and continues to be that the gospel is not according to
man! Paul's concern is with the **truth of the gospel**. Wright
substitutes ecclesiology for soteriology by failing to see that the
gospel is the issue and that ecclesiology is epiphenomenal. In
other words, Wright makes an important result of the gospel,
namely the unity of God's people both Jew and Gentile, into
the gospel itself.

It is because of the urgency of the gospel message that
Paul rehearses the events at Antioch.[3] **But when Cephas came
into Antioch, I opposed him to his face, because he was
clearly at fault**. Though we are given only a glimpse of the
incident Paul's language nonetheless reveals its seriousness.
His opposition to Peter, **because he was clearly at fault**,[4] is
explained by Peter's actions at the fellowship gathering of
the church in Antioch. There was no question in Peter's mind
that Jewish and Gentile believers should, because of the
gospel, fellowship together. Table fellowship between Jews
and Gentiles is a consequence of the work of Christ. For a
Jewish believer to separate from Gentile believers would be
a reprehensible denial of the gospel. Yet this is precisely why
Paul found it necessary to rebuke Peter **to his face**. Prior to this,
Peter had been consistent with the gospel. **For before certain
persons came from James he would eat regularly with the
Gentiles**. Peter, who had baptized Cornelius (Acts 10:47, 48)

---

[2] N. T. Wright (2005), *Paul*, Fortress Press, 111-13. The italics are in the
original. Compare J. D. G. Dunn, "The Incident at Antioch (Gal. 2:11-18),"
JSNT 18 (1983) 3-57.

[3] The church at Antioch was a mixed congregation of Jews and Gentiles
with extensive outreach among the Gentiles. A church with many gifts and
means, it was also a testing ground for the way in which genuine ministry
to all people groups would develop in the church. Thus Antioch was, next to
Jerusalem, the greatest metropolis connected with the spread of Christianity
and the fountainhead of missionary activity to the Gentiles. An important
city in its own right, Antioch was the Roman headquarters of Syria and
Cilicia and the seat of the imperial mint. It was a city in which Roman,
Greek, Syrian and Jew rubbed shoulders. It was at Antioch that believers in
Christ were first dubbed "Christians" (Acts 11:26).

[4] ὅτι κατεγνωσμένος ἦν : "clearly at fault" or condemned, blameworthy.

and had defended his actions before critical Jewish believers (Acts 11:1-18), understood full well that fellowship with Gentile believers was a consequence of the gospel. If the Jerusalem church practiced fellowship and the Eucharist in accordance with Jewish food regulations, the church at Antioch evidently did not, and Jewish believers adjusted to the change.

Therefore Peter **would eat regularly with the Gentiles,** as is possibly implied by the imperfect tense of *sunesthiō* (was eating with). **But after they came he began withdrawing and separating himself, fearing those of the circumcision party.** Who these persons designated *from James* were, we simply do not know.[5] Were they sent as James' emissaries? Did they make use of James' name to promote Jewish practices among Jewish Christians? Although we do not know much about those **from James** it must have been due to their strict observance of Jewish cleansing and dietary laws that Peter felt pressured, whether directly or indirectly, to change his approach from one of open fellowship with Gentile believers to one of distance and separation. The imperfects possibly imply that this change happened gradually (*hupestellen kai aphōridzen*). Peter began **withdrawing** and eventually **separating** altogether from table fellowship, and presumably the Lord's Supper as a part of that fellowship with Gentile believers, **fearing those of the circumcision party**. Betz thinks that Peter feared political consequences, loss of power. "Peter chose the position of power and denied his theological convictions."[6] Fear of criticism

---

[5] Martyn, in his interesting essay on "The Circumcision Party As A Group of Christian Jews In The Jerusalem Church" (236-40) says, commenting on Acts 11:2: "Apparently in addition to the usage in which 'the persons drawn from those who are circumcised' refers to Jewish Christians in general (so Rom 4:12, Eusebius, and Acts 10:45), the expression had acquired the status of a technical term in the vocabulary of the Jerusalem church, referring in fact to a *party* within that community. Unlike other members of the church, the circumcision party retained its Jewish derivation as an essential mark of its identity. And it attempted to preserve that derived identity for the whole of the church by demanding consistent and – within the church – universal separation from Gentiles at meals."

[6] Ridderbos thinks "the motive was the fear that the Jews would regard Peter as a transgressor of the law." The views of Betz and of Ridderbos are, of course, quite compatible.

and declining prestige rather than loss of power are more
likely reasons for Peter's withdrawal from table fellowship.
Compare the attack Peter experienced in Acts 11:1ff upon his
return from Cornelius.

Peter's actions influenced other Jewish Christians to
compromise the gospel message by withdrawing from table
fellowship with Gentile Christians. **And the rest of the Jews
joined with him in his pretense; so that even Barnabas
was actually led astray with them by their hypocrisy**. Peter
contradicted the gospel and its implications, doing so even
against his own conscience (**his pretense,** or **hypocrisy**). But
we never sin alone. **The rest of the Jews,** meaning Jewish
Christians of Antioch, influenced by Peter's example, **joined
with him in his pretense.** "This was *hypocrisy* on their part
and Peter's, because, although at the bottom of their hearts
convinced of Christian freedom, they, from fear of men...
concealed the more liberal conviction of which they were
conscious, and behaved just as if they entertained the opposite
view" (Meyer). Paul in utter amazement points out that even
Barnabas was not immune from the spreading compromise
of the gospel. Indeed, **even Barnabas was actually led astray
with them by[7] their hypocrisy**.

Paul could not stand by while the gospel was fundamentally
compromised. He saw that **they were not consistent with the
truth of the gospel**. The term *orthopodousin*, a New Testament
hapax legomenon, according to Preisker, seems to mean "not
to waver", indicating here "that they deny freedom from the
Law and justification by faith alone" (*TDNT*, V. 451). However,
BDAG glosses this as "walk straight, proceed directly" on the
basis of Hellenistic usage. The metaphor is that of a confused
wanderer, someone who veers from the path, such as a
staggering drunk who cannot walk a straight line. Of course,
the action of Peter and others was not an overt denial of the
gospel, but it was a denial of the gospel all the same. In view
of this Paul could not keep silent! Paul, with clear-sighted
and penetrating vision, understood that this compromise of

---

[7] See Meyer: **By** not **to their hypocrisy.** An instrumental dative.

the gospel was no small matter and must be addressed! Betz well observes that the contrast with 2:4-5 is clear. "If Paul had yielded to the pressures of the "false brothers" at Jerusalem, he would have ended up in the same situation in which he now sees Cephas and his group. He did, however, withstand in Jerusalem, as they should have done now in Antioch. The same is, of course, true now of the Galatians (see 4:8-10)."

Since Peter, the other Jewish Christians and even Barnabas **were not consistent with the truth of the gospel** Paul was conscience-bound to correct Peter there and then. **I said to Cephas before them all: "If you being a Jew live like a Gentile and not like a Jew, how can you require the Gentiles to live as Jews?"** Though a Jewish believer, Peter prior to his compromise realized that he was free to live **like a Gentile**, that is, apart from Jewish regulations. How then could he now **require**[8] **the Gentiles to live as Jews,** that is, how could he require Gentile Christians to keep the very law from which Peter had recognized that he was free? Peter's compromise was incomprehensible!

Fundamentally, Peter's compromise was a massive denial of justification by faith to which Paul now turns his attention, though this has been the focus of his concern all along.[9] **We are by birth Jews and not Gentile sinners** – the **we** is in the emphatic position at the beginning of the sentence. Peter, Paul and the other Jewish believers **are by birth Jews**, literally, "by nature" (*phusei*), possessing many remarkable privileges and are **not Gentile sinners.** "Paul is appropriating the current Jewish conception and linguistic practice" (Ridderbos) in making this distinction. However, though Peter and Paul were Jews by birth, no privilege earns merit before God. Theological conviction, **knowing,** is placed over against the privileges of

---

[8] Martyn in his comment on 2:3 points to the significance of the verb "compel" or require in Galatians. Compare 2:3; 2:14 and 6:12.

[9] It is difficult to tell whether verses 15-21 continue Paul's discourse to Peter, summarize his concerns or elaborate upon the thought content of the event. There is probably some progression from the actual words with which Paul confronted Peter, and its elaboration has the conflict in Galatia in mind.

birth (Betz): **knowing that a man is not justified by works of law**[10] **but through faith in Jesus Christ**.

Denial of table fellowship is such a serious matter because it is a compromise of *the truth of the gospel*, the core of which is Paul's teaching about justification **through faith in Jesus Christ.** By justification Paul means the gracious act by which sinners are declared judicially righteous in the sight of God on the basis of the work of Jesus Christ on their behalf. How dare Peter withdraw from table fellowship with Gentile believers? "For whatever the Jews might possess in privileged superiority to the Gentiles, they no more than the Gentiles could, on the basis of their privileged position, achieve a righteousness with God" (Ridderbos). Of this Paul is confident – **knowing.** If God's verdict upon sinners is "not guilty" and one of acceptance in His court of law by faith in Christ, who are we to act judgmentally on our brothers and to exclude from the table those God accepts?

For Paul, the language of justification refers to a forensic act. Justification is defined over against condemnation, as in Romans 5:16: "Again, the gift of God is not like the result of the one man's sin: The judgment followed one sin and brought condemnation, but the gift followed many trespasses and brought justification." Also in 2 Corinthians 3:9: "If the ministry that condemns men is glorious, how much more glorious is the ministry that brings righteousness!" Justification answers to condemnation. In Romans 3 the "righteousness of God, apart from law" comes through the propitiatory sacrifice of Christ and "is credited to (the believer) as righteousness" (Rom 4:3). See also Romans 4:3-6, 9ff.; 22-25. For this reason Paul can cite Psalm 32:1, 2 in the context of his discussion of justification in Romans 4:8: "Blessed are they whose transgressions are forgiven, whose sins are covered. Blessed is the man whose

---

[10] Where Paul does not use the definite article we have followed him in the translation. See Zerwick, paragraph 177: "In the epistle of Galatians alone the word *nomos* occurs ten times with the article and 21 times without it. Although each case is to be judged on its own merits (182), we may say in general that ὁ νόμος is the Mosaic Law, while *nomos* is simply 'law' as such (although in the context the law in question may be the Mosaic one). Cf. Rom 3,20; 5,13."

sin the Lord will never count against him." "Law brings wrath" (Rom. 4:15), but justification answers to that wrath by the imputation of righteousness, specifically, a righteousness that Paul pointedly affirms "comes from God and is by faith" (Phil. 3:9). Negatively, justification is "not counting men's sins against them" (2 Cor. 5:19). The justificatory righteousness to which Paul refers in this portion of Galatians, consistent with what he always teaches on the subject, is that in Christ, apart from law, God provides for believing sinners "the righteousness which God's righteousness requires Him to require".[11] And, if we ask where Paul has discovered his doctrine of justification, the answer is not far to seek. Paul "constantly translates into theological vocabulary what Jesus had expressed in images and parables taken from everyday life."[12] Jesus, who also used forensic language in preaching the gospel (e.g. Luke 18:14), is Paul's predecessor in this matter. It was from Jesus that Paul learned, and that the entire church has come to understand, the important matter of table fellowship. It was taught us by the One who ate with tax collectors and sinners![13]

Paul insists that **a man is not justified by works of law but through faith in Jesus Christ.** By **works of law** Paul means moralistic works performed in the hope that God will accept us. Paul insists that God will accept no sinner on the basis of his own achievements.[14] Dunn sees "the works of the law"

---

[11] These striking words of William Cunningham are cited by John Macleod (1974), *Scottish Theology In Relation To Church History*, 137.

[12] Joachim Jeremias (1965), *The Central Message of The New Testament*, Charles Scribner's Sons, 69.

[13] For the biblical theology of justification, see Edmund P. Clowney, "The Biblical Doctrine of Justification by Faith" in D. A. Carson, ed. (1992), *Right With God – Justification in The Bible and The World*, Baker, 17-50.

[14] See Betram, *TDNT*, 2. 651: "The *erga nomou* which are here at issue for Paul have become a means of self-righteousness for the Jews. Hence they are no longer an expression of the absolute requirement of God – the Law is this for Paul in Gl. 5:3 – but they spring from man's arrogant striving after self-righteousness." "The work of man cannot stand before the exclusive operation of grace." For a full discussion of "the works of the law" in Romans, see C. E. B. Cranfield, "'The Works of the Law' in the Epistle to the Romans" in *On Romans*, 1-14. His excellent essay is in many ways a

as "identity markers", food laws, circumcision, the Sabbath, distinguishing Jews from Gentiles.[15] But the point to note, as Schnelle has observed, is that "Paul virtually makes the *insufficiency of the Torah* his point of departure. This is why ἔργα cannot be separated from the Torah itself, as though Paul only intended to criticize a certain style of Torah observance, a style "that does not mean living in accord with the Torah but simply makes the halakot its point of orientation'." Paul is not concerned with individual commands (of the Torah) but with the whole orientation of human life, as indicated by the prepositions ἐκ (out of, by, from) and διά (through, by means of) in the immediate context of 2:16 and "the thrust of the letter's argument as a whole. The identity concept Paul here criticizes understands one's relation to God to be "out of" one's own act, bound up with certain privileges, whereas he casts his own vote for a concept in which one's relation to God is mediated "through" faith in Jesus Christ and/or granted by God' (282).[16] This is why the Reformers were correct to apply Galatians to the works-righteousness system of their day and

---

trenchant response to "new perspective" views on Paul and the law. Bruce cites Cranfield, "St. Paul and the Law", *SJT* 17 (1964) 43-68, especially 55, who points out that Paul did not have the linguistic equipment for what we mean by the term "legalism" and so uses "law" or phrases containing "law" to express the concept of legalism.

[15] Dunn, "The New Perspective On Paul", *BJRL* 111: "The phrase 'works of the law' in Galatians 2:16 is, in fact, a fairly restricted one: it refers precisely to these same identity markers described above, *covenant* works – those regulations prescribed by the law which any good Jew would simply take for granted to describe what a good Jew did." See also his *Galatians* on this text *passim*.

[16] Schnelle later observes, 286, that: "Adopting the practice of circumcision and the observance of a cultic calendar would, as *pars pro toto legis* (a part of the law stands for the whole), rescind" Christian freedom. "They would move from freedom back into bondage..." This is helpful. Even when Paul might focus on circumcision, for example, it is as a part of the whole. See also Ridderbos, *Paul An Outline of His Theology*, 170-74.

Westerholm, *Perspective Old And New On Paul*, 367 n. also observes: "Thus when Paul contests the view that one can be declared righteous 'by the works of the law' (Gal. 2:26), he does not mean simply, 'One is not declared righteous by [observing] circumcision and the food and festival laws' – even though these issues provoked the current crisis. What he is rejecting is the view that one can be declared righteous on the basis (of one's

why it is right that we apply Galatians, with appropriate care, to whatever forms of moralism detract from the exclusivity of the gospel in our time and setting.[17]

To works of law Paul opposes faith in Christ. **A man is not justified by works of law but through faith in Jesus Christ. Works of law** and **faith in Jesus Christ** are diametrically opposed, and cannot be compatible or mingled.[18] Faith, not works, is the "alone instrument" (*Westminster Confession of Faith*, 11.2) by which justification is received. It has become popular to interpret the genitive διὰ πίστεως Ἰησοῦ Χριστοῦ (*dia pisteōs Iēsou Christou*) as referring to Christ's own faithfulness, a subjective genitive.[19] Although this is grammatically possible, it is not likely since **and we have believed in Jesus Christ** clearly corresponds to **faith in Jesus Christ.**[20] Betz points out that that faith is not "the basis" by which justification is earned, but that justification is mediated through faith. Christ, then, is the content of faith, the object

---

observance of) the Jewish law (cf. 2:21), of which these requirements were a part."

Calvin also insisted: "Paul therefore is not wandering from the point when he begins a disputation on the law as a whole, whereas the false apostles were arguing only about ceremonies. Their object in pressing ceremonies was that men might seek a salvation in the observance of the law, which they made out to be a meritorious service. Therefore Paul opposes to them the grace of Christ alone, and not the moral law." See also his comments on 2:16.

[17] Bultmann, *Theology of the NT*, I. 283 responds to Mundle: "He maintains that when Paul rejects works, only the works demanded by the Mosaic Law are meant...Against this interpretation must be said 1. Mundle does not ask himself *why* it is, according to Paul, that 'works' do not rightwise. If the reason they do not is that man must not have any boast before God (Rom. 3:27; 4:2), then the 'works *of the Law*,' on which Paul naturally concentrates in this discussion with the Jew, represent works in general, any and all works as works-of-merit." The entire section is helpful.

[18] See Bultmann, TDNT, VI, 219ff. "The whole of Galatians combats the possible misunderstanding that *pistis* has to be supplemented by the accomplishment of certain works of the Law." See also, Shreiner, "Works of Law in Paul", *Novum Testamentum* XXXIII, 3 (1991): 217-44.

[19] E.g. N. T. Wright, *Paul*, 47, 112.

[20] Bruce comments: "The principal and, indeed, conclusive argument for taking the genitive to be objective here is that, when Paul expresses

of faith. "Faith is never put forward as a work of creativity, of mediacy, of merit. It is never given as a ground of justification" (Berkouwer, *Justification*, 80).[21] Never is a person justified by works; only through faith in Christ. The Reformers were quite correct to insist on justification by grace alone through faith alone in Christ alone. "The foundation of free righteousness is when we are stripped of our own righteousness" (Calvin).

Peter and the Jewish believers had themselves trusted Christ for their justification: **and we have believed in Jesus Christ, in order that we might be justified by faith in Christ and not by works of law.** They had not trusted their own works in order to be just in God's court of law, but they had trusted Christ alone. How, then, could they be so inconsistent by placing works of law between themselves and fellow believers in Christ? Paul's interpretation of Psalm 143:2

---

himself by the verb πιστεύω (*pisteuō*) and not by the noun πίστις (*pistis*) Christ is the undoubted object of faith, as in the clause immediately following: καὶ ἡμεῖς εἰς Χριστὸν Ἰησοῦν ἐπιστεύσαμεν (even we have believed in Christ Jesus). This determines the sense of the preceding διὰ πίστεως Ἰησοῦ Χριστοῦ (*pisteōs Iēsou Christou*) and of ἐκ πίστεως Χριστοῦ = (*ek pisteōs Christou*) in the next clause." See also Cranfield, *On Romans*, 81-97, for an outstanding discussion of the subjective/objective genitive question, and Moisés Silva, "Faith Versus Works of Law in Galatians," in *Justification And Variegated Nomism*, 2. 227-34. Silva very successfully argues for the objective genitive ("faith in Jesus Christ") on the basis of the witness of the Greek fathers, the prominence of the act of believing in the New Testament, Paul's use of the relevant terms, and the immediate context.

[21] Berkouwer adds, p. 87: "While Judaism kept a tally sheet of the works of the law, with an eye to rewards if the accounts balanced, Paul's thought excludes the possibility of such bookkeeping. If faith were to keep a record of itself, it would sacrifice its very nature as faith. For faith is disinterested in itself, and looks only to grace."

So also Greijdanus: "From this variation of preposition and case [Greijdanus is referring to passages such as Rom. 3:28 and Phil. 3:9], it appears that *pisti* in relation to justification is not in view as ground, but as instrument. Neither Paul, nor any other author of a NT book, ever says διά πίστιν [*dia pistin*], because of, on account of, faith. Besides this, the antithesis with ἐξ ἐργων νομου [*ex ergōn nomou*] can also make us aware that faith is not being considered as a ground. The substance or ground of justification lies in Christ and His work of reconciliation and salvation, 3:13, 14; Romans 3:24-25." [Translation mine]

(LXX Psalm 142:2[22]) sums up the whole matter: **because by works of law no flesh shall be justified.** "Jewish Christians and Gentile Christians thus find themselves in the same hamartiological and soteriological situation" (Schnelle, 279). The future passive of "justify" here is most likely a logical, timeless reference pointing to the "already" of justification.

Paul now answers a common objection raised in the context of preaching gratuitous justification. Since, as Paul has demonstrated, **by works of law no flesh shall be justified,** the Jew despite all his privileges is in the same position needing justifying righteousness, as do Gentile sinners. **But if while seeking to be justified in Christ we were found to be sinners, then is Christ a servant of sin?**[23] **Seeking to be justified in Christ** corresponds to **we have believed in Jesus Christ** in verse 16. There continues a stark contrast with **justified...**

---

[22] *kai mē eiselthēs eis krisin meta tou doulou sou hoti ou dikaiōthēsetai enōpion sou pas zōn.*

[23] Note the observation of Markus Barth, *Justification,* 40. He notes that Calvin and others do not see this sentence as a contrary-to-fact condition. If it is contrary-to-fact "the whole sentence affirms that Jews and Gentiles, because they are 'in Christ,' are by no means exposed as sinners." Barth thinks that the sentence is not contrary to fact and "contains without irony the assertion that precisely 'in Christ' all men, Jews and Gentiles alike, are found guilty as sinners." Barth supports this in three ways:

(1) "Other sentences in Paul have analogous structures and similar content. Every time Paul rejects a deduction drawn from a premise with the words 'Far from it!', he 'rejects the suggested thought as one which the previous premises, themselves accepted as true, do not justify.' In other words he 'accepts the premise; denies that the conclusion follows.' [Barth is citing Burton.] When Paul *does* formulate a contrary-to-fact condition, he likes to use the particle *an* in the apodosis...Applied to Gal. 2:17, this means that Paul accepts the premise that 'in Christ' we are found to be sinners, but he rejects the conclusion that Christ is therefore a servant of sin."

(2) "According to Galatians 2:15 and Romans 3:22-23, etc., the Jews as well as the Gentiles are really and actually exposed in God's judgment as sinners."

(3) "The Old Testament predecessors of the interceding Son of God quite correctly guard themselves against intending to help Israel in such a manner as to disavow or belittle her sin. On the contrary, the intercession itself reveals how great the sin is that has been committed. 'Alas, this people has sinned a great sin' (Exod. 32:31). Cf. the prayer of the high priest on the Day of Atonement ..."

by works of law. Since, then, both Jew and Gentile stand in need of the justifying righteousness that comes by means of faith in Christ, if even Jews following Torah **were found to be sinners, then is Christ a servant of sin?**[24] That is, if works of the law are unnecessary for justification does this mean that Christ encourages sin? When the gospel is faithfully preached, charges of antinomianism will inevitably arise. If sinners are justified by faith in Christ alone, providing through works of law no contribution whatsoever, then is not Christ **a servant of sin**? Isn't Paul preaching antinomianism? To this Paul responds μὴ γένοιτο (*mē genoito*), **Absolutely not!** Perish the thought![25]

Paul expands on the thought that sinners can contribute nothing to their justification and encourages consistency with the gospel of grace by arguing **for if I build again the things I destroyed, I prove myself a transgressor.** To **build again the things I destroyed** means to retrace one's steps back away from faith to works, to replace the gospel with law, to substitute righteousness obtained by our obedience for righteousness received by faith. Paul may be using the "reconstruction" metaphor in a way similar to his later use in Ephesians 2:14-15, in which the law as a division of Jew and Gentile is presented after the image of the wall in the Jerusalem Temple that separated the inner courts (Aaron, Israel, women) from the outer "court of the Gentiles". Paul would then be saying that Peter's preaching of the gospel made clear that this wall of separation, the Torah as Israel's unique treasure, has been broken down by Jesus; but now Peter's behavior in pulling back from Gentile believers is, in effect, rebuilding the wall, with Peter on the wrong side of the rebuilt wall! He is on

---

[24] ἄρα should be viewed as an interrogative particle since it is followed, as is Paul's norm, by μὴ γένοιτο.

[25] Calvin: "The Jews were mistaken in claiming any holiness for themselves outside Christ, for there was none. Hence the complaint, 'Did Christ come to take the righteousness of the law away from us, to change saints into sinners, to subject us to sin and guilt?' Paul denies it and rebuts the blasphemy with horror. Christ did not introduce sin; He unveiled it. He did not take away righteousness, but stripped the Jews of their false cloak."

the wrong side if he wants to make obedience to the law the boundary between insiders and outsiders because he has been living like an "outsider" with reference to dietary laws.[26] This is precisely what Peter attempted by withdrawing from table fellowship with fellow believers. Christians will constantly face the temptation to return to those old, dark ways of works-righteousness and of forsaking the work of Christ for us. There is a Pharisee in the hearts of all sinners tempting them to look within, to themselves, to their own "righteousness" rather than to the provision of Christ! To **build again the things I destroyed** means that **I prove myself a transgressor**, that is, "any return to the Law-service meant confinement in the role of transgressor" (Verseput, 56). What will one find when he returns to law, builds again what was destroyed? He will find that he cannot keep the law for justification, that sin multiplies, and that the one who attempts self-justification is hopelessly entangled in the damning effects of transgression.

In verse 18 Paul began to speak in first person and continues to do so through verse 21. Undoubtedly, this is a "paradigmatic" **I** by means of which Paul presents himself as "the prototypical example" of believers in Christ (Betz). Yet surely there is something more here. These verses are some of the most profound in Paul's epistles. Even though the **I** of these verses is paradigmatic, they are also Paul's personal confession. They reveal to us not only the profundity of Paul's theology but also the depth and intensity of his devotion.

In verse 19 Paul begins a series of rich, complex verses with the pronoun (**I**, *egō*) in the emphatic position, explaining the significance of life in Christ as opposed to life under law. **For I through the law died to law so that I might live for God.** The law has no power to justify. The law is the letter that kills (2 Cor. 3:6), it cannot impart life (Gal. 3:21). The law can have no role in the justification of the sinner. But how does the law lose its power? In other words, how did Paul die to the law in order to live for God? The monumental answer is that the law loses its power through the death of Christ who bore the

---

[26] This idea was suggested to me by Dennis Johnson.

law's curse (3:13). The death of Christ was **through the law**, that is, through the just demands of the law upon sinners. It was this just penalty that Christ bore for sinners on the cross.[27] To paraphrase: "in my representative," Paul is declaring, "**through the law** – its just demands having been paid by my substitute – **I died to law.** The Father's *condemnation* of Christ on the cross in my stead *condemned* the *condemnation* of the law!" See Romans 6:1ff. and 8:3.

For Paul and all believers to come to this realization about the law is crucifixion together with Christ. **I have been crucified with Christ** (*Christō sunestaurōmai*). **Christ** is placed grammatically in the emphatic position since it is to Him that a relationship with God is owed. **Crucified with Christ** is a perfect tense indicating that what Christ accomplished when He died for sinners on the cross continues to have significance for Paul and for all believers. **I have been crucified with Christ** (another way of saying **I died**) **so that I might live for God.** Through the work of Christ Paul died to the law, to the old way of life based on human merit and to the law's condemning power. But this death is a means to life. Lategan importantly observes, "Christ's representation on his behalf is so real that Paul considers himself part of that event." But we think that he overstates Paul's point in seeing the "existential consequences"of that union as "a secondary result" (Lategan, 427-28). It is not true to Paul to minimize the *ordo salutis* aspect of Paul's union with Christ in the interest of his stress on *historia salutis*. This is to separate what Paul keeps together. It is that existential, experiential aspect of co-crucifixion that Paul will next emphasize – it is nothing less than Christ living in Paul.

---

[27] Machen: "'The law,' Paul probably means, 'caused me to die to the law, because the law, with its penalty of death upon sin (which penalty Christ bore in our stead) brought Christ to the cross; and when Christ died I died, since he died as my representative.' In other words, the death to the law of which Paul here speaks is the death which the law itself brought about when it said, 'The soul that sinneth it shall die.' Christ died that death, which the law fixes as the penalty of sin, when He died upon the cross; and since He died that death as our representative, we too have died that death; the penalty of the law is for us done away because that penalty has been paid in our stead by the Lord Jesus Christ."

Paul continues, **it is no longer I who live, but Christ lives in me.** Paul, having already indicated that he died **so that I might live for God**, now says that in a certain sense he does not live.[28] The **I** who was the old Paul, living under the judgment of the law and under the condemnation of God's wrath, no longer lives (compare 6:14). In Romans 6 Paul says this in different terms by speaking of the death of the "old self". Paul could not speak of the total change in his point of view and way of life more radically than he does. Paul, the old Paul, the Paul of the law, no longer lives, **but Christ lives in me.**[29] Paul's life is completely redirected and reoriented by the wonderful thing that Christ has done for him. **Christ lives in me** indicates how extensive is the transformation brought about in Paul's life by the gospel! So extensive is this reorientation that the reader must remember Paul's opening remarks on the resurrection of Christ (1:1). The resurrection of Jesus is determinative for his theology. The entire section is permeated with eschatology. Implicit in the passage is the confession that the believer not only died with Christ but also was raised with Christ.[30] The Christian life is resurrection life.

Paul does not equate union with Christ with a loss of personal identity. He continues to live life, but a new life in Christ. He adds: **and the life I now live in the flesh**[31] **I live in faith of the Son of God who loved me and gave Himself for me.** The new life of faith is one of **faith of the Son of God** who atoned for sin. Faith in Christ is founded upon His once-for-all achievement on the cross, His self-sacrifice for His people. The aorists, **loved, gave** (ἀγαπήσαντός, *agapēsantos*; παραδόντος,

---

[28] Bruce notes that "so completely is self dethroned in the new order that in this context Paul will not *egō zō* but 'it is no longer I who live; it is Christ who lives in me...'"

[29] Betz: "The underlying assumption is that the resurrected Christ (1:1) is identical with the 'Spirit' (2 Cor. 3:17a) which is given to the Christians, and which dwells in them and provides 'life for God' for them." This "identity" is, of course, not ontological but economical.

[30] See Silva, 175.

[31] Betz: "This statement, simple as it is, may be polemical. It rejects widespread enthusiastic notions, which may have already found a home in Christianity, according to which 'divine life' and 'flesh' are mutually

paradontos) do not themselves alone point to the completed act of Christ's sacrifice but its finality is a truth derived from Paul's theology as a whole.[32] Christ is the sole object of faith, and Christian living is based on His achievement. But this Christ who sacrificed Himself for sinners also indwells those who by faith have trusted in Him alone for salvation.[33] By Christ's work on the cross and indwelling, Paul continues to insist that salvation is not according to man!

Paul concludes by emphasizing once again that there is nothing that sinners can do for their own justification. **I do not nullify the grace of God. For if righteousness is through law, then Christ died for nothing.** The Judaizers invalidate the grace of God by requiring works of the law for justification. Paul will have nothing of that point of view! **I do not nullify the grace of God.** It is possible that Paul is refuting a charge to the effect that he nullifies grace by setting aside the law. Betz argues that if one's view of grace included Torah, then Paul could be accused of denying grace. But the opposite is the case. It is his opponents who invalidate the grace of God by requiring works of the law of Gentile believers. **For if righteousness,** that is, if justification, **is through law, then**

---

exclusive, so that those who claim to have divine life also claim that they have left the conditions of mortality. The Christian life 'in the flesh' is at the same time 'in faith'…In other words, the 'divine life' which the Christian receives through the indwelling of Christ expresses itself as 'faith'."

[32] Lategan, 429,430 points out that, while "he loved me" and "gave himself for me" links 2:20 with 1:11-12, it also anticipates the theological and ethical sections in chapters 3–4 and 5–6. "He loved me" "is an abbreviated description of the ethical content of the gospel, as personified in Christ and his 'Verhalten', and which forms the content of chapters 5 and 6." "He gave Himself for me" "describes the theological or soteriological basis for the Christian existence and its ethical content, and is the subject matter of chapters 3 and 4." "Therefore, 2.20 not only links 1–2 in an integrated way to 3–4 and 5–6, revealing an amazing unity of construction and content, but appeals to Christ in a double way: his cross not only makes the new existence of the believer soteriologically possible, but at the same time demonstrates the ethical content of the gospel by the style of this existence as selfless giving."

[33] Lategan, 428, 429: "It would appear then that 2:20 is linked to Paul's preceding argument in two ways – structurally and content-wise.

Christ died for nothing. If there is anything that sinners can do to contribute to justification before a holy and righteous God, then why did Christ die? Indeed, His death would have been in vain. "God would be guilty of throwing Himself away" (Berkouwer, *Justification*, 78).

In this section of Galatians Paul has continued to sound the theme that salvation is by grace and is not according to man. "The entire segment, vv. 15-21, thus serves a single theme, proving that the Law-service does not result in righteousness before God. Why, then, Paul asks, should one force the Gentiles to judaize (v. 14b)?" (Verseput). In 3:1ff., Paul will continue this theme with specific application to the Galatians' own knowledge of Paul's preaching of the gospel and their professed belief in that gospel.

Structurally, the link is with 1.4, which anticipates what is to follow in 2:20 and which already prepares the scene for the focus on Christ, not Paul, that is, underlining the *theological*, rather than the biographical nature of Paul's argument. Regarding content, the tension between God and man is sustained right through the argument up to 2:20, when the dramatic denouement takes place and where Paul can show that the usual nature of the gospel implies that true human existence is possible only in co-operation and co-existence with God, not in opposition and resistance to God.'

6.
By Law or Through Faith in Christ?
(3:1-5)

Translation
O foolish Galatians! Who has bewitched you before whose eyes Jesus Christ was placarded as crucified? This one thing I desire to learn from you, was it by works of law or by believing the message you heard that you received the Spirit? Are you really so foolish? Having begun in the Spirit, are you now ending in the flesh? Have you experienced so much for nothing – if indeed it was for nothing? Well then, the one who bountifully supplies the Spirit to you and works miracles among you, does he do this by works of law or by believing the message you heard?

Summary
Paul passionately argues the sufficiency of the gospel in view of the Galatians' "foolish" abandonment of the good news of Christ crucified. His questions are intended to remind them of their own experience. Since the Spirit of God invaded their lives by grace, any attempt to add legalistic components to the gospel must be wrong. The Spirit is operative by faith in Christ and not by "works of law". "Are you really so foolish?" Paul asks. "Having begun in the Spirit are you now ending in the flesh?" Paul wishes to know if their experiences of gospel living were "for nothing"? The presence of the Holy Spirit

and miraculous signs done among them were evidences of
the eschatological reign of Christ. Living by law is a thorough
contradiction of their gracious experience!

Comment

To this point Paul has defended grace alone from his experience. He now begins a series of arguments based upon the
experience of the Galatians and upon Scripture. His purpose
remains the same, to defend the freedom of grace over against
works of law. Paul earnestly desires to bring again to life the
memory of the gospel he first preached to the Galatians and
to see them grounded in that gospel.

Unconcerned with diplomacy in view of the grave and
perilous circumstances confronting the Galatians Paul
begins his argument with a passionate plea! **O, foolish
Galatians! O** is important to the translation. The vocative
O indicates Paul's "indignant astonishment" (Zerwick, 35)
at the Galatians' defection from the truth of the gospel.[1]
Foolish (*anoētos*) expresses the folly of the Galatians' lack of
spiritual discernment. REB translates as **You stupid Galatians!**
Moffatt translates as **O senseless Galatians...** and Phillips as
O you dear idiots of Galatia. These translations demonstrate
attempts to get at Paul's sheer exasperation. Indeed, Paul is so
frustrated that he can only view their defection as some sort
of bewitchment! We should remember, however, that we have
here a passionate plea but not anger as such toward Paul's
converts. As Ramsay points out, behind Paul's words is an
authoritative tone but the feeling is that of sorrow and pathos.
He notes: "they who talk so much about his indignation in

---

[1] Zerwick, 35: "In classical usage, the vocative is regularly introduced by
the particle ὦ, whose omission constitutes an exception into whose reasons
one may profitably inquire. In Hellenistic usage the contrary is the case:
the omission of the particle has become the rule (and hence has no special
significance), so that where ὦ is exceptionally used in the NT one is justified
in supposing that there is some reason for its use. In fact ὦ apart from
the Acts, occurs in contexts suggesting deep emotion on the part of the
speaker...This is but a little particle, but it casts such a light on the state of
mind of Our Lord and of His apostles, that no one, surely, in reading the
Scriptures, would wish to neglect its indications."

Galatians are missing the real emotion that drives him on: it is intense and overpowering love and pity for specially beloved children" (*Historical Commentary*, 312).

O foolish Galatians! Who has bewitched you is an expression of Paul's bewilderment over the Galatians' traitorous stance toward the gospel he had preached to them. **Bewitched** (*ebaskanen*) was a term drawn from the popular concept of the evil eye (Moulton and Milligan, 940). So unwise and foolish was the Galatians' attitude toward the gospel that Paul expresses total disbelief! Their actions are unaccountable. It is as if they had been put under a spell! How could they **before whose eyes Jesus Christ was placarded as crucified** allow themselves to be influenced by the Judaizers? By the use of the aorist passive (*proegraphē*) Paul reminds them of his initial preaching. Did he not preach the truth of the gospel so vividly that Christ was **placarded, portrayed**[2] as crucified? Was not the compelling exhibition of Christ crucified the definitive moment in their lives, the time at which all other claims to right-eousness were laid aside? In view of the wounds of Christ, His loving sacrifice and atoning death, how could the Galatians now entertain any other gospel than that of free grace? "This placard ought to have kept their eyes from wandering, and so to have acted as a charm...against all Judaic sorceries" (Lightfoot). Paul's exclamation makes plain that the heart of the matter is the sufficiency of the cross of Christ. When all is said and done, the Judaizing position makes Christ's death needless (2:21). Placarding Christ as crucified, as the full and sufficient atonement for the sins of sinners, remains the task of the minister of the Word.[3]

---

[2] Betz: "One of the goals of the ancient orator was to deliver his speech so vividly and impressively that his listeners imagined the matter to have happened right before their eyes." Calvin: "They had a knowledge that could almost have given them a sight of Him...By this he suggests that the actual sight of Christ's death could not have affected them more than his preaching." For examples of public notifications, see Moulton and Milligan, *prographō*, 4270.

[3] Calvin: "Let those who want to discharge the ministry of the Gospel aright learn not only to speak and declaim but also to penetrate into consciences, so that men may see Christ crucified and that His blood may flow."

Paul will expand the essential content of that awesome and wonderful proclamation in the verses that follow, especially in verses 10-13.

Paul next asks: **This one thing I desire to learn from you, was it by works of law or by believing the message you heard that you received the Spirit?** The point of Paul's question is to remind them of their own experience and to drive them to the conclusion of grace. The Galatians **received the Spirit** without any element of law-keeping.[4] Since the Spirit of God invaded their lives by grace, surely any attempt to add legalistic components to the gospel at this stage must be wrong. The Holy Spirit was not operative in their lives by **works of law** but **by believing the message**[5] of Christ crucified. The same gospel by which they came to faith in Christ is the same gospel by which they should continue to grow in Christ. Paul also makes this point in Colossians 2:6-7.

Therefore, Paul adds **Are you really so foolish? Having begun**[6] **in the Spirit, are you now ending in the flesh?** It is **foolish**, utterly senseless for the Galatians, having begun in the Spirit, to regress to **the flesh**. Paul's use of *sarx* (flesh) here is deprecatory and ethically negative (see 5:19ff.). It implies living according to the old order of things (**the present evil age**, 1:4), a forgetfulness of Christ's redemption and a return to old, dark ways of self-dependence. **Ending in the flesh** (*sarki epiteleisthe*, see Phil. 1:6) implies more than a poor finish. Paul's contrast between life that finds its origin in the Spirit and life under the law as a means of salvation is total.

---

[4] Morris: "The verb *receive* points to the truth that the Spirit is given to believers, not acquired as the result of some merit they possessed."

[5] On the translation of *ex akoe pisteo*, see Silva, "Faith Versus Works of Law In Galatians," 234-36. "The word πίστις (*pistis*) in vv. 2 and 5 bears the closest possible relationship to the clause that *immediately* follows in verse 6, Καθὼς Ἀβραὰμ ἐπίστευσεν (*kathōs Abraam episteusen*), while the latter is inseparable from οἱ ἐκ πίστεως (*hoi ek pisteōs*) in verses 7 and 9. That the three expressions allude to the same basic concept is quite apparent; one would need extraordinarily persuasive evidence to the contrary before setting aside the clues Paul himself is providing for us."

[6] Morris: "We should not miss the point that the gift of the Holy Spirit is not reserved for those who have made great progress in the Christian faith, but is a gift conferred on every true believer."

It is possible that *epiteleisthe* should be translated "being perfected". Fung thinks that Paul is "making an ironic reference to the Judaizers' claim to 'make perfect' the Pauline version of Christianity which the Galatians had received by insisting on their 'keeping the law' as a necessary complement."

Paul continues his argument asking **Have you experienced so much for nothing?** The verb *paschō* can refer to suffering of various kinds, but here it probably means "experience". Paul is likely referring to the gift of the Spirit and attendant miraculous gifts mentioned in the context (3:5). Hence, *BDAG* suggests: *have you had such remarkable experiences in vain?* Context should decide the meaning of the verb. Since *paschō* here is surrounded by the blessings of the preached Word and the gift of the Spirit it seems best to interpret Paul's meaning positively, an experience of blessings and not of suffering. **If indeed it was for nothing** – Paul is still hopeful that the Galatians will see the folly of the Judaizing error and that their experience will not have been **for nothing.**[7]

Concluding this argument Paul repeats in expanded form the question of verse 2. **Well then, the one who bountifully supplies**[8] **the Spirit to you and works miracles among you, does he do this by works of law or by believing the message you heard?** God's gift of His **Spirit** and attending **miracles** among the Galatians was not a result of law keeping (**works of law**) but of faith (**believing**) in the gospel (**the message you heard**). Paul's emphasis on **the Spirit** in this context is telling. Life in the Holy Spirit contradicts life in the flesh (5:16-25; 3:2, 3). The presence of the Holy Spirit is the blessing of eschatological promise (3:14) and the sustainer of eschatological hope (5:5). The miraculous signs done among the Galatians were signs of the kingdom, evidences that the world to come has broken

---

[7] Ridderbos' interpretation, "if indeed *in vain* is strong enough to suggest what it is," does not seem to me to be tenable. Paul's purpose in reminding the Galatians of their experiences is to draw them back to the true gospel from the false gospel to which they are defecting. Paul's attitude seems to be that expressed in 5:10.

[8] For my translation of *epichorēgōn* by *bountifully supply*, compare 2 Corinthians 9:10.

into their lives through Jesus Christ. Therefore living by
law, as a means of justification and acceptance with God, is
contrary to the Christians' identity as *pneumatikoi* (6:1) –
those gifted with the eschatological Spirit! The readers should
remember the lame man at Lystra (Acts 14:9), the disciples at
Antioch filled with the Holy Spirit (Acts 13:52), and the signs
and wonders performed at Iconium (Acts 14:3). Hence Paul's
arguments are based in reminiscence. (See Ramsay, *Historical
Commentary*, 327, 329).

7.
When Curse Turns To Blessing
(3:6-14)

Translation

As it is written, Abraham believed God and it was counted to him as righteousness. Know then that those who believe are Abraham's sons. The Scripture, foreseeing that God would justify the Gentiles by faith, proclaimed the gospel in advance to Abraham, that "in you shall all the nations be blessed". Therefore those who believe are blessed with believing Abraham. For as many as rely on works of law are under a curse, for it is written: "Cursed are all who do not continue to observe everything that is written in the book of the law to perform its requirements." That no one is justified before God by law is evident, because "the righteous shall live by faith". Now the law is not based on faith, but "he who practices the precepts of the law shall live in them". Christ redeemed us from the curse of the law by becoming a curse instead of us, just as it is written, "Cursed is everyone who is hung upon a tree". The purpose of this was that, in Christ Jesus, the blessing of Abraham might come to the nations, so that we might through faith receive the promise of the Spirit.

Summary

Paul begins his argument from Scripture by appealing to God's grace given to Abraham. Abraham's justification is not unique but paradigmatic, as seen in Genesis 15:6. Just as

Abraham was justified by faith, so those who believe in Christ are justified and are "Abraham's sons". The blessing promised to the nations through Abraham was a promise of the gospel in advance. From Abraham's justification by faith and from the promise that the Gentiles would also be justified by faith, Paul concludes: "Therefore those who believe are blessed with believing Abraham."

Indeed, the law cannot justify but brings its curse to bear upon all who attempt acceptance with God by its terms. Paul appeals to Deuteronomy 27:26 to show that anyone who fails to adhere perfectly to the law's demands will find the law's curse for his efforts. The implicit argument is that sinners do not obey all that is written in the book of the law because they are incapable of doing so. Paul cites Habakkuk 2:4 in order to demonstrate that justification is by faith and also Leviticus 18:5 to confirm his pervasive argument that law and gospel are antithetical ways of relating to God.

Paul then moves from plight to solution, once again citing the Old Testament. Pointing to Deuteronomy 21:23, he presents Christ as the sinner's substitute who was hanged as a criminal on the cross to bear and redeem us from the law's curse. The fruition of Christ's death is the blessing of Abraham upon the nations and reception of the Spirit through faith.

Comment

In 3:1 Paul has described the Galatians as **foolish**. To follow the Judaizing viewpoint deserts the only way to God, exchanges grace for the bondage of works, what is free for relentless demands, good news from heaven for the bad news of human effort, and the infinite merit of Christ for man's total demerit. At this point Paul begins his argument from Scripture by appealing to God's grace given to Abraham. In pointing back to Abraham Paul makes clear that there is, and always has been, one way for acceptance with God. Abraham's way is not peculiar to him, but is paradigmatic.

The passage begins with an "introductory formula", *kathōs*, meaning **as (it is written)** (Betz). Paul focuses on Abraham's faith rather than his faithfulness: **As it is written, Abraham believed God and it was counted to him as righteousness.**

Since the Jews viewed Abraham as a proto-law keeper, Paul's approach was revolutionary.[1] This crucial Pauline understanding of Abraham, the man of faith, is further expounded in Romans 4:3 and in the surrounding context in which Paul demonstrates that Abraham was counted righteous "before he was circumcised" (Rom. 4:10). Paul, in Romans 4, stresses "to the one who does not work but trusts him who justifies the ungodly, his faith is counted as righteousness" (4:5). Also, in Galatians 3:6 Paul introduces Abraham in order to counter the works-righteousness of the Judaizers' false gospel.

Undoubtedly the Judaizers had also appealed to Abraham. But their use of Abraham as a proto-law keeper led them to emphasize Abraham's *faithfulness* as a law keeper rather than his *faith* and, further, led to the assumption that being a child of Abraham meant to be circumcised and to obey the law. This is why Paul turns to Genesis 15:6: *And he believed the LORD and he counted it to him as righteousness.* In this passage God's grace and not Abraham's work is the salient feature – God's grace to which Abraham responded by faith.

Paul undoubtedly intended for his hearers to recall the context of Genesis 15:6. In this passage God assures Abraham of his promise that Abraham would possess the land and have an heir. When Abraham asks, "O LORD God, how am I to know that I shall possess it [the land]?" God responded by a ceremony in which He passed through the severed pieces of sacrificial animals thus, in essence, taking an oath of self-malediction: "Let this happen to Me if I fail to keep My word!"

---

[1] Morris: "We should notice that Jews often had a very different picture of Abraham. They revered him very highly, but not for the same reasons as Paul. Thus ben-Sirach wrote, 'Abraham was the great father of a multitude of nations, and no one has been found like him in glory; he kept the law of the Most High' (Ecclus. 44:19-20, RSV). The law was not given for centuries after his time, but ben-Sirach sees the greatness of Abraham in that he complied with the provisions that later would be laid down in the law. Others stressed Abraham's obedience when he was instructed to take his son Isaac and offer him in sacrifice (Gen. 22). What endeared Abraham to many Jewish thinkers were his virtues and his deeds. They understood him to have kept the law before it was written. Paul's emphasis on Abraham's faith must have come as a complete surprise to the Galatians."

It is this word of promise (ultimately fulfilled in the sacrifice of Christ) that Abraham believed.

Recalling the context of Genesis 15 adds significantly to Ridderbos' prudent observation that the justification of which Paul speaks negatively means "being placed outside the state of guilt" and positively "to be in harmony with the divine standard of judgment". He adds: "The big assumption underlying it is that God accomplished the punishment which His righteousness demands in Christ on the cross, and that by being included in Christ the believer can arrive at acquittal."

The salient point is that in the context of justification, Paul stresses Abraham's faith rather than his faithfulness. Moreover, the truth that the gospel is not according to man is accented no less by the fact that Abraham's faith **was counted to him as righteousness.** Comparing Paul's use of **was counted to him as righteousness** with the parallel passage in Romans 4 helps us to understand the significance of Paul's declaration.

Firstly, in Romans 4, **justified by works** is contrasted with Abraham's faith that was **counted to him as righteousness** (vv. 2, 3). The contrast between works and justifying righteousness could not be clearer. Further, **works** that are **counted** as a **wage** and one's **due** are plainly contrasted with **faith** that is **counted as righteousness** which, again, is described as **the blessing of one to whom God counts righteousness apart from works** (vv. 4-6). In 4:5 Paul describes God as **the God who justifies the ungodly.** Contrary to Jewish portrayals of Abraham as a proto-law keeper, Abraham is **the ungodly** whose only hope for justification rests in God's mercy rather than in meeting the law's demands. Abraham the ungodly! This idea, unthinkable to Jewish ears, demonstrates that God justifying the ungodly, the very thing that Israel's judges must never do, is the only hope for sinners. Thus, Paul magnifies God's grace! To those who believe the gospel **righteousness** is **counted to them as well** (v. 11). Paul's argument is rounded off with the immediate application of the imputation of righteousness to his readers: **But the words "it was counted to him" were not written for his sake alone, but for ours also. It will be counted to us who believe in him who raised**

from the dead Jesus our Lord, who was delivered up for our trespasses and raised for our justification (vv. 23-25).

It is apparent that, for Paul, the matter of counting or reckoning a sinner righteous by faith is to be viewed in the sharpest contrast to works, merit and human attainment. Heidland correctly remarks that "here we have a radical break with Judaism at the very point of the understanding of" λογίζομαι [*logidzomai*, to count, reckon, impute]. Rather than this "Jewish recording of merits" Paul proclaims "a gracious gift given to those who abandon all the claims that works might have and trust in the God who justifies sinners who have no claims". He adds: "One might equally say that faith is acknowledged to him for righteousness, or even better that righteousness is allotted to the believer. Moreover, the seat of judgment is in the gracious will of God, and this makes it quite impossible for human insight to anticipate the judgment in terms of merit. What faith is intrinsically is of no relevance. This is the one answer to the question why faith is declared to be righteous. The very question is rejected as false. Attention is directed away from human weakness or supposed human strength to the grace of God. Everything depends on this" (*TDNT*, IV, 290, 291).

As we have seen, Paul cites Genesis 15:6 to point to Abraham's justification by belief in the promise, the gospel in prospect. "Abraham was not justified merely because he believed that God would multiply his seed, but because he embraced the grace of God, trusting to the promised Mediator, in whom, as Paul declares elsewhere, 'all the promises of God are Yea and Amen'." (Calvin) From Genesis 15:6 Paul next argues the significance of this for the controversy with the Judaizers. The implication for the Galatians is most understandable on the assumption that the Judaizers themselves referenced Abraham as a proto-law keeper. Over against the Judaizing assumption that children of Abraham are those who are naturally descended from Abraham, are circumcised and keep the law for justification, Paul argues that Abraham's sons are those who believe the gospel. **Know then that those who believe are Abraham's sons.** On this he is insistent (**Know** is

an imperative followed by an inferential particle, **then**). Not
those who obey the law for justification but those who believe
in Christ are justified and are **Abraham's sons**.[2]

What makes a person a son of Abraham? Is it physical
descent, circumcision, or observance of feast days? None
of these things, says Paul, make people Abraham's sons.
Abraham's sons are those who believe in Christ. The promise
given to Abraham was the gospel in prospect. This promise
Abraham believed and in believing this promise he was
justified. We who now read Paul's letter believe the promise
in retrospect, the substance of which is Christ himself. When
a sinner believes in Christ he is justified. This is what it means
to be Abraham's son. The method of grace is altogether that of
faith and not works. The Damascus road experience, his new
understanding of Christ and of his gospel, made Paul into the
great redemptive-historian and determined his Christocentric
reading of the Old Testament. Paul saw that the gospel has
always been the only way in which God accepts sinners. Only
those who believe, and not those who are relying on works of
law, are Abraham's sons.

The gospel determined the meaning and significance of
the promise given to Abraham in Genesis 12:3. **The Scripture,
foreseeing that God would justify the Gentiles by faith,
proclaimed the gospel in advance to Abraham, that "in you
shall all the nations be blessed"**. Paul's personification of
Scripture, **the Scripture foreseeing,** acknowledges God as
the ultimate author of Scripture[3] and presses upon his readers
God's authority in this matter of justifying righteousness. It is
God's word to Abraham that Paul references and this word

---

[2] Zerwick, 41: "A certain intimate relation to a person or thing is
expressed in a manner not indeed exclusively Semitic, but in our literature
certainly prevalently so, by 'son', υἱός, followed by a genitive. This extended
usage of the word 'son' is more readily understood when it is a question of
certain relationships to a person. Thus he who reproduces and expresses in
his own way of life that of another is called a 'son' of the latter; thus 'sons
of Abraham' Galatians 3,7…" Ramsay, *Historical Commentary*, 337-44 argues
that Paul references a metaphor drawn from Greek law.

[3] See B. B. Warfield (1970) "It Says:" "Scripture Says:" "God Says" in
Inspiration and Authority of The Bible, Presbyterian and Reformed Publishing,
299-348.

of promise was a **foreseeing that God would justify the Gentiles by faith** and a proclamation of **the gospel in advance to Abraham.** What Abraham heard by way of God's voice and received by faith was God's proclamation of **the gospel in advance.**[4] "The promise to Abraham was an *anticipation of the gospel,* not only as an announcing of the Messiah, but also as involving the doctrine of righteousness by faith" (Lightfoot). Abraham, in believing the promise, trusted in Jesus Christ and was justified by faith. But the gospel was not for Abraham alone, nor only for his progeny. Scripture foresaw that God promised in advance to **justify the Gentiles by faith.** This promise is found in Genesis 12:3 and 18:18 and is summarized by Paul: **"in you shall all the nations be blessed".** Thus Paul recognizes that God has always come to sinners as "an 'evangelical' God" (Duncan) and that as far back as Father Abraham the promise of imputed righteousness has been a promise to be received **by faith** and not by works. "What happened in Abraham's day was, in fact, a forecast of the future. The faith element in God's method of justification is therefore timeless" (Guthrie).

Since the promise given to Abraham included the nations and since that promise was one of justification **by faith,** the Judaizers were standing squarely against the gospel that had been proclaimed in advance to Abraham by adding works of law to the promise. Requiring works of law for Gentile converts as necessary for justification bled the gospel of its life. Requiring works of law for justification turns the gospel into its opposite.

From Abraham's justification by faith and from the promise that the Gentiles would also be justified by faith Paul concludes: **Therefore (*hōste*) those who believe are blessed with believing Abraham**. Having already demonstrated that sons of Abraham are those who believe as Abraham believed, Paul now concludes that whoever believes – and Paul's particular reference is to Gentiles – are **blessed with believing Abraham**. All who are accepted by God must be accepted just

---

[4] Meyer: "This promise was a gospel *before* the gospel."

as Abraham was accepted, not by works of righteousness, but by faith in Christ freely offered in the gospel.

"Not being blessed is the same as being cursed" (Betz). Having demonstrated that justification is and always has been only through faith in Christ Paul makes the same point from another perspective. Law cannot possibly be a means of justification **for as many as rely on works of law are under a curse. For as many as** is comprehensive, including both Jew and Gentile.[5] Paul wrote this way rather than simply writing "the Jews" because "he wanted to draw a generalized conclusion from the proof-text of Deuteronomy and apply it to others as well as the Jews. These others he had in view must have included both the Jewish *Christian* agitators (cf. 2:16) and the Galatian (i.e., Gentile) Christians attracted to the agitators (cf. 3:2,5)" (Kim, 139, 140).[6]

---

[5] Betz: "It would include also the Galatians if they would carry out their present plans to come under the Torah. Thus the curse must be connected with Paul's own curse in Galatians 1:8-9. The logic behind Paul's words, therefore, is simply that exclusion from 'blessing' (cf. 6:16) equals 'curse'."

[6] Kim, *Paul and The New Perspective*, 139, 140. Kim is writing in opposition to Scott and Wright's theories of extended exile. According to this theory, the Jews of second temple Judaism, though they had returned from Babylonian captivity, nonetheless considered themselves as still in exile due to foreign domination. In this context, Deuteronomy 27–30 with its threats of disobedience and promise of blessing was foundational. Since Paul has in view this passage in Galatians 3:10 the theory proposes that Paul is declaring the Jewish nation is under the curse for its disobedience and Galatians 3:13 is viewed as promise of restoration. Redemption from the curse of the law would then mean redemption from exile. But, as Kim points out, among his several devastating arguments (140, 141): "why is it that 'all those who are of the works of the law are under a curse?' For anybody who operates on the basis of the covenantal curses and blessings of Deuteronomy 27–30, the exactly opposite inference from Deuteronomy 27:26 would be in order: 'all those who are *not* of the works of the law (i.e. all those who do not keep the law) are under a curse.' Therefore, on the assumption of a well-established theory of continuing exile, Paul's Judaizing opponents in Galatia would have the better of the argument here: just as Israel was cursed and sent into exile for her disobedience to the law, so all those who do not keep the law will be cursed. Hence, the need for observance of the law!" This theory demonstrates once again how far skewed interpretations of Galatians become when severed from the purpose of Paul, which is to demonstrate that the gospel is not according to man and that salvation is all of grace.

Paul once again confirms the comprehensive curse function of the law by appealing to Scripture: **for it is written: "cursed are all who do not continue to observe everything that is written in the book of the law to perform its requirements."** Paul's appeal to the curses of Ebal in Deuteronomy 27:26 is for the purpose of showing that any failure to adhere perfectly to the demands of the law incurs the law's curse. Moreover, since no one can keep the law of God, any one who attempts acceptance by God on the basis of law will find only the curse of the law of God for his efforts.[7] Here Paul anticipates the categorical statement of 5:3 that "to every man who lets himself be circumcised that he is obligated to obey the whole law."

Seyoon Kim has seen the precise logic of Paul's argument: "Why is it that 'all those who are of the works of the law are under a curse'? On what premise would the quotation from Deuteronomy 27:26 be a logical support for the statement? Deuteronomy 27:26 (cited also in 3:10) is a statement in negative form of the principle of Leviticus 18:5 (cited in 3:12): He who keeps the law will have life in it (Lev. 18:5), but he who does not keep it will be cursed (Deut. 27:26). According to this scheme, when it is said that 'all those who are of the works of the law are under a curse,' it must be because they are thought of as not keeping the law although they are 'of the works of the law.' But are not 'those of the works of the law' by definition law-keepers? But then in what sense are they thought of as not keeping the law so as to incur a curse? This line of reasoning seems to lead us inexorably to the word *pasin* in Deuteronomy 27:26 and cited in 3:10: 'those of the works of the law' are thought of as not keeping the law because they do not keep '*all things* written in the book of the law.' The phrase,

---

[7] See Thomas R. Schreiner, "Is Perfect Obedience To The Law Possible? A Re-examination of Galatians 3:10", *JETS* 27/2 (1984): 151-60. Schreiner argues, correctly we think, for the reading that we have found at least as far back as Calvin, namely, that there is an implied proposition that it is impossible to keep the law perfectly. The text must be read in this way: (1) All who do not obey the law perfectly are under the curse of the law; (2) the implied proposition, no one is able to keep the law perfectly; (3) Therefore, all who rely for justification on works of law are under a curse.

'those of the works of the law,' implies their commitment to keep the law. But then why, in spite of that commitment, do they not keep '*all things* written in the book of the law'? The only answer available appears to be because they *cannot* keep '*all things* written in the book of the law'. Thus, the premise implicit in the declaration of 3:10a seems to be that no one can keep the law perfectly (cf. Gal. 5:3)" (Kim, 141).

And so, Paul teaches that the way of law is antithetical to the way of faith. And this is just as relevant in preaching the gospel today, as it was when Paul first proclaimed it. "He only can be happy under a dispensation of law," wrote Weinel, "who can live a life-long lie."[8] The gospel comes to break that commitment to a life-long lie, and to open our hearts to the truth of God's grace in Christ.

Paul's point in citing Deuteronomy 27:26 is to insist that anyone who does not perform the works of the law in minute detail and with perfection will know its curse. The law's curse contrasts with blessing (vv. 8, 9) in the same way that law and faith contrast, that is, in absolute terms. Failure to **continue to observe everything that is written in the book of the law to perform its requirements** brings the sinner under the law's awful and relentless curse. Ridderbos' pertinent summary is almost overpowering, all the more so since it is true to Paul: "The ὑπὸ (under) makes of the κατάρα (curse) a real power which reigns and brings devastation upon those subjected to it. The curse is the

---

[8] Cited by B. B. Warfield (1989), *The Plan of Salvation*, Simpson, 31, 32. The entire section is interesting to read in the light of the New Perspective on Paul. Weinel continues: "But proud, downright, consistent natures cannot be put off with a lie. If they are unable to resist, they die of the lie; if they are strong, it is the lie that dies. The lie inherent in the law was the presumption that it could be fulfilled. Every one of Paul's associates understood that the commandment could not be kept, but they did not own it to themselves." Warfield interestingly adds: "This is a true picture of the Middle Ages. Men knew very well that they could not earn for themselves salvation, or even the incitement of the grace of God; they knew very well that they failed in their 'good works,' at every stage; and yet they kept the ghastly fiction up." In this context the Reformation should be viewed as "nothing other than Augustinianism come to its rights: the turning away from all that is human to rest on God alone for salvation."

sovereign utterance of the living God, effective, charged with power."[9]

The preacher in preparing to expound this text will do well to summarize man's plight. One way of getting at this is to note that Jesus, in Matthew 5:21-22; 27-28 and context, does precisely what Paul is doing in this passage in Galatians. In these verses Jesus knocks the props out from under all attempts at self-justification. The curse of the law means judgment pure and simple. The law sentences us to death. The greatness, majesty, holiness and sovereignty of God are the great presuppositions of the text. Yet men's minds are not duly impressed with this theme in large measure because these themes are so seldom preached!

Paul's portrait of man under the curse of the law is congruous with the revelation of Scripture as a whole that presents mankind, fallen in Adam, guilty before God, and each totally unable to recover himself from his fallen state. We are hopeless in ourselves. One tragedy attending self-righteousness is that the self-righteous exclude themselves from the hearing of good news because the self-righteous person thinks he is in no need of such news from heaven. The gospel comes to sinners. Charles Bridges' statement on this matter accords fully with what Paul teaches in Galatians: "Ignorance of the law is the root of self-deception. An acquaintance with its spirituality unveils the hidden world of guilt and defilement, brings down self-complacency, and lays the sinner prostrate before the cross."[10]

The law, then, shows us what we are really like and what our true need is before God. Paul's point is that we need a perfect record to stand in God's court of law. Could there be a worse dilemma for sinful man? How can an unholy human being stand in the presence of the living and true God, absolutely holy in His being? Paul would have us see that, if one attempts to stand before God in his own righteousness,

---

[9] Duncan also summarizes the desperation saying that: "the issue is plain that *they must either find a way of keeping the Law or else come under its curse.*"

[10] Charles Bridges (rpt., 1976), *The Christian Ministry,* Banner of Truth, 365.

he will perish in his sins eternally, under the "curse of the law". This is why Paul is so passionate in his opposition to the legalistic compromises of the gospel aimed at by the Judaizers. "Because Paul is supremely concerned about the absolute necessity of meeting in some real way the legal demands of God, he pours contempt on the futile efforts of Judaism in this direction."[11]

Paul continues to argue for grace and against merit by citing Habakkuk 2:4. **That no one is justified before God by law is evident, because "the righteous shall live by faith."** The law demands perfect, personal obedience to its precepts for justification. No sinner can meet those demands. Justification before God is not achieved by the personal merit of sinners. On the contrary, **the righteous shall live by faith.** Paul also cites Habakkuk 2:4 in Romans 1:17 where it is crucial to his argument for justifying righteousness in that epistle.[12] Paul, both in Romans and in Galatians, reads the passage in view of the gospel. He reads the passage here in order to continue the argument of verse 10. Righteousness by faith is contrary to the law with its curse. Paul's mind swirls with the glad tidings of justification by faith and its Old Testament anticipation.

In verse 12 Paul adds Leviticus 18:5 to his mounting argument from the Old Testament. **Now the law is not based**

---

[11] Geerhardus Vos (2001), "The Alleged Legalism in Paul's Doctrine of Justification" in *Redemptive History and Biblical Interpretation,* Presbyterian and Reformed, 390.

[12] Paul reads Habakkuk 2:4 in view of the gospel. Ridderbos comments on Paul's use of Habakkuk 2:4 noting that the "passage is one of the few Old Testament examples in which faith is presented as the one thing necessary for redemption. In Habakkuk 2:4 this faith is not set in contrast to the works of the law, however, but over against the arrogance and self-confidence of the wicked. Positively seen, though, the faith intended in Habakkuk 2 and Galatians 3 is essentially the same. It is a resting in God without regard to human care and effort." Guthrie comments: "The words undoubtedly had a deeper meaning for Paul than for Habakkuk, but the germinal ideas were there. Thus 'faith' becomes faith in Christ, 'righteous' means accounted righteous in God's sight, 'living' refers to the highest form of life, embracing eternal life." Also, Calvin's observation is helpful: "By faith he (Habakkuk) simply means the quiet assurance of a conscience that relies on God alone. Therefore Paul uses this quotation aptly."

on faith, but **"he who practices the precepts of the law shall live in them."** The reference to Leviticus 18:5 simply confirms Paul's pervasive argument in this section, that law and gospel are antithetical ways of relating to God. This is why he insists that **the law is not based on faith**. Faith is by free grace, unconditional, but the law is conditional. The way of faith leads to justification but the law to condemnation. The two ways of law and faith are incompatible as ways of acceptance with God. Therefore, when Paul cites the Levitical passage he is insisting that failure to obey any part of it brings curse, as he has already pointed out explicitly in verse 10 and will bring out again in verse 13, because the law demands that its adherents live in its precepts, and keep its commandments perfectly. Paul's use of this passage is based upon his understanding that no sinner can keep the law's demands. "We admit," says Calvin in the spirit of Paul's concern, "that the doers of the law, if there were any, would be righteous. But since that is a conditional agreement, all are excluded from life because none offers the righteousness that he ought."

It is in line with this thought, the demands of the law and the inability of a sinner to meet those demands, that Paul now moves to his most important argument from the Old Testament and demonstrates the only hope of sinners in life and in death. That hope is in the redemption of Christ alone! **Christ redeemed us from the curse of the law by becoming a curse instead of us, just as it is written, "Cursed is everyone who is hung upon a tree."** With no intervening particle Paul immediately brings his readers to the one solution and only hope for sinners – Christ and his redemption. The abruptness with which Paul moves from the plight of sinners to Christ indicates his eagerness to present the only hope for redemption. **Christ redeemed us** – both Jew and Gentile. Duncan's view that "it is by the deliverance of Israel from the curse of the Law that God made it possible for the blessing promised to Abraham to extend to the Gentiles" fails to recognize that the continuation of the theme of redemption in verse 14 clearly includes Gentiles **(so that we might through faith receive the promise of the Spirit)**.

Paul's term for redemption here (ἐξηγόρασεν, *exēgorasen*) refers to purchase but Ridderbos correctly notes that "a more particular thought is attached to this redeeming than simply that of the emancipation of a prisoner. At issue here is satisfaction of violated justice, as is evident from the phrase: *from the curse of the law.*" Paul will use this term again in Galatians 4:4-5. Here Christ redeems believers from the law's curse; there he redeems "those under law" to bring us into the freedom of adulthood. Similarly, Büchsel notes that, though the word represents a transfer to freedom, "the essential point is that it confers both an actual and also a legally established freedom ensuring against any renewal of slavery. The claim of the law is satisfied.2 Indeed, "the curse of the Law is an ordinance of God which truly corresponds to His holy will towards the sinner… as is shown by the fact that it remains eternally valid and effective in relation to the lost." Büchsel adds significantly: "The fact that the holy will of God expressed in the Law and its curse finds true and full recognition in the transition to divine sonship and justification by faith, so that no man can find forgiveness in Christ unless the judgment on his sinfulness is also revealed in the experience of Jesus as the Crucified is what Paul expresses" in his use of ἐξαγοράζω, *exagoradzō* (*TDNT*, I. 126, 127).

The enslavement from which Christ has redeemed sinners is that of the **curse of the law**. With what astonishment, therefore, we read in Burton "this is not the judgment of God. To miss this fact is wholly to misunderstand Paul. But if the curse is not an expression of God's attitude towards men, neither is the deliverance from it a judicial act in the sense of release from penalty, but a release from a false conception of God's attitude, viz. from the belief that God actually deals with men on a legalistic basis." How could one reading Paul come to this conclusion? What can account for such a view but surrender of the intellect to the contemporary *zeitgeist*? On the contrary, Paul is teaching precisely what Professor Burton assumed that he did not. Disobedience to God's law brings with it curse (Deut. 27:9-26). By saying that **Christ redeemed us from the curse of the law by becoming a curse instead of**

us Paul is teaching substitution, vicarious atonement – Christ in our place paying the debt that we owed.[13] To put it another way, what is implicit here is made explicit in those passages in which Paul teaches the "great exchange", the imputation of our sin to Christ and of his judicial righteousness to believers. The ὑπέρ, *huper*, of the text means "instead of".[14]

Moreover, Paul's reference to Deuteronomy 21:23, "anyone who is hung on a tree is under God's curse," is intended to stress the substitutionary nature of Christ's atonement. The passage from Deuteronomy refers to the exposure of a criminal's corpse. When a crime deserved death the criminal was hung in the open as one cursed by God and was buried the same day (see Joshua 10:26ff.) In John 19:31-42 Jewish authorities are represented as insistent that the bodies of the crucified not be left till the next day, so profaning the Sabbath. Bruce points to the significance of Numbers 25:4 where during the apostasy of Baal-peor God's wrath is shown in a plague which was averted when the chiefs were hanged (παραδειγματίζω, *paradeigmatidzō*) "in the sun" before him. Bruce observes that the verb not only implies public exposure but also making a public example, "to effect atonement for covenant-violation". See also 2 Samuel 21:6. Bruce adds "The curse of Deuteronomy 27:26 was pronounced at the end of a covenant-breaking renewal ceremony and had special reference therefore to the covenant-breaker. Christ accordingly underwent the penalty prescribed for the covenant-breaker."

---

[13] Lightfoot: "The expression is to be explained partly by the Hebrew idiom, ...but still more by the religious conception which it involves. The victim is regarded as bearing the sins of those for whom atonement is made. The curse is transferred from them to it. It becomes in a certain sense the impersonation of the sin and of the curse. This idea is very probably in the scape-goat, Leviticus xvi. 5..."

[14] See, for example, A. T. Robertson (1977), *The Minister and His Greek New Testament*, Baker, 35-42 in which Robertson traces the use of *huper* in the business documents of the papyri, demonstrating that "the presumption is now in favor of the use of ὑπέρ for the idea of substitution." Zerwick, 91, also observes that *huper* "generally means 'for' in the sense 'in favour of,' but not rarely covers also 'for' in the sense 'in place of,' e.g. John 11,50 ...or Galatians 3, 13..."

This is precisely Paul's point. Christ took the penalty of covenant breakers. Christ in his atonement satisfied the claims of the law upon the sinner and so "brought freedom" for the believer. The REB captures the flavor of the passage: "Christ bought us freedom from the curse of the law by coming under the curse for our sake; for scripture says, 'Cursed is everyone who is hanged on a gibbet'." Calvin observes: "Now [Paul] does not say that Christ was cursed, but something more, that He was a curse, signifying that the curse of all was placed on Him. If this seems harsh to anyone, let him be ashamed also of the cross of Christ, in the confession of which we glory. God was not ignorant of what death His Son would die when He pronounced, 'Cursed is everyone who hangs on a tree'." I take Calvin to mean that Christ was not cursed in His person, that is, He did not personally deserve the curse, but was cursed by substitution, by bearing the curse due us for our sins.

Many commentators point out that the text does not say that Christ was cursed "by God". Fung, for example, thinks that "it is significant that Paul avoids using of Christ the expression that is used in the LXX of Deuteronomy 21:23 ('accursed by God'): the implication of such an expression would conflict with Paul's view of Christ's death as his supreme act of obedience to God's redemptive will (cf. Rom. 5:19; 2 Cor. 5:19)." While this concern is certainly to be appreciated, we must not allow it to obscure the fact that the law is God's law, a reflection of His nature, and that Christ was placed by the Father under the curse of His law for our sakes in a way that does not in the least detract from Christ's voluntary obedience to the Father. In this way Paul's teaching here is to be seen in continuity with Isaiah 53:10: "Yet it was the will of the LORD to crush him; he has put him to grief" (ESV).

In this passage, therefore, as in Galatians as a whole, Paul is vitally concerned with "how one gets saved".[15]

---

[15] N. T. Wright (1991) *The Climax of the Covenant*, T & T Clark, 150, commenting on the context surrounding 3:11: "Paul is not here speaking of those problems with which existentialist theologians have wrestled – 'achievement', 'accomplishment' and the like; nor yet with those traditional in Protestantism, 'legalism' (or 'nomism'), 'self-righteousness', and so forth.

2 Corinthians 5:21 forms the closest parallel to Paul's meaning here: "God made Him who had no sin to be sin for us, so that in Him we might become the righteousness of God." And on the basis of a correct understanding that Paul is teaching penal, vicarious atonement Luther observes that God heaped the sins of sinners upon Christ and said to Him: "Be Peter the denier; Paul the persecutor, blasphemer, and assaulter; David the adulterer; the sinner who ate the apple in Paradise; the thief on the cross."

Justification comes to sinners who believe on the sole ground of the atoning work of Christ, His vicarious, penal substitution, His achievement of the salvation of sinners in His obedience, cross and resurrection. Therefore it is no small loss if one follows Burton, or modern theories of atonement, that deny penal substitution, or at least some versions of the "new perspective on Paul". The difference is the difference between salvation and damnation. If Christ did not die in my place to save me from the penalty of God's broken law, then I am lost forever. This is the theme of Galatians, the message of Paul in the controversy with the Judaizers who attempted to mingle faith and works for acceptance with God. And this theme continued to echo into the time of the Protestant Reformation and continues to this day to be the grand theme sinners need to hear. As the church is faithful to her calling she will continue to proclaim with clarity this necessary note until Christ comes again.

The conversion of Charles Simeon, who ministered at Holy Trinity Church in Cambridge for fifty-four years, illustrates the importance of this point. Having lived outside of Christ and for himself, he was faced with fulfilling a school requirement to partake of Communion.[16] Struck by the thought – "Satan himself was as fit to attend as I" – he immediately began to prepare, in the flesh, for the assignment, making himself quite ill with reading, fasting and prayer. He thought to prepare better before returning

---

Nor is he offering an abstract account of 'how one gets saved'." On one thing we can agree: Paul offers no "abstract" account! His account is as concrete as the cross of Christ!

[16] For what follows, see Handley C. G. Moule, *Charles Simeon*, IVP, 24-29.

to the table at Easter. In God's providence, as he read Bishop Wilson on the Lord's Supper during Passion Week, he met with an expression to the effect that "the Jews knew what they did, when they transferred their sin to the head of their offering." "What, may I transfer all my guilt to another? Has God provided an Offering for me, that I may lay my sins on His head? Then, God willing, I will not bear them on my own soul one moment longer." Simeon testifies, "I sought to lay my sins upon the sacred head of Jesus; and on the Wednesday began to have hope of mercy; on the Thursday that hope increased; on the Friday and Saturday it became more strong; and on the Sunday morning, Easter-day, April 4, I awoke early with those words upon my heart and lips, 'Jesus Christ is risen today! Hallelujah! Hallelujah!'"

Is Simeon a mere example of a passing application of the gospel, of the introspective conscience of the West that is now dispensable? No, Simeon is an example of the multitudes of men, women and children who have come to see themselves under the curse of the law, in need of a Redeemer, and who have been "enabled to see that all my sins were buried in my Redeemer's grave". Handley Moule says "Luther's 'article of a standing or falling church' was for Simeon the article of a standing or falling soul, in unalterable personal conviction." And so must it be for all who have entrusted themselves to their curse bearer. For it is in Christ that infinite curse has turned to infinite blessing. The sinner, who views sin as a breach of God's law and who understands that "the death of Christ is a most solemn exemplar of the last judgment,"[17] will cry out for and find mercy on the basis of the merit of the sinless substitute. The suffering of the Son of God can deliver the sinner from the infinite debt that he has incurred for having broken the law of God since the infinite nature of Christ gave to his finite suffering infinite value. When the sinner trusts Christ, in the language of the hymn, "justice smiles and frowns no more".[18]

The purpose of this was that, in Christ Jesus, the blessing of Abraham might come to the nations, so that we might through

---

[17] John Owen, *Works*, 2.106.
[18] James Denney (1904), *Studies in Theology*, Hodder and Stoughton, 128: "The condemnation of our sins in Christ upon His Cross is the barb on the

faith receive the promise of the Spirit. Paul firstly clarifies the fruition of Christ's death by declaring that the blessing of Abraham might become universal, **might come to the nations.** The nature of salvation history is now such that the gospel promise given to Abraham has been extended to the Gentiles.

Then, secondly, he says that **we might through faith receive the promise of the Spirit** – an objective genitive meaning "the promised Spirit". Consequently, Paul brings full circle his argument in the early verses of chapter 3 that the presence of the Spirit in the Galatians' lives is by grace and not by works. Remarkably, the presence of the Spirit received by the Galatians at their conversion (3:2-5) is in fulfillment of the gospel promise given to Abraham. The presence of the Spirit, therefore, is an eschatological fulfillment evidencing that the new age has arrived in Christ.

Therefore, to repeat, living by law, as a means of justification and acceptance with God, is contrary to the Christians' identity as *pneumatikoi* (6:1) – those gifted with the eschatological Spirit! All that we have as Christians we have **in Christ** and, therefore, **through faith.**

So Paul's conclusion abounds with words indicating the sovereignty of grace – demonstrating that the gospel is not according to man. The Spirit is *received*, not attained by our efforts. The Spirit is in our lives as a result of *promise* received by *faith.* It is all of grace from first to last.[19]

---

hook. If you leave that out of your Gospel, I do not deny that your bait will be taken; men are pleased rather than not to think that God regards them with goodwill; your bait will be taken, but you will not catch men. You will not create in sinful human hearts that attitude to Christ which created the New Testament. You will not annihilate pride, and make Christ the Alpha and the Omega in man's redemption." This is an excellent remark despite Denney's unfortunate view of the canon reflected here.

[19] Bruce cites M. D. Hooker, 168: "Paul does not explain how one who is made a curse becomes a source of blessing: but since it is 'in Christ' that the blessing comes, and since it is by being identified with the one true descendant of Abraham that Jews and Gentiles receive the promise, it is clear that the curse has been annulled – transformed into blessing. This can only be through the resurrection: the judgement of the Law – that Christ was under a curse – has been withdrawn; God himself has vindicated his Son as righteous, and those who have faith in him are reckoned righteous and live."

8.
The Law and the Promise
(3:15-25)

Translation

Brothers, let's take an everyday example. Just as when a human covenant is ratified no one annuls or adds a codicil to it. But to Abraham the promises were spoken and to his seed. Scripture does not speak of his seed, as of many, but as of one, "and to his seed", who is Christ. This is what I mean: The law that has come into force 430 years later cannot annul a covenant previously ratified by God thus invalidating the promise. For, if the inheritance were by law, it would be no longer according to promise. But God graciously granted it to Abraham through a promise. Why then the law? It was added because of transgressions, until the promised seed should come to whom the promise was made, ordained through angels in the hand of a mediator. Now the mediator is not of one, but God is one.

Is the law then contrary to the promises of God? Absolutely not! For if a law were given that could impart life, righteousness then would be by law. But the Scripture confines everyone under sin so that the promise that is by faith in Jesus Christ might be given to those who believe.

Before the faith came we were held in confinement under law until the intended faith should be revealed. So then the law was our disciplinarian appointed to lead us to Christ, in order that we might be justified by faith. But now that the faith has come we are no longer under a disciplinarian.

Summary

Paul now addresses the place of the law in redemptive history. He takes as his example a "human covenant" which, once ratified, no one can cancel and to which no codicil can be added. Paul is demonstrating that the law which came later cannot alter God's promise to Abraham. God's covenant is inviolable and reliable.

Next, Paul argues on the basis of the singular "seed" that the promise made to Abraham finds fulfillment in Christ and that if human covenants are inviolable then certainly God's covenant is. The law codified at Sinai cannot alter God's covenant promises! Law does not invalidate promise or the inheritance given on the basis of God's promise. If salvation were through law-keeping, then law would annul the promise!

"Why then the law? It was added because of transgressions, until the promised seed should come." The law was not given to provide life but to demonstrate sinners' need for grace! The law cannot provide righteousness; the law shows the need for righteousness. Paul argues that the law came "third hand" (Neill), but the gospel of promise comes directly from God.

In view of this it is understandable that Paul asks, "Is the law then contrary to the promises of God?" He answers, "Absolutely not!" The law does not contradict God's way of salvation by promise. The law was never intended to justify sinners but to confine people under sin in order to make clear that the way of salvation was through God's gracious promise. The law imprisons but cannot provide escape. Indeed, the law functions to point to faith in Christ as the way of salvation. Before Christ came, sinners were "held in confinement". The law functioned as a "disciplinarian appointed to lead us to Christ, in order that we might be justified by faith". Since Christ has come, full maturity has been reached and the disciplinary function of the law, from the standpoint of redemptive history, is no longer necessary. In Christ the curse of the law has ended, and its custodial role is now obsolete. In view of all this, how can the Judaizers pursue righteousness by works?

Comment

Though Paul's tone is quieter his purpose is not less passionate. He acknowledges the communion of the saints and his concern for the **brothers** (cf.1:11; 4:12, 28, 31; 5:11, 13; 6:1, 18). His love for Christ's church always shows through! Indeed, it is Paul's love for the gospel and for Christ's church that moves him to write. Having insisted that sinners are not saved by obedience to the law but through the achievement of Christ alone Paul now must address the place of the law in redemptive history.

He reasons with them: **Brothers, let's take an everyday example. Just as when a human covenant is ratified no one annuls or adds a codicil to it.** There has been a great deal of debate over precisely to what Paul's **everyday example** might have referred. The discussion has revolved around the meaning of **a human covenant.** Since *diathēkē* can mean either "testament" or "covenant" translations vary. However, there are a number of reasons for viewing the proper translation of the term as "covenant".

First, *diathēkē* is the term used in the LXX for "covenant". Further, everywhere else that Paul uses *diathēkē* it means "covenant" (Rom. 9:4; 11:27; 2 Cor. 3:6, 14; Eph. 2:12). Most importantly, since Paul's discussion in its larger context is concerned with the Abrahamic covenant, one is predisposed to translate *diathēkē* by the term "covenant". This weights the decision so much in its favor that it is difficult to see how it cannot determine the question. Paul is discussing the significance of God's covenant by comparing it to a human covenant. The human covenant simply points beyond to the greater, more significant, covenant made by God (v. 17).

William Ramsay provided the best argument for translating *diathēkē* by the term "will" or "testament" (*Historical Commentary*, 349-55). He maintained that the decision in favor of this translation should be determined by the reference to "inheritance" in 3:18. However, the inheritance granted to Abraham was not related to a "will", so Ramsay's argument here seems to be without substance. Ramsay further argued that, since Paul is speaking "after the manner of men", he was "employing the word in the sense in which it was commonly used as part of the ordinary life of the cities of the East', and this demands the concept of "will" or "testament". But surely Paul could have used the term "covenant" to refer to irrevocable business arrangements between two parties as analogous to God's covenant with Abraham. Nonetheless, Ramsay and those who have followed him have recognized Paul's point regarding the irrevocable nature of the arrangement to which Paul refers. Paul, says Ramsay, assumes "*Diathēkē* as irrevocable from the moment when it was properly executed and passed through the Record Office of the city" (*Historical Commentary*, 370). Fung thinks that the legal terminology links the word to "testament", but he concludes that "whatever the precise background of the human analogy, Paul's point is plain: even a human legal settlement is irrevocable in nature."[1]

What K. M. Campbell has argued regarding *diathēkē* in Hebrews 9:16, 17 might be applicable to Galatians 3:15, namely, that the ideas of "covenant" and of a "will" might not be so far removed from one another as generally supposed. He notes "it has been demonstrated that from about the sixth century B.C. it became customary for a wealthy individual who had no issue publicly and officially to adopt a son to be his heir." The document drawn up and witnessed was a *diathēkē*. Campbell thinks that the essential idea of the Old Testament covenant and the contemporary Greek usage of *diathēkē* are fundamentally at one. Quoting W. D. Ferguson he notes that "in the Scriptures it is God who takes the initiative, and in the inscriptions it is the testator. In both there is some disposition made. It is also similar in that, in both, certain duties are enjoined upon the children or heirs. The one making the διαθήκη [*diathēkē*] always assumes the right to command, and to withhold his bequest if the conditions to it are not fulfilled."[2]

Whatever one decides about the precise nature of *diatheke* Paul's point is clear: once the *diathēkē* is ratified no one has

---

[1] Ramsay argues that this was the nature of a "testament" in Hellenized Asia Minor: "the testator, after adopting his heir, could not subsequently take away from him his share in the inheritance or impose new conditions on his succession."

[2] K. M. Campbell, "Covenant or Testament? Hebrews 9:16, 17 Reconsidered," *EQ* 44 (1972), 107-11. Betz notes that Paul might be utilizing the Jewish idea of *mattenat bari* which "designates a transaction of property from donor to

the right to cancel or add a codicil to it. The law coming later cannot alter God's promise given to Abraham. "Hence no one may make the fulfillment of the promise dependent upon the keeping of the law. That would be to do violence to the unconditional character of the promise, and would be like modifying covenants, something which even among people is regarded as unauthorized and impossible" (Ridderbos). Paul's illustration from human life serves to point to the reliability of God's greater covenant promise. The law coming later simply cannot abrogate the gospel promise given to Abraham.[3]

Paul's primary application of the irrevocable nature of the covenant promise will come in verse 17, but first Paul underscores the Christocentric character of the covenant context. **But to Abraham the promises were spoken and to his seed. Scripture does not speak of his seed, as of many, but as of one, "and to his seed", who is Christ.** God himself spoke the promises (hence they are irrevocable) to Abraham **and to his seed.** Paul's argument is based upon the singular **seed** which, even though it is a collective noun, he sees as an indicator of the one person in whom the gospel promises of God to Abraham are concentrated, namely, Christ. **Scripture does not speak of his seed, as of many, but as of one, "and to his seed", who is Christ.** Even if Paul's argument is to a degree rabbinic,[4] his motive is redemptive-historical. Promises made to Abraham and to his offspring (Gen. 13:15 ff; 17:7 ff.) find their fulfillment in Christ. The collective aspect of **seed**, however, does not completely fall away. He

---

donee, which takes place at once and is not conditional upon the donor's death, although he may retain his right to usufruct during his lifetime. The disposition, however, cannot be canceled or changed." This, however, raises the question how a primarily Gentile audience would be familiar with such an arrangement. Perhaps, Betz suggests, it was more widespread than supposed.

[3] Eadie notes: "To add to a covenant is virtually to annul it; the Judaistic dogma, under the guise of a supplement, was really an abrogation of the original promise or covenant."

[4] But is Paul's argument rabbinic? Duncan is surely right in saying that "for Paul the only true interpretation of this or any other Scripture passage was one which was in accordance with the revelation of God in Christ." The thought of John Murray on Matthew's use of Hosea 11:1 (Matt. 2:15 "Out of Egypt have I called my son") comes to mind. See John Murray, *The Unity of The Old and New Testaments,* in *Collected Writings* 1. 25, 26. He notes "it is easy to allege that this

tells us in verse 29 that those belonging to Christ are **Abraham's seed** (see also 3:14). But his point for the present is that the gospel promises given to Abraham find their concentration and focus in Christ Himself. It is essential that the Galatians hear, because of Judaizing error, that the Scriptures and their promises find their fulfillment in Christ. Ultimately, "Paul is not basing a truth on a small point of grammar. He has a deep spiritual appraisal of the real nature of Abraham's covenant" (Guthrie).

Having established the redemptive-historical, Christo-centric matrix of the covenant promises, Paul now proceeds to apply the point of verse 15. **This is what I mean: The law that has come into force 430 years later cannot annul a covenant previously ratified by God thus invalidating the promise.** If human covenants are inviolable, then certainly God's covenant is. The law coming years later[5] can do nothing to alter the covenant promises that were given by God and ultimately given with God's own Son in view! The Judaizers argued for the priority of law, but on what basis? The fulfillment of the promise did not depend upon the law given at Sinai but upon God's own free and unconditional promise. The law could do nothing to set that promise aside.

Law does not invalidate the promise. **For, if the inheritance were by law, it would be no longer according to promise. But God graciously granted it to Abraham through a promise.** Paul introduces new vocabulary, **the inheritance.** The promise of grace made to Abraham fulfilled in Christ as a cornucopia of

---

is an example of unwarranted application of Old Testament passages to New Testament events particularly characteristic of Matthew. But it is Matthew, as other New Testament writers, who has the perspective of organic relationship and dependence. The deliverance of Israel from Egypt found its validation, basis and reason in what was fulfilled in Christ. So the calling of Christ out of Egypt has the primacy as archetype, though not historical priority. In other words, the type is derived from the archetype or antitype. Hence not only the propriety but necessity of finding in Hosea 11:1 the archetype that gave warrant to the redemption of Israel from Egypt."Applying such thoughts to Paul could be fruitful and it seems to me that we are only on the outer limits of understanding redemptive history with anything like the depth of Paul.

[5] 430 years according to the LXX reading in Exodus 12:40. Included in the 430 years is the patriarchs' sojourn in Canaan and their posterity's stay in Egypt.

blessing on God's people is **the inheritance. The inheritance**, the Judaizers claimed, came **by law.** But Paul will have none of this. If the inheritance were gained by law-keeping, then the principle of grace would be set aside, and the inheritance **would be no longer according to promise.** Salvation by law-keeping sets aside promise and effectively cancels the covenant made with Abraham. If salvation were through law-keeping then law-keeping would annul the promise. Duncan is correct in seeing here an antithesis between Paul and the Judaizers. Two conflicting principles are at work – legalism and evangelicalism. In 3:18, **Abraham** is in the emphatic position, undoubtedly so that the way of promise may be underscored. In the instance of God's promise to Abraham the initiative is God's and not Abraham's. "If in the case of Abraham God took the initiative and of His own free grace *promised* to him the inheritance, why should the sons of Abraham think they are called to *earn* it by a process of legal obedience?" (Duncan).

But if the inheritance did not come by law, what then is the purpose of the law? What was its design? **Why then the law? It was added because of transgressions, until the promised seed should come to whom the promise was made, ordained through angels in the hand of a mediator.** What does Paul mean that the law **was added because of transgressions?** He means that law provides the context for Christ's achievement. The law is given to show sin and to reveal transgressions (Rom. 3:20; 4:15; 5:13; 7:7, 8). By **added**, Paul means that the law as given at Sinai was given after the promise.[6] **The promised seed**, Christ, comes against the backdrop of law. Law, far from saving, providing life or righteousness,

---

[6] See C. E. B. Cranfield, "St. Paul And The Law," *SJT* 17 (1964): 46ff. Cranfield points out that the law "not only increases sin in the sense that it makes it more sinful, it also *increases sin in the sense that it makes men sin more.*" He adds: "*In particular, the law makes men sin more, in that it establishes the possibility of legalism.* The very existence of the law is necessarily for sinful man a temptation to try to use it as a means to the establishment of a claim upon God, and so to the defence of his self-centredness and the assertion of a measure of independence over against God. He imagines that he can put God under an obligation to himself, that he will be able so adequately to fulfill the law's demands that he will earn for himself a righteous status before God."

demonstrates the sinfulness of sin and the need of grace. That was its function in redemptive history, a function that is now fulfilled, that continued **until the promised seed should come.** This does not mean that the sinfulness of sin is no longer revealed through the law but only that this structure of redemptive history for Israel is now fulfilled in the coming of Christ (3:22-25). In this sense "the law does not outlast the curse" (Lührmann). The law, therefore, was not given to provide life but to demonstrate sinners' need for grace! The law does not provide righteousness, rather "law brings wrath" (Rom. 4:15). Indeed, "the law was added so that the trespass might increase" (Rom. 5:20).[7]

It was added because of transgressions, until the promised seed should come to whom the promise was made, ordained through angels in the hand of a mediator. By stating that the law was **ordained through angels in the hand of a mediator,** Paul underlines the inferior position of law to promise, its subordinate role. Unlike the promise the law did not come directly from God to his people but **through angels**[8] (a tradition anchored in the LXX of Deut. 33:2; see also Heb. 2:2; Acts 7:38, 53) in **the hand of a (human) mediator.** Though Moses is meant, his name is conspicuous by its absence here and throughout Galatians. Christ is the crux of history and not Moses.

Verse 20 is difficult and the interpretations of the verse have been numerous. Literally the text reads, **now the mediator (or intermediary) is not of one, but God is one.** Among the

---

[7] Duncan notes that men may sin in ignorance but they transgress "only when they have a recognized standard of what is right, and it was to provide such a standard that the Law was brought in." He points out that, by showing sinners their need, God was not deviating from the principle of faith.

[8] Duncan suggests an interesting possibility: "Undue devotion to the ordinances of the Law seemed to Paul to imply a worship of angels rather than of the living God, and thus to have affinities with paganism." See also Schnelle, 289 note 82: "Cf. Deut. 33:2 LXX; Josephus, *Ant.*15.136; *Jub.*1:29; *T. Dan.*6:2; and elsewhere. Rabbinic evidence is given in Strack and Billerbeck, *Kommentar,* 3:554ff. Martyn, *Galatians,* 354-65, points out that *diatassō* is never connected with *nomos* in the Septuagint. Paul thus also shows semantically that he places the origin of the law in a special category while in fact taking the tradition that the Torah was given by angels, originally meant in a positive sense, and presenting it *negatively.*"

suggestive translations are Moffatt: "(an intermediary implies more than one party, but God is one)"; TEV: "But a go-between is not needed when there is only one person; and God is one"; REB: "but an intermediary is not needed for one party acting alone, and God is one."[9] The interpretation of the passage requires that we see the point of connection with the preceding argument. The law came **through angels in the hand of a (human) mediator**, meaning Moses. The law is in an inferior position to the promise and the mode of its deliverance demonstrates its subordinate place in the history of redemption. The promise, however, was given without such intermediaries. The method of its deliverance corresponds to its superior and determinative position in God's economy. Therefore, the passage may be paraphrased in this expansive way: **The law given through the mediator requires more than one party, but God gave the promise directly without such parties.**[10] The meaning of the passage seems to be well summed up by Stephen Neill: "the promise came to Abraham first-hand from God; and the law comes to the people *third-hand* – God – the angels – Moses the mediator – the people."[11]

In view of what he has said in verses 19-20 concerning the relationship between law and promise, Paul asks: **Is the law then contrary to the promises of God?** Did God change His approach to how sinners are saved by giving the law? Is the law in that sense **contrary to the promises of God?** Does the giving of the law indicate another way to salvation, a way that is different from the way of promise, a legalistic as opposed to

---

[9] Phillips' paraphrase is provocative: "The Law was inaugurated in the presence of angels and by the hand of a human intermediary. The very fact that there was an intermediary is enough to show that this was not the fulfilling of the promise. For the promise of God needs neither angelic witness nor human intermediary but depends on him alone."

[10] Eadie: "The clause, 'but God is one,' does not announce dogmatically the unity of the Godhead, as do several similar utterances in the Pentateuch. Whatever doctrinal ideas the words might suggest, they are here used on purpose to deny all duality in the bestowment of the promise..." For an example of the viewpoint that Paul refers here to the concept of God's unity, "the dogma of monotheistic religion," see Betz.

[11] In personal correspondence Dennis Johnson has suggested, following his colleague Steve Baugh, that Paul appeals to Deut. 6:4-5 in this passage and

an evangelical way to knowing God? This would be a complete misunderstanding of Paul's theology and to this question he responds: *mē genoito*, Absolutely not!

The giving of the law certainly does not contradict God's way of salvation by the promise. A distinction in function does not imply that God's purpose in the law contradicts His promise. Indeed, Paul argues, **For if a law were given that could impart life, righteousness then would be by law.** Righteousness would have been *ek nomou* (by law) if the law had been empowered to impute it. But the law was totally incapable of justifying sinners and it was never intended for that purpose! The law was not intended to be the source of life[12] or of justification. The law cannot bring life; the law can only demand that we obey its precepts. Paul's entire argument is predicated on the view that no sinner is capable of keeping the righteous requirements of the law for justification. The law demands perfect, personal obedience, but it cannot empower anyone to so obey. The law shows that we are not righteous; it cannot be the source of righteousness. Rather than providing life and justifying righteousness, Paul tells the Galatians that the law's subordinate function was to confine men under sin in order to make clear that the way of promise and grace is the way of salvation.

---

that it means: "God is the sole party responsible for the fulfillment of covenant blessing here (unlike the reciprocal obligations entailed in the blood sprinkling ceremony of Exod. 24) because the divine Son undertakes to become incarnate to fulfill the covenant obligations on our behalf...so that the promise to Abraham is solely guaranteed by the unilateral commitment of the one God." While I favor the exposition given above, that the method of deliverance of the Abrahamic covenant corresponds to its superior and determinative position in God's economy, the suggestion of Steve Baugh via Dennis Johnson is very attractive and deserving of ongoing consideration.

[12] Betz: "It is one of the principal doctrines of Judaism that God gave the Torah for the purpose of providing a way for Israel into eternal life. We can safely conclude that Paul's opponents agreed with the Jewish position, or they would never have required the Galatians to accept circumcision and Torah. Also, it is obvious that Paul himself denies the doctrine. For him, life is given through the Spirit. Indeed, according to Paul it is false to expect life from the Torah, since it was never given for that purpose. If, however, life does not come from the Torah, neither does righteousness." Meyer notes that "the ζωη [life] is the eternal life which is manifested at the *Parousia* (Col. iii.3 f.), and therefore in reality the κληρονομία [*klēronomia*] (vv. 18, 29)."

But the Scripture confines everyone under sin so that the promise that is by faith in Jesus Christ might be given to those who believe. Beginning with the adversative *alla* **(but)** Paul emphasizes that the Scripture does not grant the possibility of a righteousness provided by law, rather, it **has shut up** or **confines (***sunekleisen*, BDAG *sugkleiō*, "to confine to special limits, *confine, imprison*"**) everyone under sin.**[13] *BDAG* suggests the translation "has locked everything in under the power of sin." REB: "But scripture has declared the whole world to be prisoners in subjection to sin..." The law, then, serves God's purpose of grace by hemming in, closing off, imprisoning. "It shuts up all men under accusation and therefore, instead of giving, it takes away righteousness" (Calvin).[14] The law provides no avenue of escape; rather, it is a prison from which – by its very provision – there is no exit![15]

But why has the law been established to function in this confining way? Paul answers that question by means of a purpose clause, **so that the promise that is by faith in Jesus Christ might be given to those who believe.** That is, that the only means of salvation would stand in *bas-relief*. "Belief is opposed to works, as the principle of grace is to merit. This, therefore is the full-fledged break-through of the nomistic scheme of redemption" (Ridderbos). The law confines so that salvation by promise might be **given to those who believe.** Faith, not works of the law, is the means appointed to receive the promise. Not merit

---

[13] Guthrie rightly, we think, suggests that the neuter *ta panta* "all things" should be interpreted in a personal way. "A clear parallel to this personal use of the neuter to bring out the idea of comprehensiveness is found in John 6:37, 39."

[14] Calvin continues: "The reasoning is most powerful. 'You seek righteousness in the law. But the law itself, with the whole of Scripture, leaves nothing to men but condemnation; for all men and their works are condemned as unrighteous. Who then shall live by the law?' He is alluding to 'He who shall do these things shall live in them.' Shut out by guilt, I say, from life, we seek salvation in the law in vain. By saying *all things* he conveys more than if he had said 'all men'; for it embraces not only men but everything that they have or can put forward."

[15] Michel, *TDNT* VII, 746: "One should not forget the element of polemical distortion in the argument of Gl. 3:23 that the Law does not bring about a holy and blessed enclosing but a shutting up which renders man helpless and

but the empty vessel of faith. "The marvelous fact is this, that *the way of salvation is the way of faith just because it is only in faith that the exclusiveness of divine grace is recognized and honored....* As penitence excludes all merit, so too faith, directed only to divine mercy, excludes all worthiness" (G. C. Berkouwer, *Faith and Justification,* 189). As the law cried out "condemned", God's intent was to lead His people to faith which cries out for grace.

Paul as the great redemptive-historical theologian under-scores the temporary, provisional character of the law as the dominant factor in the old administration of the covenant. This temporary, provisional character of the law is what Paul intends by **before the faith came**. By **the faith** Paul means Christ him-self, that is Christ and the benefits brought into this present evil age by the in-breaking of the kingdom with all its newness.

Keeping the redemptive-historical thrust in mind **the faith** is a full and encompassing way of expressing the newness, sparkle and freshness of the kingdom inaugurated by Christ in His resurrection. Paul is thinking of "faith centered in Christ" (Guthrie).[16] In contrast to the atmosphere of freedom in which the Christian now lives believers in the old administration **were held in confinement under law until the intended faith should be revealed.** Just as sin seen in view of God's law was in verse 22 the "jailer", so now Paul declares the law itself to be the method of confinement until Christ should come. The law, then, is a great pressure pushing sinners onward in confined helplessness till

---

captive like imprisonment." Bruce observes: "The law does indeed produce transgressions, and by that very fact it demonstrates its inability to lead to justification and life. Those who use it as a way to justification and life are in fact misusing it; it is this misuse that nullifies the promise. What the law does is to bring to light the universal human plight: all are 'under sin'. If, realizing this, men and women look round for a way of deliverance from their plight, they find it in the promise. Believing the promise, and the one who has made it, they are justified – justified by faith in Jesus Christ, in whom the promise and its fulfillment are embodied. Far from being against the promises, then, the law drives men and women to flee from its condemnation and seek refuge in the promises."

[16] Fung: "The faith in question, referred to three times in vv. 23 and 25 as '*the* faith' (articular), is the faith in Christ just spoken of in v. 22; it is the principle (and means) of salvation opposed to law and at the same time stands for the new order of eschatological salvation itself. The coming of faith is therefore

the only One who could deliver should come.[17] "To change the metaphor, the law functions, like blinders on a horse, to point Israel in one direction – to the advent of the new age and the fulfillment of the promise" (Cousar). Liberation from bondage comes by means of the saving achievement of Christ. Christ alone could break open the prison doors. The law could not bring righteousness but only hold in confinement, closing all of man's prideful means of self-escape, until the righteousness demanded by the law should appear. Paul's use of the term **revealed** should remind us of 1:12, 15-16. "As in 1:12, 16, *revelation* designates here the separation of two worlds, which for Paul himself had been accomplished at Damascus, but even there he understood it in principle as the final end of the law" (Lührmann).

So then, writes Paul, **the law was our disciplinarian appointed to lead us to Christ, in order that we might be justified by faith.** Paul describes the function of the law by the term *paidagōgos*, variously translated as "tutor" (A.V.), "wards in discipline" (Moffatt), "attendant" (Goodspeed), "a strict governess" (Phillips), "instructor" (TEV), "custodian" (RSV), "disciplinarian" (NRSV) and "guardian" (ESV). The NIV simply translates "so the law was put in charge to lead us to Christ"; the REB translates "the law was thus put in charge of us until Christ should come, when we should be justified through faith". Those translations of *paidagōgos* that view the

---

identical with the coming of Christ, who is the object of faith; it is the coming of Christ, making possible the coming of faith, which is the decisive point in salvation history."

[17] Ridderbos: "The apostle speaks in the first person plural, even though he is speaking not only for the Jews, but also for the more numerous Gentile readers (cf. 4:9). For the Gentiles, too, though outside the pale of the revelation of Israel, were co-subject to the law with the Jews, and were not without knowledge of it (Rom. 2:14-16)." Bruce notes that Gentiles and Jews alike are "confined under sin" in verse 22 so "Gentiles and Jews are included in the reference to 'being under law'. G. Howard…maintains that the law of Moses, whether Gentiles or Jews are said to be under it – not in the sense that all are subject to its specific demands, but in the sense that 'the law is a suppressor and a restrainer of mankind'; men and women are suppressed under its tyranny, but are released from that tyranny by Christ. The law kept the Gentiles out of the privileges of the people of God and kept Israel apart from the rest of mankind; this divisive force has been overcome by the unifying effect of Christ's redemptive act."

function of the law as instructional, e.g. "tutor", are least able to convey the meaning of the text, while those translations emphasizing the custodial and disciplinary purpose of the law best express Paul's meaning.

A *paidagōgos* in antiquity was not a "teacher" (*didaskalos*) in the strict sense of the word, but an attendant who, in wealthy Greek and Roman homes, was put in charge of a son's behavior and actions until he reached puberty. The *paidagōgos*, usually a slave, was a custodian in charge of administering the father's discipline during the time of immaturity until the child grew into mature manhood.[18] Therefore, when Paul describes the law as **our disciplinarian appointed to lead us to Christ, in order that we might be justified by faith** he means that the law, far from providing righteousness and salvation, disciplined sinners to come to the Savior who only can justify. The law cannot justify; it can only demonstrate the sinner's need of justification. Justification comes by faith and not by law-keeping.[19]

But now Christ has come. There is something new under the sun! Therefore, what difference does it make? **But now that the faith has come we are no longer under a disciplinarian.** Since Christ has come full maturity has been reached and the disciplinary function of the law, from the standpoint of redemptive history, is no longer necessary. In Christ the curse of the law is fulfilled, the supremacy and control of the law has ended, and its disciplinary and custodial role has been rendered obsolete. How then can the Judaizers pursue righteousness by works? Indeed, the function of the law was to lead sinners to Christ who alone can justify. Moreover, from a redemptive-historical perspective, to teach the dominion of the law is to regress into the pre-Christian era (Cousar).

---

[18] See especially R. N. Longenecker, "The Pedagogical Nature of the Law in Galatians 3:19–4:7," *JETS* 25 (1982): 53-61; and D. J. Lull, "'The Law Was Our Pegagogue': A Study in Galatians 3:19-25," *JBL* 105 (1986): 481-98.

[19] Ridderbos speaks of the law as leading to "a growing passion for freedom because of the oppressive yoke. The law makes man unsatisfied, teaches him how he will *not* get to the freedom of life. In this sense the law drives to Christ, in order that we should be justified in Him through faith – justified, that is, emancipated from the curse and the impotence wrought by the law."

9.
Sons of God through Faith
(3:26-29)

Translation

For you are all sons of God through faith in Christ Jesus. Well then, since all who have been baptized into Christ have clothed themselves with Christ, there is no Jew nor Greek, no slave nor freeman, and no male and female;[1] for you are all one in Christ Jesus. So if you are Christ's, then you are Abraham's seed and heirs according to promise.

Summary

Since Christ has come we are not to view our position as that of prisoners or minors, but as adopted sons of God through faith in Christ. Paul connects the dominant theme of union with Christ with baptism which is the sign of faith common to "all" believers. "Those who have been baptized into Christ" have in that baptism "clothed themselves with Christ".

---

[1] The pattern of the preceding phrases is changed from a negative conjunction *oude* to *kai* – "male *and* female". Lightfoot suggested that Paul alludes to Genesis 1:27. Fung cites Witherington in asserting that Paul's purpose was to oppose the rabbinic concept that a woman must be connected to a circumcised male to have a place in the covenant community, and that "in Christ, marriage, with its linking of male *and* female, into a one flesh union, is…not a requirement for believers". For these reasons we have opted to translate "male and female" rather than the usual "male or female".

The implications of this union are sweeping. Paul emphasizes the consequences of union with Christ for the community of faith: "there is no Jew nor Greek, no slave nor freeman, and no male and female; for you are all one in Christ Jesus." Former religious, social and sexual distinctions are irrelevant so far as spiritual privileges are concerned. Now, in Christ, such distinctions are abolished.

Paul concludes the argument begun in 3:6 by insisting that all believers are "Abraham's seed and heirs according to promise." Believers are, in Christ, the spiritual seed of Abraham and, therefore, heirs according to the promise. This is not the result of law but of grace!

Comment

God is holy. His nature is contrary to all sin. But the last of the law's threatening thunderclaps has cracked over our Savior's head and God says to us, "Be at peace". In the cross God shakes hands with us sinners, indeed embraces us. The cross is the basis of our justification, for God's reconciling of the world unto himself and also for our adoption into His family. **For you are all sons of God through faith in Christ Jesus.** Since Christ has come we are not to view our position as that of prisoners under law or of minors awaiting maturity. By faith in Christ believers are full **sons of God.** "No tongue, either of men or of angels, could proclaim the glory of this magnificently enough"(Luther).

This sonship by which the Father receives us is the accomplishment of His Son and is ours by virtue of our union with Him. The text may be translated "for you are all sons of God through faith in Christ Jesus" (as I have done) or "For you are all sons of God in Christ Jesus through faith." Since Paul, in this section, stresses union with Christ many have opted for the latter translation. It is also favored by the fact that Paul uses here the preposition *en* rather than *eis*, whereas typically in Paul "believing" or "faith" is *eis* (into) Christ. It is in Christ Jesus that we are accounted sons; it is through faith that we are in Christ. On the other hand Paul has stressed faith in Christ all along and it may seem best to translate the passage by keeping that in the forefront. In any case this at best is a matter of subtle nuance. Union with Christ is the theme stressed here along with faith in Christ.

Why does Paul connect the theme of union with Christ to baptism?[2] What does he mean by saying **all who have been baptized into Christ have clothed themselves with Christ**? Paul's concern is to show that baptism visibly represents the union of the believer to Christ. Paul certainly does not mean for us to interpret baptism *ex opera operato*. Baptism does not possess efficacy apart from the gospel. That view would contradict all that Paul has argued till now and would require viewing baptism in place of circumcision as a "plus" to the gospel. But baptism is not an addition to the gospel; rather, it finds its rightful place in the church only when viewed in the context of the gospel of grace through faith in Christ and as a sign of union with Him.

Paul, then, means to stress that baptism is common to **all** Christians whether Jew, Gentile or from whatever standing in society, and that sonship is not limited to Jews. The sign of faith allows for no discrimination but belongs to everyone who is in Christ and has faith in Him. Those **who have been baptized into Christ** have in that baptism **clothed themselves[3] with Christ**. In baptism Christians have put on Christ as one would put on an identifying garment.[4] Believers in Christ have been given a new identity. Christ himself is the believer's clothing. "Just as a garment which one puts on…quite envelops the person wearing it, and identifies his appearance and his life, so…the person baptized in Christ is quite entirely taken up in Christ and in the salvation brought by Him" (Ridderbos).

The implications of union with Christ and of baptism, which marks **all** believers without exception as God's sons, are vast and sweeping. Here Paul expresses the social consequences

---

[2] Whether or not Paul is referencing an early church baptismal liturgy does not seem to me to be provable from the data we presently possess. At any rate, it should not determine to any great degree how we understand Paul's meaning.

[3] Or perhaps "are clothed upon with Christ". See Oepke, *TDNT*, II.320.

[4] Morris: "If they had reflected on what their baptism signified, the Galatians would not have been misled by the false teaching that led them to circumcision."

of the gospel of grace for the community of faith. Union with Christ implies an astonishing unity among **all who have been baptized into Christ.** What distinguishes believers is union with Christ rather than those cherished social and political distinctions common to the world of Paul's day and often of our own. Consequently, Paul insists **there is no Jew nor Greek, no slave nor freeman, and no male and female; for you are all one in Christ Jesus.** The old status prior to baptism defined by this present evil age is now abolished and "it is significant that Paul makes these statements not as utopian ideals or as ethical demands, but as accomplished facts" (Betz).

The religious distinction between Jew and Gentile has no place in the Christian church.[5] No sinner can earn deliverance. Freedom has come through Jesus' shed blood. Therefore **there is no Jew nor Greek.** Justifying righteousness and sonship belong to all equally who have entrusted themselves to Christ and are in union with Him. As Paul would later write: "For there is no difference between Jew and Gentile – the same Lord is Lord of all and richly blesses all who call on him, for, 'Everyone who calls on the name of the Lord will be saved'" (Rom. 10:12; compare 1 Cor. 12:13; Col. 3:11). We should also keep in mind Ephesians 2:14-16 in which Paul speaks of the law as a "wall of separation" between Jews and Gentiles that was removed by Christ's atonement.

Moreover, the social distinctions prevalent in Paul's day present no barrier to spiritual privilege. There is **no slave nor freeman.**[6] Though these distinctions were common in

---

[5] Compare Eduard Lohse (1971), *Colossians and Philemon*, Fortress Press, 143, 144, on Colossians 3:11: "What separates men from one another in the world – which of course still exists – has been abolished in the community of Jesus Christ... he speaks about men of completely diverse origins who have been gathered together in unity in Christ through allegiance to one Lord. True, they also continue to live in the roles that the world assigns to them as Greeks or Jews, slaves or free. But where the Body of Christ exists and where his members are joined together into a fellowship, there the differences which separate men from one another are abolished."

[6] Morris: "To recognize that a believing slave was just as important in God's sight as the highest among the nobility was to point to a radical abolition of a distinction that was taken for granted throughout Paul's world. These words mark a revolution."

the society of Paul's day and even among Christians in the social order, these distinctions do not exist within the freedom purchased for God's people by Christ. Union with Christ makes it impossible for one of higher rank to claim a greater share in God's grace because of that status. In this respect union with Christ is the great equalizer in the church.

Even the distinction of sex provides no ground for elitism so far as spiritual blessings are concerned. There is, in this regard, **no male and female**.[7] From the standpoint of redemption in Christ this along with the other distinctions mentioned by Paul are totally irrelevant. To both men and women the gospel has been preached, the gift of the Spirit has been given, and baptism has been administered. Neither maleness nor femaleness provides any advantage so far as these things are concerned. In Paul's day, when women were often despised or certainly not valued appropriately, his statement must have come as a powerful corrective to those in the church who might be tempted to view the matter after the old order of things. For surely, Paul's viewpoint is the eschatological one that has been apparent all along and he is working out the implications of the new creation to which

---

[7] Guthrie: "There was particular point in the mention of the absence of distinctions of sex for Jewish readers or those influenced by them. The Jew tended to despise the woman. But the same approach was true of the majority of the Gentile world (Macedonia was an exception). There is no doubt that few outside the Christian Church in Paul's day would have maintained any form of equality of the sexes. The apostle himself drew some distinctions between the sexes as far as their functions with the Church were concerned, but no distinctions over their position in Christ."

Ramsay, *Historical Commentary,* 389, 390, suggests that this passage is "one of the many little touches throughout this Epistle which place the reader in the Graeco-Phrygian cities of Asia Minor. Among them the position of women was unusually high and important, and they were often entrusted with offices and duties which elsewhere were denied them. Hence, the allusion to the equality of the sexes in the perfect form which the Church must ultimately attain, would not seem to the people of these Graeco-Phrygian cities to be so entirely revolutionary and destructive of existing social conditions as it must have seemed to the Greeks. The Greeks secluded respectable women, and granted education to them only at the price of shame; but few Phrygian cities were fully Hellenised in this respect."

believers presently belong (Gal. 6:15). Let the rabbis insist that a woman might find a place in the covenant community by virtue of her connection to a circumcised man. Not so in the true covenant community, the church of the Lord Jesus Christ! Males and females are both privileged with membership in the community by faith in Christ![8]

The interpretation of Paul's words as androgynous misses the point as does the application of the text to the question of female office-bearers in the church. Paul is not teaching the removal of all distinctions within the church. Paul does not say that male and female are identical, but that they are one. His purpose is to state that spiritual privileges belong equally to all within the church without exception. The sort of elitism represented by the Judaizing party or other kinds of spiritual elitism that might be based upon additional distinctions have no place in the church. Moreover, it is inappropriate to apply this verse to the question of female office-bearers. This is certainly not Paul's purpose in the passage. Elsewhere Paul insists upon male leadership grounded in creation (1 Tim. 2:11-15). In addition, a consistent application of this sort of argument might do away with all office in the church. We must strictly adhere to Paul's purpose in the passage which is to insist that spiritual privileges belong to all who have union with Christ. Ordination is not a common privilege but is a calling to a particular office within the church. Therefore applying this text to the question of female office-bearers in the church is misplaced.

Spiritual privileges, then, belong to all equally in the church of Christ **for you are all one in Christ Jesus.** Formerly distinctions of religious heritage, class, and sex have divided and have been used as excuses to exclude others from spiritual

---

[8] S. Lewis Johnson, "Role Distinctions in the Church," in John Piper, Wayne Grudem ed. (1993), *Recovering Biblical Manhood and Womanhood*, Crossway, 164: "There is no reason to claim that Galatians 3:28 supports an egalitarianism of function in the church. It does plainly teach an egalitarianism of privilege in the covenantal union of believers in Christ.... Questions of roles and functions in that body can only be answered by a consideration of other and later New Testament teaching."

privileges. But now, in Christ, such distinctions are abolished. Those who have formerly opposed one another and gloried in distinctions are **one in Christ Jesus**[9] or, as Paul says in Ephesians, form "one new man" in Christ.

Paul has shown a powerful application of this reality for church life in Galatians 2:11ff. in which he rebuked Peter for his failure to recognize that table fellowship must be extended without exception to all who are justified by faith in Christ. Paul could not stand by while the gospel was compromised by Peter nor does he stand by idly while the gospel is compromised by the Judaizers. Moreover, Paul's instruction on the reality of union with Christ and of His people forearms us to be guardians of this principle within the church today. The basis upon which God receives us in Christ is the same basis upon which we are called to receive one another. Denying that is a denial of the gospel.

Paul concludes his argument begun in 3:6 by saying **so if you are Christ's, then you are Abraham's seed and heirs according to promise.** In 3:7-9 Paul refers to believers as the seed of Abraham to whom the promises were made (v. 16). All believers (**if you are Christ's**) are **Abraham's seed and heirs according to promise.** They all belong to Christ the promised seed and are, therefore, Abraham's seed. They are all heirs of the promise.[10] "This κληρονόμοι (heirs) is the *triumph* of the whole, accompanied with the seal of *divine certainty* by means of κατ' ἐπαγ (according to promise); the two together forming

---

[9] Guthrie: "If all people, to whichever of the previously mentioned classes they belonged, are regarded as on an equal footing, it is because in Christ everyone appears the same, as if one all-inclusive man includes every other Christian. The full force of the masculine gender of *heis* (one) should be retained, for the idea is not of a unified organization, but of a unified personality."

[10] Morris: "*Heirs* is an important word in the present discussion. The Jews were very proud of the fact that they were the descendants of the great patriarch and physically his heirs. But more important than this was the fact that all who had faith, whether Jews or Gentiles, were heirs *according to promise*. God had made great promises to Abraham, and for Paul it was crystal clear that those promises were fulfilled in believers, not in those who could claim no more than physical descent."

the final death-blow to the Judaistic opponents" (Meyer). Christians are part of the people of God throughout the ages. We are, in Christ, the spiritual seed of Abraham and therefore in Christ heirs according to the promise.

Ridderbos well says: "With this last link in the chain, it becomes clear in what sense Christ could be called the seed of Abraham (v. 16): in a corporate sense, that is, as Head of the body and of the new covenant. Always and again this one thing is reconfirmed: that belonging to the seed of Abraham is not determined by physical descent, but by faith. Essentially, in principle, the seed of Abraham is spiritual seed. If on the one hand this represents a limitation of the concept, on the other hand it represents a tremendous broadening of it. It is this broadening of the concept of Abraham's seed that is the subject in this context."

10.
No Longer a Slave but a Son
(4:1-7)

Translation
This is my point: as long as the inheritor is a minor, he is no better off than a slave though he is lord over all. But he is under guardians and stewards until the time appointed by the father. So it was with us: when we were children we were enslaved under the basic elements of the world. But when the fullness of time came, God sent His Son, born of a woman, born under law, in order that He might redeem those under the law, so that we might receive adoption. That you are sons is evident since God sent the Spirit of His Son into our hearts, crying out, "Abba, Father!" So you are no longer a slave but a son; and if a son, also an heir through God.

Summary
   Having shown that believers are Abraham's seed and heirs according to promise (3:29) Paul now explains more fully what it means to be an heir. He illustrates this by means of a Roman legal practice wherein a minor lives in hope of possession of a future inheritance. The heir is potentially the legal owner but does not yet possess it "until the time appointed by the father". All who were "enslaved under the basic elements of the world" were in an analogous position until in "the fullness of time" God signaled the end of bondage for those under law.

"The fullness of time" corresponds to the incarnation of the Son sent by the Father for our redemption, "born of a woman, born under law". The slavery, from which we are redeemed, corresponds to Paul's illustration of the minor who is "under guardians and stewards until the time appointed by the father". Now believers live in the reality of their inheritance.

The purpose for which God sent His Son was to redeem sinners under law. An accompanying and concomitant purpose, as indicated by the second portion of the double purpose clause, was "so that we might receive adoption". Adoption roughly corresponds to the concept of inheritance in Paul's earlier illustration and stresses the gratuitous nature of the believer's relationship to God through Christ. The Spirit of adoption, also sent by the Father, cries out "Abba, Father!" from within the hearts of believers. Paul brings full circle an argument begun in the early verses of chapter three demonstrating that salvation is by grace. Indeed, the Spirit cries out to the Father, passionately exulting in God's redemption. "So you are no longer a slave but a son; and if a son, also an heir through God." Believers are heirs, adopted sons, through the grace of God. The Trinitarian structure of the passage underscores the divine origin, accomplishment and application of redemption.

Comment

We must not allow the chapter division to hinder us from grasping the flow of Paul's argument. Having shown that believers in Christ are Abraham's seed and heirs according to promise (3:29) he now works out more fully what it means to be an heir. He does this by pointing to a legal situation that must have been familiar to the readers, in which a minor lives in the hope of the possession of a future inheritance. **This is my point:[1] as long as[2] the inheritor is a minor, he is no better off than a slave though he is lord over all.**

Much discussion has focused around the precise legal circumstance to which Paul draws the Galatians' attention. It

---

[1] Literally, *But I say*.

[2] ἐφ' ὅσον χρόνον (*eph hoson chronon*), as long as.

is reasonable to follow Betz's suggestion that Paul refers to a practice in Roman law called *tutela impuberis* ("guardianship for a minor"), or more precisely, *tutela testamentaria* ("guardianship established by testament") wherein the *paterfamilias* appointed guardians for his children who would inherit the father's property after his death. Betz points out that during the time in which the heir is a minor he is potentially the legal owner of the inheritance though he does not yet possess it.[3] Ramsay, on the other hand, sees this as referring to Anatolian and specifically South Galatian custom (*Historical Commentary*, 392).

Whatever the precise reference Paul's point is plain. So long as the believer is a minor he does not yet enjoy his inheritance; indeed, **he is no better off than a slave though he is lord over all.** Before Christ's coming God's people did not enjoy fully the gospel privileges God planned for them. They were, like the heir, **under guardians and stewards until the time appointed by the father.** *Epitropoi* "is the regular term in Greek law for the guardian of the infant, appointed by the father, or by the law in default of the father's nomination. It was also the regular translation of the Latin *tutor*" (Ramsay, *Historical Commentary*, 392). Ramsay suggests that the second term, *oikonomos*, which is less easily understood, refers to one who, as the name implies, regulates the household and business affairs of the infant.[4]

---

[3] Betz adds: "To be sure, this comparison must be taken *cum granu salis*. This similarity between the minor and the slave is one of appearance only. The point Paul wants to make is, however, clear: both, the minor and the slave, lack the capacity of self-determination." Bruce cites an interesting illustration from the will of one "Eudaemon of Oxyrhynchus (AD 126), relating to two of his sons who were minors: 'If I die before the said Horus and Eudaemon have completed twenty years, their brother Thonis and their maternal grandfather Harpaesis, also called Horus, son of Thoris, shall be guardian (ἐπίτροπος) of each of them until he completes twenty years.' Here the twentieth birthday anniversary is the προθεσμία τοῦ πατρός."

[4] Ramsay, *Historical Commentary*, 392-93, suggests that there are no direct parallels in Roman law and that in pure Greek law this arrangement was unknown. "But the law and manners of the Graeco-Phrygian cities (and of the Seleucid cities generally) were not pure Greek. They were Hellenistic, having the form which Greek ideas assumed, when they went forth to conquer the East and were inevitably modified in the process. Accordingly,

That this illustrates the position of Israel under the law is apparent. Israel's full appreciation of gospel freedom could not be known until Christ came. But Paul's concern is not limited to Israel but to all who **were enslaved**[5] **under the basic elements of the world** (4:3, 9) which includes Gentile sinners who also may be Abraham's seed and heirs according to promise (3:29).[6] Paul's point, then, is that the supervisors of the minor continue until the time appointed by the father. That his point is applicable to all Christians may be indicated by Paul's use of the first person plural.[7]

What does Paul mean by enslavement **under the basic elements of the world** (τὰ στοιχεῖα τοῦ κόσμου, *ta stoicheia tou kosmou*)? These **basic elements** can mean the ABCs of a given world-view, in this case, of the religious principles held by those to whom Paul is writing. On this interpretation Paul would have in mind the elements of knowledge, the basic teachings of false religion which have held Jew and Gentile in bondage. Others see this as referring to

---

everything becomes clear when we look at the Syrian Law-book. The same distinction is there drawn as in Rome: a child is subject to an *Epitropos* up to fourteen, thereafter he is able to make a Will and dispose of his own property, but the practical management of the property remains in the hands of a *curator* till the ward reaches the age of twenty-five. But the Syrian law differs from the Roman in permitting the father to appoint both *epitropos* and *curator* by Will. This is exactly the state of things which Paul speaks of; and the probability is that the distinction of *epitropos* and *oikonomos* dates back to the old Seleucid law, and this persisted both in Syria and in South Galatia. In Syria, however, as time went on, Roman law affected native custom; and so the name *curator* was substituted for *oikonomos*. Thus, once more we find that we are placed amid Seleucid, and therefore South Galatian, not among North Galatian, manners and law."

[5] Fung points out that "the periphrastic pluperfect...emphasizes the continuous state of slavery more than the simple pluperfect ...would."

[6] Meyer: The child who is to inherit "represents, not the people of *Israel*; but, according to the connection with iii. 29 (compare iv. 3), *the Christians as a body*, regarded in their earlier *pre-Christian* condition. In this condition, whether Jewish or Gentile, they were the *heir apparent*, according to the idea of the divine predestination...in virtue of which they were ordained to be the Israel of God (vi. 16), the true σπέρμα of Abraham".

[7] Betz: "what he has to say applies to *all* Christians, whether Jewish or Gentile in origin."

elemental powers, the stars, or cosmic spirits.[8] Most modern commentators take the reference in Galatians 4:3, 9 and in Colossians 2:8 to refer to spirits related to astral bodies. On the other hand **basic elements** can refer, as Delling puts it, to "the 'basic materials' of which everything in the cosmos, including man, is composed" (*TDNT*, VII, 684), that is the basic elements thought to have made up the world – earth, air, fire, water.

De Boer points out that the idea of **basic elements** as earth, air, fire, water was the common meaning, "especially when complemented by the genitive τοῦ κόσμου (*tou kosmou*). The full phrase thus seems to have attained the character of a technical term for the four elements from which the universe was thought to be composed."[9] This, evidently, is how Paul's readers would have understood the term.

How, then, does this definition mesh with what Paul teaches the Galatians in this passage? De Boer demonstrates four ways in which this definition of **basic elements** fits into Paul's argument:

Firstly, he points out that existence under the **basic elements of the world** was tantamount to existence under the law (see 4:8-11). The Galatians had once worshiped these "gods". Desiring to come under the legal demands of the Judaizers is tantamount to wanting once again to be enslaved to the **basic elements.** This is the functional equivalent of returning to the gods they left behind upon profession of the gospel. "Surely," Paul insists, "you do not want to return there again!" (4:9)

---

[8] The term is used in Hebrews 5:12 as elemental teaching and in 2 Peter 3:10 it refers apparently to physical elements.

[9] Martinus C. De Boer: "The Meaning of τὰ στοιχεῖα τοῦ κόσμου (*ta stoicheia tou kosmou*) in Galatians," *NTS* 53.2 (2007): 207. More fully he writes that J. Blinzler (in 1963), E. Schweitzer (in 1988), and D. Rusam (in 1993) "have shown conclusively that *BDAG*'s meaning no. 2 (the basic elements from which everything in the natural world is composed, namely, earth, air, fire, water) is really the only one possible. Their researches show that this was by far the most common meaning of the term στοιχεῖα (*stoichea*) and then especially when supplemented by the genitive τοῦ κόσμου (*tou kosmou*).The full phrase thus seems to have attained the character of a technical term for the four elements from which the universe was thought to be composed."

Secondly, the **basic elements** are "weak and impotent just like the law" (De Boer, 215). Just as the law cannot save but can only enslave (4:3), so the "gods" formerly worshiped by the Galatians were really no gods at all – they could not save but could only enslave (4:8, 9).

Thirdly, "to return to the observance of the Law is to return to the veneration of the *stoicheia*" (De Boer, 215). This is in principle a return to the gods they had previously worshiped. So, "in Paul's mind the observance of the Law and the veneration of the *stoicheia* were in some sense functionally and thus also conceptually equivalent." De Boer concludes that the **basic elements** are the gods once worshiped by the Galatians and that there must have been some similarity between that enslavement and the enslavement under the law. At least one of those similarities leads to the fourth point.

Fourthly, De Boer points out that Paul's words were chosen as a reference to calendrical observances. "Paul has here chosen words that could cover both Jewish and pagan calendrical observances. The Galatians are wanting to turn to the Law and the calendrical observances the Law prescribes." This is tantamount to returning to the **basic elements** and to the calendrical observances associated with them. They are not different in kind, whether pagan or Jewish. Paul's point is that "by returning to the Law they are going back to where they came from" (De Boer, 217).

De Boer's line of reasoning is that *ta stoicheia tou kosmou* is, in Galatians, "an instance of metonymy whereby Paul refers in summary fashion to the religious beliefs and practices associated in Galatia with the four elements (earth, air, fire, water) of the physical universe" (De Boer, 223). In addition, the four elements are the gods once worshiped by the Galatians, which involved a pagan calendar. This helps us to see the point of Paul's biting criticism of the Judaizers. What they offer the Galatians as a fuller, deeper commitment to God is, in essence, no different than paganism![10]

---

[10] Lührmann on 4:8-9 adds: "The term *elements of the world* calls to mind the theory developed by Empedocles that the world can be reduced to the four basic elements: earth, air, fire, and water. In cosmological terms

We should avoid rigidly interpreting **the basic elements**. Even though De Boer's interpretation seems to put us on the right path, other viewpoints are possible. The debate and search for a precise understanding of Paul's meaning will continue in the hope of arriving at a consensus. What is crucial, however, is Paul's solemn warning that following the program of the Judaizers with its required calendar is enslaving idolatry! This contradicts the eschatology of the gospel, the rich meaning of **the fullness of time**, and the freedom purchased for us by Christ. De Boer's viewpoint need not stand alone but could be easily connected with Esser's conclusion, cited by both Bruce and Fung, that for Paul the *stoicheia* was a summary for "all things in which man places his trust apart from the living God revealed in Christ; they become his gods, and he becomes their slave."

Over against the enslaving idolatry of legalistic Judaism stands the gospel in all its freedom. **But when the fullness of time came, God sent His Son, born of a woman, born under law, in order that He might redeem those under the law, so that we might receive adoption.**[11] **The fullness of time** corresponds, in Paul's analogy, to **the time appointed by the father** (4:2). Just as the minor comes into the full possession of his inheritance at the time legally specified by the father, so the coming of Christ is the emergence of the new age. Once again, Paul's stature as the great redemptive historian comes to the fore. Here Paul contemplates the predetermined plan of God to redeem the world, the scheme with which he began the epistle, and the two-ages that should determine the Christian's approach to life. With this in mind, the coming of **the fullness of time** should signal the end of all Judaizing tendencies and the beginning of a new way of life. The

those are the basis materials of which the world consists, and the human being, as microcosm, is likewise put together from these basic materials. Mythologically, they may be gods understood as earth, sky, sun, and sea, whose worship is necessary in order to assure the harmony of the cosmos, or as angelic beings in Judaism, which knows no other gods but the one God. Paul discounts the devotion of the Galatians to the law as idolatry of the same kind."

[11] Dunn points out the close parallel with Romans 8:3-4.

expression "designates the arrival of the present dispensation of time at its predetermined goal of fulfillment through the appearance of the Messiah."[12] This is the time of fulfillment, as Paul says elsewhere, the time when the old has gone and the new has come (2 Cor. 5:17), when that which once was hidden has now been manifest (Col. 1:26; Rom. 16:26), the very end of the ages that has come upon us in Christ (1 Cor. 10:11). This is the time in which the beautiful motet has broken into the dissonance of the world filling us with beauty and calling us onward (see on Gal. 1:4).

The fullness of time was signaled by the historic entrance of the incarnate Christ in this world and by His achievement. **God sent His Son, born of a woman, born under law**. In saying **God sent His Son** Paul presupposes a purpose for which the Son was sent by the Father. He also contemplates the Son's pre-existence[13] (2 Cor. 8:9; Phil. 2:6; Col. 1:15), while **born of a woman** stresses his genuine incarnation. The Son became man, born of a woman. In condescending to be born of a Jewish mother the Son of God was **born under law**, a necessity if He was to accomplish the salvation of those under the law.[14] "He entered into the prison-house where his people were held in bondage so as to set them free" (Bruce).

The purpose of the incarnation of the Son of God and His existence under law is explained by two purpose clauses in verse 5. The Son came into this world in the manner Paul has

---

[12] Vos, *The Pauline Eschatology,* 26. Lührmann: "Intended here is the time of the change from the one world to the other – which Paul calls revelation in 1:12, 16; 3:23 – the end of the age of the law and the opening of the age of faith in the Christ event. Thus it is a question of a break between ages, not a fulfillment in the sense of logical culmination."

[13] "Does the 'sending' of the Son imply his pre-existence? If the Spirit was the Spirit before God sent him, the Son was presumably the Son before God sent *him*." For a critique of Eduard Schweizer's argument that "God sent his Son" was a sending formula derived from Torah-Wisdom-Logos speculations of Alexandrian Judaism taken over by Hellenistic Christians, see Longenecker, 167-70.

[14] Morris: 'Paul is objecting to the Galatians becoming subject to the law, but he does not minimize its place in the divine plan. The law was important, as is seen by the fact that the Son of God became subject to it. But it did not occupy the place that the Galatians were supposing.'

described in order that he might redeem those under the law, so that we might receive adoption. The purpose for the incarnation of the Son of God under the law was the redemption of sinners under the law. The Son of God must bear the yoke to free us from it; he must take our chains if we are to be unloosed.

It is good to remark that redemption from sin is not only a matter of the death of Jesus in the place of sinners on the cross, as essential and indispensable as that death was. Redemption also relates to the life that the Son of God chose to live under the law of God for us sinners who had broken it. Though the concept is unfortunately rarely heard nowadays, the words of Paul in this passage have rightly provided for theologians a plank in the doctrine of Christ's "active obedience". By "active obedience" theologians have not meant that there are two different kinds of obedience, one "active" and another "passive". No, what is meant is that the entire life of Christ culminating in His death on the cross was entirely one of obedience in the place of sinners, obedience both to the requirements of God's law as well as submission to its penal obligations.

Historically, the recognition of this two-fold character of the one obedience of Christ was based upon the Bible's teaching that God's demand of fallen man was perfect obedience to the law and that mankind was under penalty for breaking it. Our redemption, then, requires a Redeemer who both obeys the law's positive requirements and pays the penalty for our sins vicariously. This passage in Galatians does not of itself fully address the matter of Christ's "active obedience" but in teaching that the Son was **born under law** it does provide one strand of evidence, along with other passages and considerations, for the teaching that our redemption depends upon both Christ's vicarious obedience to the requirements of the law and on his vicarious payment of the law's penalty.

The word **redeem** here is used in the New Testament only by Paul. *Exagoradzō* [15] means "buy back" (see on 3:13). Paul is emphasizing the cost of our redemption as well as the liberation which results from His purchase. The law cannot redeem; only Christ can. Morris is surely right in saying, particularly

---

[15] In addition to 4:5, see 3:13; Ephesians 5:16 and Colossians 4:5.

when we remember that **basic elements** are applicable to both Gentile and Jew, that "the apostle has in view all those who come under condemnation from whatever law they serve; they will be without any hope of saving themselves."[16] The slavery, from which we are redeemed, corresponds as well to Paul's illustration of the minor who **is under guardians and stewards until the time appointed by the father.** Since Christ came, believers live in the reality of the inheritance, which belongs to them through Christ's redemption.

This leads to the second portion of the double purpose clause **so that we might receive adoption.** Since Christ has come, believers are like sons whose legal position is no longer that of minors waiting for their inheritance but instead of those who have arrived at the appointed time and entered into their inheritance. Adoption is the result of the redeeming work of Christ. The parallel to the minor who has entered into his majority and that of adoption is not exact. But adoption does correspond to the concept of inheritance and stresses the gratuitous character of the believers' relationship to God through Christ.

The question arises: what is the background to Paul's concept of adoption? Does he find the matter for this in Greek practice, Roman adoption or in the Old Testament? W. M. Calder assumed that the only legal system familiar to the recipients of Paul's letter was Graeco-Seleucid and, following Ramsay, that the legal terms of chapter four were intelligible to the readers because they were culturally Greek. "St. Paul himself, as Jew, citizen of Tarsus, and *ciuis Romanus,* was of course acquainted with three legal systems, and knew exactly what he was doing when he adopted legal phraseology in addressing converts acquainted with only one of the three."[17] On the other hand, Lyall has argued that the Greek law of adoption was inadequate to provide the background of Paul's concept ("the Greek law of adoption was a pale shadow of the

---

[16] Morris: "The absence of the article here means that Paul is speaking of more than the law under which the Jews tried to live their lives (cf. Rom. 2:14-15)."

[17] W. M. Calder, "Adoption and Inheritance in Galatia," *JTS* 31 (1930): 372-74. This quotation is found on 373.

Roman, existing more as a succession device than anything else"), and that the evidence for a Jewish concept of adoption is inadequate. Roman law alone is suitable to explain adoption in Paul's epistles.[18]

Others, however, have argued that the Old Testament provides the background for Paul's concept of adoption. Rossell contends against the consensus that Paul is alluding to Graeco-Roman practice, which thinks that adoption is not clearly found in the Old Testament, and argues that scholars have not given adequate attention to Romans 9:4 ("who are Israelites; to whom *pertaineth* the adoption, and the glory, and the covenants, and the giving of the law, and the service *of God*, and the promises", AV). He also argues that Paul's use of Abba helps to confirm that his ideas on adoption are Semitic and not Graeco-Roman.[19]

Ridderbos also, while admitting that the term *huiothesia* (adoption) stems from the Graeco-Roman legal world, thinks that its content is derived from Old Testament redemptive-historical background, more precisely from the adoption of Israel as son of God. He finds Romans 9:4 to be of special significance in this regard and also the fact that Paul applies 2 Samuel 7:14 to the church in its new covenant setting (2 Cor. 6:18; cf. Rom. 9:26). "From this original significance of sonship as the special covenant relationship between God and Israel it is also to be explained that Paul alternately and in very much the same sense speaks of 'children of God' and 'children' or 'seed of Abraham' (Rom. 9:7, 8; Gal. 3:26; 4:6, 7, 28, 29). It is the peculiar privilege of Israel as nation that, in conformity with the Old Testament promises of redemption (cf. 2 Cor. 6:16-18), passes over to the church of the New Testament and there receives a new, deepened, significance" (*Paul*, 198).

Ridderbos' conclusion makes perfect sense because of Paul's consistent redemptive-historical focus. Witness how

---

[18] Francis Lyall, "Roman Law in The Writings of Paul – Adoption," *JBL*, 88 (1969): 458-66. This quotation is found on 465.

[19] William H. Rossell, "New Testament Adoption – Graeco-Roman or Semitic?," *JBL*, 71 (1952): 233–34. Rossell admits that "the only possible allusion to Graeco-Roman custom seems to be in Galatians 4:1-3", 234.

thoroughly Paul has up to this point argued for the gospel in
this epistle against the Old Testament backdrop. For Paul, the
Old Testament redemptive-historical setting is paramount and
it would be difficult to think that this is not the case when he
thinks of adoption. Yet when we consider with Lyall the apparent connections between Paul's writings and the Roman legal
world, it seems impossible to dismiss an association between
them.[20] Is there a solution to this problem? Does Paul have one
view of adoption in mind to the exclusion of the rest?

I suggest that Paul's work as a missionary helps to clarify the
matter. While for Paul himself the Old Testament redemptive-
historical background is fundamental, yet he finds in Graeco-
Roman legal terminology and concepts parallels ready at
hand to describe the essentials of his theology. So, in any given
context in which Paul utilizes the concept of adoption, or in
which the term *huiothesia* is used (Gal. 4:4-6; Rom. 8:15, 23;
9:4; Eph. 1: 4, 5), Paul might allude to one or more elements
familiar to his audience while at the same time keeping the
Old Testament theme secure in his own mind. This might,
in part, explain the use of Abba in a context that might also
allude to Roman law, and in Galatians 4 might also explain

---

[20] Lyall, 466: "The adoptee is taken out of his previous state and is placed
in a new relationship with his new *paterfamilias*. All his old debts are canceled,
and in effect he starts a new life. From that time the *paterfamilias* owns all the
property and acquisitions of the adoptee, controls his personal relationships,
and has rights of discipline. On the other hand he is involved in liability
by the actions of the adoptee and owes reciprocal duties of support and
maintenance." He adds: "The Christian doctrines of election, justification,
and sanctification imply that the believer is taken out of his former state, and
is placed in a new relationship with God. He is made part of God's family
forever, with reciprocal duties and rights. All his time, property, and energy
should from that time forth be brought under God's control. The Roman law
of adoption, with concept of *patria potestas* inherent in it, is a peculiarly useful
illustration of these doctrines in action. I conclude that Paul's use of the term
'adoption' in Romans, Ephesians, and Galatians was a deliberate, considered,
and appropriate reference to Roman law." See also the entry "Adoption" in
The Oxford Classical Dictionary, 13: "The effect of both *adoption* and *adrogatio*
was to place the adopted person for all legal purposes in the same position
as if he/she had been a natural child in the power of the adopter. The adoptee
took the adopter's name and rank and acquired rights of succession in his
new family, losing those held in the old family."

why the parallel to the Roman idea of *tutela testamentaria* and of adoption do not precisely correspond.[21] Paul as preacher and missionary, with a mind fully stocked with Old Testament redemptive history, might well grasp hold of adequate though not exact parallels in the culture to which he ministers in order to proclaim his message meaningfully.[22]

Paul's chiastic thought in verses 4 and 5 subjects our hearts to the debt of love we owe to the Son of God through whom we are redeemed. God sent His Son who became man that we might become sons of God; the Son was subject to the law so that those under the law might be redeemed. Now, in verse 6 Paul adds to this astonishing truth by telling us that the Father also sent the Spirit. In both cases the Father is the initiator which rivets Paul's theme of grace even more deeply into the fabric of his argument. **That you are sons is evident since God sent the Spirit of His Son into our hearts, crying out, "Abba, Father!"**[23] Paul wants his readers to remember what he has said in 3:26 (**For you are all sons of God through faith in Christ Jesus**) and also his argument from their experience in 3:1-5. There he had asked: **This one thing I desire to learn from you, was it**

---

[21] C. F. D. Moule, "Adoption," *IDB* 49: "Galatians 4:5 is somewhat perplexing. If the context were a straight contrast between servitude and *hiothesia* it would be simple to interpret it to mean that, though *naturally* slaves, we are *adopted* (or possibly are destined to be adopted) into the status of sons by God's graciousness. But, in fact the argument seems to be rather that, naturally sons, we are nevertheless like slaves unless and until we 'come of age'." He adds that it is not clear whether "the date set by the father...is an allusion to an actual law by which the father could determine in advance when his child was to come of age, or whether it is an artificial adaptation to the theological meaning of the full arrival of the time (v. 4) when God brought his Son into the world."

[22] To extend the thought one might remember how Stephen Neill (1988), *The Interpretation of the New Testament*, Oxford, 287 points out that: "A missionary, who is also a theologian, has great advantages in making the attempt to understand the New Testament, since, far more than the scholar in a Western Church, he stands in a relationship to the original facts which greatly helps to make them intelligible." Neill is utilizing this concept to illumine Luke's view of history. I am suggesting that as we think like missionaries and remember that Paul was a missionary his thought becomes more intelligible.

[23] Zerwick, paragraph 34: "The nominative with the article is thus found for the vocative even in classical use; but where it occurs in the NT it is

**by works of law or by believing the message you heard that
you received the Spirit? Are you really so foolish? Having
begun in the Spirit are you now ending in the flesh?**

In 4:6 Paul is speaking of all Christians, having changed
from second person plural to first person plural. **God sent the
Spirit of His Son into our hearts.**[24] Perhaps frequent reading
of this passage hinders us from understanding its power and
from feeling its full impact. It is an understatement to say that
Paul's language is remarkable: **God sent the Spirit of His Son
into our hearts, crying out, "Abba, Father!"** Using a triadic
pattern Paul points to the Spirit's new covenant work.[25] The
Spirit cries out **"Abba, Father!"** We have already remarked
that Paul likely has in mind the Old Testament background
of adoption and that the Aramaic and Greek reference to God
the Father may be one of several pointers in that direction.
That is not to question, however, that the expression probably
already was in wide use. Indeed, Paul may have introduced it
to them (Lührmann) when he preached among them.[26] Meyer
argues that **"Abba, Father!"** was so familiar that it had become

---

rather to be referred to Semitic influence." Hence, ἀββα ὁ πατήρ. On the
question: whether Paul here saying adoption is the reason God sends the
Spirit (seeing *hoti* as causal) or that the sending of the Spirit demonstrates
that we are God's children it is best to keep in mind Guthrie's observations:
'this appears to give the basis on which the Spirit is given. But realization
of the full privileges of sonship can only come through the Spirit. Rather is
Paul making clear that adoption and the gift of the Spirit are concomitant.
Moreover, verse 5 is stated as potential, but verse 6 as an actual, experience.
The Christian has already experienced the Spirit. That is an indisputable
evidence of sonship."

[24] Ridderbos: "The operation of the Spirit is characterized by this, that He
brings the believers to the Father, and grants them the assurance of kinship,
just as the Son Himself lives in unbroken communion with the Father.
Hence at one time the sonship of believers may be called the ground for the
receiving of the Spirit; at another, the gift of the Spirit may be designated as
the means through which the believers become conscious of their kinship
(cf. Rom. 8:15). In this there is no contradiction but the evidence of the
reciprocity of the gift of the Spirit and sonship."

[25] On triadic patterns in the New Testament, see Robert Letham, *The Holy
Trinity*, 52-72.

[26] An interesting suggestion of K. E. Kirk (1937), *The Clarendon Bible: The
Epistle To The Romans,* Oxford, 212, should be considered: "It is interesting

in effect a proper name since the conjunction of the two had become habitual in prayer. Be that as it may, there can be little doubt that the ultimate background for the expression is the preface to the Lord's Prayer. Behind the Greek *Pater* lay the Aramaic diminutive *Abba*. How remarkable that the disciples were being taught by the Lord Jesus to address God by the same endearing expression used by Him, God's unique Son, in prayer to His Father! See Mark 14:36. And now Paul adds a new depth dimension to the expression by associating it with our redemption from sin and the indwelling of the Holy Spirit.[27]

God sent the Spirit of His Son into our hearts, crying out, "Abba, Father!" But what does this **crying out** mean? Here in Galatians 4:6 it is the Spirit who cries out, whereas in Romans 8:15 Paul writes that believers by the Spirit cry out **"Abba, Father!"** Who can exhaust the meaning of this prayerful cry since it is, in both instances, the strange and mysterious work of the Holy Spirit? Nonetheless, we can say that the Spirit sent **into our hearts** indicates God's new covenant communion with His people, His effectual desire to fellowship with us, freeing us from the law's bondage and the slavish fear that accompanied it. The cry of the Spirit, **"Abba, Father!"** indicates intimacy, and in this case, the access of the indwelling Spirit to the Father's throne on our behalf. It is the Spirit's cry, the third person of the Trinity, but who also enables us to cry out with intimacy to the Father (Rom. 8:15). The Holy Spirit **cries out** in the fullness of His eternal relationship with the Father as the third person of the Trinity and now also enables us to cry out in all the extremity of our need – not to some black hole, but to a Father who loves and receives us in the merit of Christ. Moreover, the Spirit's cry is passionate

---

to notice that *adoption* was not a Jewish but a Greek practice, yet it gives the right to utter the *Jewish* child's cry, 'Abba, Father'. S. Paul thus delicately insinuates once more that Jew and Greek are one in Christ." Understanding adoption as Roman would not alter the observation.

[27] For the significance of "Abba" in the prayers of Jesus and of the early church it is still best to begin with Joachim Jeremias (1965), *The Central Message of The New Testament,* 9-30, and Joachim Jeremias (1979), *The Prayers of Jesus,* Fortress Press. Compare also J. Barr, "Abba Isn't 'Daddy',", *JTS* 39 (1988): 28-47.

and exultant. *Kradzein* means to call out, to cry aloud. In this context in which redemption from sin and the law is the theme, that cry can be nothing less than one of exultant joy. God is not distant or remote, but the Spirit of the living Lord indwells us and exults in God's redemption.

So you are no longer a slave but a son; and if a son, also an heir through God. Paul is calling his readers to know the unknowable and to grasp the ungraspable. He wants the Galatians to understand that God the Son came down and exchanged places with sinners so that God's wrath was exhausted in Him, and that the Father adopts sinners who believe, and are now set free from tyranny.

Paul now speaks in the second person singular personalizing the gospel: **So you are no longer a slave but a son**. The **no longer** refers to their prior legal bondage, whether to the Judaizing viewpoint or to paganism. This is why God sent His Son into the world, and freedom is the result of the Spirit's application of the gospel to your life. **No longer slaves but sons**! This is what the Galatians believers need to comprehend and appreciate! Moreover, the believer as son is **also an heir through God**, as has also been pointed out in 3:29. The believer is no longer in his minority but has arrived at the time of fulfillment. You are no longer an inheritor who is a minor, under guardians and stewards awaiting your inheritance. The Father sent His Son and the Spirit of His Son so that even your future inheritance is a present possession. You are no longer a slave, no longer in bondage to law; you are a son of your Father through his redemptive intervention. "The age of the curse of the law is over; the age of blessing has dawned, and its signs are Spirit, righteousness, life and adoption as children.... None of this is achieved by the law, in spite of being asserted by the law itself and by the new teachers in Galatia" (Lührmann). You are an heir to all that was promised through Abraham of old. It is all of grace from first to last. Indeed, the Trinitarian structure of the passage serves to underscore the divine origin, accomplishment and application of our redemption.

11.
Slaves to Those who by Nature Are Not Gods
(4:8-11)

Translation
In the past, when you did not know God, you were enslaved to those gods which were really not gods at all. But now that you have come to know God, or rather are known by God, how is it that you turn again to those weak and poverty-stricken elements? Do you wish to be enslaved under them all over again? You regard days and months, and seasons and years. I am truly afraid that I have toiled for your sakes in vain!

Summary
Paul continues the appeal begun in 3:1-5. He describes reversion to legalism as a return to idolatry! He reminds the Galatians of their past when they "did not know God" and were "enslaved to those gods which were really not gods at all". To their former commitment he contrasts their acceptance of the gospel. Now they "know God". To remind them of the gratuitous source of that knowledge he adds, "or rather are known by God". This contrast makes their reversion to legalism utterly incomprehensible.

How can the Galatians become enslaved once more to those "weak and poverty-stricken elements", those things they once trusted as their master? Part of that past enslavement included calendrical observances and to this they are returning, but now in the guise of the Jewish calendar. This reversion should be interpreted in light of Galatians 2:21: "I do not nullify the grace of God. For if righteousness is through law, then Christ died for nothing."

The sharpness of Paul's attack upon the Judaizers could not be missed by his readers. In adopting the Jewish calendar the Gentile believers are abandoning the gospel. They are being enslaved all over again! Indeed, so serious is this that Paul fears he has toiled for their sakes in vain!

Comment

Paul remonstrates with the Galatians, returning to the passionate appeal begun in 3:1-5. The Galatians' conversion to the true gospel makes turning to the legalism of the Judaizers incomprehensible. The intrepid Paul states his passionate plea in a daring and arresting manner. Paul does not describe reverting to legalism as turning to something new but as returning to something old, namely, the Galatians' previous idolatrous way of life! **In the past, when you did not know God, you were enslaved to those gods which were really not gods at all. But now that you have come to know God, or rather are known by God, how is it that you turn again to those weak and poverty-stricken elements?**

Paul reminds the Galatians of their **past** when they **did not know God**. This past corresponds to their former participation in the old aeon, "the present evil age", in which they were once immersed. Of course, as Paul makes plain in Romans 1:18-23, there is a sense in which all people know God while sinfully suppressing what they know to be true. But here when Paul reminds the Galatians of their past ignorance of God he means that they did not have a saving relationship with God, and did not know Him personally, by faith through Christ. This is Pauline missionary language (Acts 17:23; 1 Thess. 4:5) – the Gentiles do not know God. In this miserable condition of ignorance of God the Galatians **were enslaved to those gods which were really not gods at all.** There is but one true and living God and the **"gods"** to which the Galatians were once **enslaved** were **really not gods at all** (lit. "by nature not gods" referring to their essence). Compare especially 1 Corinthians 8:4-6. Paul understands that pagan gods do not exist, and believers have been freed from "mute idols" (1 Cor. 12:2, niv).[1] But the fact that these false gods do not exist does not alter the fact that those worshiping them, as the Galatians once did, are enslaved to them!

In contrast to the old life of enslavement to false gods, the Galatians **have come to know God or rather are known by God.** The Galatians have embraced the gospel, have trusted in Christ, and have come to know God through Jesus the mediator. Paul has already described the Galatians' justification and adoption; this is what it means to **know God.**[2] But Paul is not content to say that the Galatians **know God.** He wants the Galatians to remember the gratuitous source of that knowledge and so inserts **or rather are known by God.** "For Paul, there is no real distinction between being known by God and being chosen by him" (Rom. 8:29) (Bruce).[3] See also Amos 3:2. In this way, Paul keeps the sovereignty of grace before his readers in contrast to the works-righteousness of his opponents. "Paul reminds the Galatians whence the knowledge of God had come to them. He states that they did not obtain it by their own exertions, by their mental acuteness or industry, but because, when they were at the furthest possible remove from thinking about Him, God prevented [read: went graciously ahead or interposed on behalf of] them with His mercy" (Calvin). Duncan suggests an additional shade of meaning. He thinks that Paul is not only pointing to the divine initiative in salvation but that "knowledge" means "acknowledge-

---

[1] Bruce adds: "In Paul's mind these so-called gods were thoroughly 'demythologized'; they were non-entities, as the 'men of knowledge' in the Corinthian church recognized (1 Cor. 8:4). But what those 'men of knowledge' did not sufficiently recognize was that, on people who still believed, or even half-believed, in them, these idols continued to exercise a sinister, indeed demonic, influence (1 Cor. 8:7)." Similarly, Fung: "these so-called entities are actually non-entities, though behind them may lurk demonic influences (cf. 1 Cor. 8:4; 10:19-21)."

[2] An ingressive or inceptive aorist suggesting a state.

[3] Bruce also thinks that Paul may intend "not only to stress the divine initiative in this reciprocal knowledge, but also to exclude any gnostic inference from his words."

ment" (cf. 1 Cor. 8:3; 2 Tim. 2:19). Paul's point then is "that the Galatians have not merely come to know God as Father, but have (by the Spirit) been brought into such filial relationship with Him that they are acknowledged by Him as sons."[4] In any case Paul contrasts who the Galatians were with who they now are in Christ. This contrast makes reversion to legalism utterly incomprehensible.

But now that you have come to know God, or rather are known by God, how is it that you turn again to those weak and poverty-stricken elements? Do you wish to be enslaved under them all over again? Paul does not speak of the Galatians turning to something new but of their turning back to their old way of life! Turning to Jewish legalism is tantamount to turning again **to those weak and poverty-stricken elements** (*stoicheia*). We have already pointed out (see on 4:3) that, for Paul, *stoicheia* was a summary for "all things in which man places his trust apart from the living God revealed in Christ; they become his gods, and he becomes their slave" (Esser). Further, part of that slavery included the bondage of calendrical observances. So Paul questions their sanity for wanting to return to the enslavement of **those weak and poverty-stricken elements** – not **weak and poverty-stricken** because they are powerless to enslave, but because they are powerless to save, powerless to impart a true knowledge of God! An evidence of how far they have gone on this road is that the Galatians **regard days and months, and seasons and years**, that is, they adopt and observe the Jewish calendar! Note also Romans 8:3-4 in which Paul says that the law, weakened by the flesh, was powerless to bring about genuine conformity to the law's righteous requirements. Only the grace of God in the gospel can set hearts at liberty to obey out of love.

Bruce points to the similarity between Paul's language and Genesis 1:14 and points out that the list in Galatians proceeds from shorter to longer time divisions. By observing **days** is probably meant feast and fast days (see also Col. 2:16).

---

[4] The REB reads: "But now that you do acknowledge God – or rather, now the he has acknowledged you – how can you turn back to those feeble and bankrupt elemental spirits?"

Months is a probable reference to new moon observances (Num. 28:11-15). **Seasons** refers to festival seasons (Lev. 23) while **years** might mean Sabbatical years or (Fung) New Year celebrations. Bruce cites one source saying, "in the short time since their evangelization, the Galatians could scarcely have got around to the observance of special years." To this view, Bruce contrasts Ramsay, who "after his conversion to an earlier date of the epistle than that which he had adopted in his *Historical Commentary*, made the attractive suggestion that a report has newly reached Paul that they were observing the sabbatical year A.D. 47/48" – a suggestion made by Ramsay in his *St. Paul the Traveller and the Roman Citizen*.

The context of Paul's concerns about calendrical observances must be kept in mind if we are to interpret Paul's other statements about the observance of special days, for example in Romans 14:5,6, in proper relation to the meaning of this passage. In Galatians Paul does not have in mind the positions of weaker and stronger brothers and their communion in the body of the church. Personal convictions of conscience and preferences are not the issue here as they are in Romans. The observance of days as part of legal requirements for justification is Paul's concern in Galatians. Therefore in Galatians Paul must strictly condemn them. We can also agree with J. C. Kirby, as cited by Bruce, who notes that Paul is not, in Galatians, forbidding all festivals but is "forbidding only those which have lost their meaning" and become a mere "shadow" (Col. 2:17). Bruce concurs: "He is not forbidding the Galatians to have any festivals whatever; he is deprecating their scrupulous observance as something imposed by law."[5] Interpreters of this matter should not forget Paul's earlier remarks in 2:21: **I do not nullify the grace of God. For if righteousness is through law, then Christ died for nothing**. Adopting legalism, with the bondage of the Jewish calendar, in place of the gospel is a practical denial of the atoning work of Jesus Christ.

The sharpness of Paul's attack upon the Judaizers' viewpoint could not have been missed by his Gentile readers. To go the

---

[5] This observation has implications for the debate regarding the permissibility of observance of Christmas and Easter.

route of observing the Jewish calendar was not just adding to the gospel message, it was abandoning the gospel message. It was not an enhancement but a return to former idolatry. Paul identifies, in essence, Torah-keeping for justification with the Galatians' former paganism! They have forgotten that they live in the new age of Christ's resurrection, the fullness of time, and only dimly remember their emancipation in Christ! To adopt the Judaizing religion is **to be enslaved under** the former idolatry, summarized in the term *stoicheia*, **all over again**! In desperation Paul pleadingly complains: **I am truly afraid that I have toiled for your sakes in vain!** Every leader with a true pastor's heart can identify with Paul's fear that those who seem to turn back from the gospel are fruitless and that therefore his labor has been useless. Paul is not content with telling them the truth without also pleading with them from his heart. By expressing his apprehension he calls them to respond to his ardent call to the gospel!

12.
I Am At a Loss to Understand You!
(4:12-20)

Translation
Become as I am, because I have become as you are, brothers. You never wronged me. Rather, you know that through illness I preached the gospel to you originally, and even though you endured trial because of my illness you did not despise me nor were revolted by me, but you received me as an angel of God, as Christ Jesus. Where is your happiness? For I bear witness to you that if you had been able you would have gouged out your eyes and given them to me! So have I now become your enemy by telling you the truth? They are ardently devoted to you, but not for any good purpose. Indeed, they wish to shut you out from the gospel so that you might enthusiastically embrace them. It is good to be made much of for good purpose at all times and not only when I am present with you. My children, for whom I again suffer birth pangs until Christ be formed in you, I could wish to be with you now and change my tone of voice, because I am at a loss to understand you.

Summary
Paul's passionate concern shows most clearly here. Just as Paul has been freed in Christ to live as a Gentile, so the Galatians should follow his example and live in freedom from the law. Following the Judaizers denies God's grace, and is also a

failure to follow Paul, the follower of Christ. The Galatians should become like Paul and live by grace.

Paul wants to recall the blessing of his former visit. Paul had originally stayed with them due to illness. Even though his ailment was a trial to them they had received Paul "as an angel of God, as Christ Jesus."

Now he contrasts this former agreement on the gospel with their present attitude. "Where is your happiness?" The joy felt by the Galatians on Paul's visit, when no sacrifice seemed too much for them, has dissipated. He must now criticize their present course. The Judaizers are zealously devoted to them, but their devotion is disingenuous. They wish to shut the Galatians out from all that would influence an acceptance of free grace. To be zealous about genuine love and community is always good, but the Judaizers are insincere.

Paul suffers for the Galatians as a mother in birth pangs, that Christ be formed in them. He longs to be with them, though the epistle must suffice. Paul anguishes over the Galatians' defection from grace. "I am at a loss to understand you."

Comment

Despite the difficulties in interpreting details, the gist of this passage is immediately apparent. Paul's pastoral heart breaks over the Galatians' defection. His plea is personal and loving. **Become as I am, because I have become as you are, brothers.** Just as Paul has become free in Christ to live as a Gentile, so they should follow his example and live in Christ's freedom apart from the enslavement of the law.[1] We would do well to think more deeply about the thoroughness of Paul's conversion, the depth of his understanding of and love for the gospel, and how faithful he was to his calling as apostle to the Gentiles. When Paul came to know Christ he was converted from all that had previously defined him, the things that made Saul to be Saul, his whole way of life. Now he finds his identity in

---

[1] Meyer: "*Become as I,* become free from Judaism as I am, *for I also have become as you;* for I also, when I abandoned Judaism, thereby became as a Gentile (ii. 14; Phil.iii.7f.), and placed myself on the same footing with you who were then Gentiles, by non-subjection to the Mosaic law. Now render me the *reciprocum,* 'reciprocity,' to which love has a claim."

Christ. For this reason Paul can boldly call upon the Galatians to **become as I am**. Ultimately, his appeal is not so much about Paul as it is about Christ.

I almost translated: **Identify with me, just as I also identify with you** – this does not miss the mark by much, especially considering Betz's view, that Paul expresses his personal concern in Hellenistic rhetorical "friendship" style. To follow the Judaizers is not only, however, a denial of friendship, but of the gospel of grace. To deny the gospel is no longer to be like Paul! Neither Paul nor the Galatians may appeal to law for justification. In effect this is an appeal to abandon any hope of salvation but through the grace of Christ. If the Gentiles take that stance they will have **become as I am.** We should not miss that Paul continues to regard the Galatians as **brothers.**

In order to deepen his personal appeal he reminds the Galatians of his former visit among them. He tells them, **you never wronged me.** The implication is, of course, that to follow the Judaizers now *would* wrong Paul! Indeed, following the Judaizers denies his gospel. However, he desires them to recall the blessing of the gospel proclamation that accompanied him on his former visit in which there was love and camaraderie. The Galatians could not fail to detect Paul's anguish over their defection.

The Galatians did not wrong Paul on his visit. On the contrary they treated him with the utmost respect. They did Paul no injustice, **rather**, he reminds them, **you know that through illness I preached the gospel to you originally, and even though you endured trial because of my illness you did not despise me nor were revolted by me, but you received me as an angel of God, as Christ Jesus.** *Proteron* means "on the former of two occasions", hence, on his first visit,[2] Paul

---

[2] *To proteron* can mean "originally" as well as "the first time", implying a second visit. Some think that the grammar is not decisive. Turner, 3. 30 *Syntax*: "*originally* (but the true compare. sense is possible: *the first time*." Fung states that in Hellenistic Greek *(to) proteron* "lost its strict meaning and came to mean only 'originally,' 'at the first.' This is the sense which the phrase often bears in the NT (e.g. Jn. 6:62; 7:50; 9:8; 2 Cor. 1:15; Eph. 4:22; 1 Tim. 1:13; 1 Pet. 1:14) and probably has in the present verse as well."

had preached **through illness**, which seems to mean that Paul was detained among them contrary to his plan, because he was sick or indisposed.[3] Ridderbos thinks that Paul refers not to illness but to an exhausted condition resulting from what he suffered from his enemies when he brought the gospel to the province of Galatia (Acts 14:19ff., 2 Tim. 3:11). That view is possible, or an illness might have resulted from his mistreatment at the hands of his opponents. Ramsay's view is well known. He supposes that Paul contracted a fever during his first missionary journey and left the low country of Pamphylia for the sake of his health in favor of the high country of Pisidian Antioch in the province of Galatia (Acts 13:13-14). What the precise circumstances of Paul's journey among the Galatians and the nature of his ailment were we simply do not know.[4]

What we do know is that Paul was detained because of his indisposition, preached the gospel among the Galatians, and that they gladly heard the message and eagerly received him. He writes: **even though you endured trial because of my illness you did not despise me nor were revolted by me, but you received me as an angel of God, as Christ Jesus.** Paul's physical ailment was a **trial** not only to Paul but also to the Galatians, who did not push him aside in his need but received him joyfully. **You did not despise me nor were revolted by me.** The term translated **revolted** (*ekptuō*), as has been demonstrated often, means "to spit out". Spitting was considered a prophylactic against disease or demons. Schlier comments: "It is not used here in the metaphorical sense of 'to expose,' 'to despise,' 'to reject' etc., but quite literally in the sense of the ancient gesture of spitting out as a defense against

---

[3] Ramsay, *Historical Commentary*, 421 (see the entire discussion 417-28): "Accordingly, we see what was the actual fact. They changed their plan, and they entered the Galatic Province; but the reason was not simple desire to evangelize there, it was some other compelling motive. Here the Epistle clears away all doubt. In it Paul clearly intimates, as his words must be interpreted, that his first visit had been caused not by a desire to preach to the Galatians, but by bodily disease. This cause satisfies all the conditions."

[4] However, see Ramsay, *Historical Commentary*, 422ff., where he makes a compelling case that Paul suffered from malarial neuralgia.

sickness and other demonic threats" (*TDNT*, 2. 448). That may be the case and, if so, it is also possible to read "temptation" for "trial" as does Schlier who theorizes: "The Galatians resisted the temptation to see in Paul someone demonically possessed because of his sickness, but received him as an angelic manifestation, indeed, as Christ Jesus Himself."

Rather than despising him, the Galatians, says Paul, **received me as an angel of God** ("angel", not "messenger", cf. 1:8; 2 Cor. 12:7). Indeed, as they believed his message, the Galatians received him not simply as an angel but **as Christ Jesus.** Such had been their esteem for Paul and their reception of the gospel he preached!

Paul contrasts the former glowing time of friendship and communion in the gospel with the Galatians' present coldness by asking: **Where is your happiness?** By this Paul seems to mean the happiness or joy which the Galatians felt due to Paul's presence among them and their joy in the gospel he preached to them, even though he was ailing. Indeed, in those days there seemed to be no sacrifice too great for the Galatians to make for Paul and his gospel. **For I bear witness to you that if you had been able you would have gouged out your eyes and given them to me!** Paul is probably not referring to a particular ailment that caused his stay among the Galatians, specifically an eye ailment, but speaks in glowing terms of their love for him and bond in the gospel. This is how they loved Paul! The Galatians would have given up those things dearest to them to promote his welfare as an apostle and unique representative of Christ. Now that Paul finds it necessary to criticize their present course, has all of that changed? **So have I now become your enemy by telling you the truth?**

Behind the Galatians' change of direction, and the damage to their relationship with Paul that accompanies it, are the Judaizers. **They are ardently devoted to you, but not for any good purpose.** *Zēlousin,* found three times in verses 17 and 18, has been variously translated. "They make much of you, but for no good purpose; they want to exclude you, so that you may make much of them" (NRSV). "Oh, I know how keen these men are to win you over, but can't you see that it is for their own ends? They would like to see you and me separated altogether, and have you all to themselves" (Phillips). Betz translates "pay zealous court" and thinks "it belongs to the erotic vocabulary describing stratagems of the lover to gain control over the beloved." The Judaizers' devotion to the Galatians was not altruistic but was a strategy to win them to their false gospel. "Has the search for their security of salvation made the Galatians so blind that they can no longer distinguish between a good old friend and new false friends, and that they end up as victims of one of the oldest games of human manipulation?" (Betz).

Paul continues to assault the disingenuous motives of the Judaizers by insisting that, **indeed, they wish to shut you out from the gospel so that you might enthusiastically embrace them.** Their aim is, literally, a wish "to shut you out". What does Paul mean? From whom or what do the Judaizers wish to shut the Galatians out? My translation, **to shut you out from the gospel**, assumes that the ultimate purpose of the Judaizers, the substitution of a false gospel for the true gospel, is Paul's meaning. Ridderbos thinks that Paul specifically has in mind the Judaizers' attempt to isolate the Galatians from other churches and influences contrary to their own. Ridderbos adds: "Presumably the first of these other influences is that of Paul and his preaching of the gospel." Ultimately, the aim of the Judaizers was seen clearly by Paul as a purpose to isolate the Galatians from the truth **so that you might enthusiastically embrace them.** Of course, another possibility, not unrelated to the foregoing, is that Paul is saying that the Judaizers want to shut you out of membership in the covenant community unless you receive circumcision. Therefore, you are outsiders who have only "believed" in Jesus.

Paul is not opposed to zeal in good relationships that develop gospel community! This seems to be the meaning of verse 18: **It is good to be made much of for good purpose at all times and not only when I am present with you.** To develop encouraging relationships and to be loved by the Galatian Christians is a good goal, for Paul or any other sound teacher of the truth. To be zealous about genuine love and community, as well as faithfulness to Paul or other gospel teachers, is good. But the Judaizers are not sincere but insincere, and that is the whole point.

When Paul abruptly appeals to the Galatians as his children he is zealously pursuing them for the good purpose of the gospel, even though not present with them: **My children, for whom I again suffer birth pangs until Christ be formed in you, I could wish to be with you now and change my tone of voice, because I am at a loss to understand you**. Here, in this incomplete sentence in the Greek text, the yearning heart of Paul for their good takes unusual shape. Paul thinks of the Galatians as his children and thinks of himself in motherly terms. Paul elsewhere compares his pastoral role to that of a nursing mother (1 Thess. 2:7) and to that of a father (1 Thess. 2:11; 1 Cor. 4:15; Philem. 10). His comparison to a mother in childbirth is commensurate with his painful longing for them to know Christ and his gospel!

The almost bizarre mixing of metaphors in which Paul is mother and the church embryo, and then the church is the mother and Christ the embryo, reflects Paul's heightened state of mind and excited argument. Moreover, it is difficult to determine Paul's precise meaning. By *en humin* (in you), Paul might mean that he suffers birth pangs until Christ be formed "in you" or "it can refer to the creation of the Christian community as a living organism, the 'body of Christ'" (Betz). If he means the former, the idea is that Christ might be formed in the Galatians as a fetus, inviting thought of growth and maturity over time. If he means the latter, Paul has in mind the community of believers formed after Christ's pattern, the manifestation of Christ in their midst. Betz is probably right in saying that there is no need to decide between these possibilities.[5] "Paul probably maintains both concepts at the same time." In either case the Galatians "in accepting circumcision put themselves, as it were, back into the womb"

---

[5] Lührmann interestingly suggests, "perhaps this image already anticipates the quotation from Isa. 54:1 used in v. 27. The gospel, whose content is Christ, is realized in the church as the body of Christ (cf. 3:28)."

(Cousar). Paul must endure **again** these painful **birth pangs** for the Galatians' good![6]

This section of pastoral expostulation is concluded by an expression of exasperation. **I could wish to be with you now and change my tone of voice, because I am at a loss to understand you.** Paul does not mean that he would change the tone of voice if he could be with them, but that the epistle is second best to his personal presence.[7] Paul's wish to be with them is not possible; his letter must suffice and he longs for them to heed what he has written! As things stand, Paul is at a loss to understand the Galatians. Moffatt translates this ending of Paul's anguished appeal: "I am at my wits' end about you!" Do we have anything like the love for the church which Paul, bent over in anguish, displays in this appeal?

Paul's anguish over the Galatians' plight arises from the revelation of God's grace to his own heart. "When Paul's eyes were first opened to the gospel, he saw against the background of his own former life that the law was fatal." Therefore, "his opposition to every method of obtaining salvation by means of a legal formula is obstinately intense because he sees such techniques as competitors to Christ" (Berkouwer, *Faith and Justification*, 70, 77). Paul's intense pastoral alarm is raised because he is thoroughly convinced that salvation is not according to man!

---

[6] Morris notes that "it is unnatural for the Galatians to behave in such a way that he has birth pangs twice!"

[7] Betz: "The expression 'exchange the voice' would then indicate Paul's suggestion that he could talk to the Galatians better orally than by the poor substitute of the letter." Ridderbos: "Very probably we are to think of the advantages that the living voice has over the written word. The point is not that he would be less exacting, but that in a personal conference with them he could make the readers feel what it is that moves him in their regard."

13.
Freedom versus Bondage
(4:21-31)

Translation

Tell me, you who wish to be under the law, do you hear the law? For it is written that Abraham had two sons, one by the slave woman and one by the free woman. Now the son of the slave woman was born according to the flesh, whereas the son of the free woman was born through the promise. These things are an analogy. The women represent two covenants, one from Mount Sinai engendering slavery, which is Hagar. Now Hagar corresponds to Sinai, a mountain in Arabia. She stands for the present Jerusalem, with her slave children. But the Jerusalem above is free, and she is our mother. For it is written:

"Be glad, O barren woman who has not given birth, break forth in joy and cry out, she who has experienced no birth pangs; because the children of the deserted woman are more than of the one who is married."

Now you, brothers, like Isaac, are children of the promise; but just as then the son born according to the flesh persecuted the son born according to the Spirit, so it is now. But what does the Scripture say? "Cast out the slave woman and her son. For the son of the slave woman will not inherit with the son of the free woman." Consequently, brothers, we are not children of the slave woman but of the free woman.

Summary

Paul again references the Abrahamic narrative against the Judaizers. He turns the Galatians to the law in order to drive them to grace. Those departing from the gospel cannot possibly understand the Torah. "Tell me, you who wish to be under the law, do you hear the law?"

To sharpen the law/grace distinction Paul directs their attention to the story of Isaac and Ishmael. The two sons represent a fundamental contrast shaping the whole of redemptive history. Ishmael's birth "according to the flesh" and Isaac's birth "through the promise" demonstrate the contrast of law and grace. Ishmael was born in the ordinary way by a slave woman whereas Isaac was born by promise and the intervention of grace. The contrasts – slavery/freedom, flesh/promise – are at the forefront of Paul's concern.

Paul refers to this narrative as an "allegory", but we should be careful not to read into the term a meaning that it might not have had for Paul. Indeed, his approach is typological and is summarized by his use of the term "correspondence".

The two mothers represent "two covenants", by which Paul means two antithetical approaches to salvation. There is no third option between those of Law and Gospel. Hagar points to Sinai (literally "is" Sinai) and stands for the present Jerusalem with its legalism. Sarah, by implication, points to the heavenly Jerusalem, that is the realm and method of grace. This free Jerusalem is our mother. Those who belong to Christ belong to this Jerusalem. Freedom comes through Christ's redemption from the law's bondage.

Paul next cites Isaiah 54:1 (LXX), evidently expecting his readers to know the context, which makes plain that "the theological importance of the barrenness of Sarah and thus of the Jerusalem above…is that their offspring are born as a result of God's faithfulness to his promise" (De Boer).

This gracious intervention with its promise of fruitfulness is now applied to believers who "like Isaac, are children of the promise", like "the son born according to the Spirit". Even though legalists will persecute believers, just as Ishmael persecuted Isaac, we also live in the expectancy of the inheritance of grace, as did Isaac. "Consequently, brothers, we are not children of the slave woman but of the free woman." There are two kinds of people, those like Ishmael who rely on law, children of slavery, and those like Isaac who are children of grace and freedom. Paul calls upon the Galatians not to sacrifice the gospel of grace for the enslavement of the law!

Comment

Paul fires a final volley of evidence from the Abrahamic narrative against the Judaizers. This is the apex of his biblical arguments and, as Ramsay notes, the one that "would probably outrage Jewish prejudice more than any other" (*Historical Commentary*, 430). If those who are tempted to submit again to the yoke of the law would return to the Torah and understand its meaning, they would not be drawn to law but to gospel. Those who are departing from the gospel do not understand the law! **Tell me, you who wish to be under the law, do you hear the law?** So Paul turns the Galatians to the law in order to drive them again to grace.

He begins by directing their attention to the story of Abraham and his two sons. **For it is written that Abraham had two sons, one by the slave woman and one by the free woman.** That Abraham had more sons (Gen. 25:1-6) is not relevant to his argument. Rather, as becomes apparent, he is concerned to contrast two sons, Hagar's son, Ishmael, and Sarah's son, Isaac. These two sons represent a fundamental contrast shaping the whole of redemptive history. **Now the son of the slave woman was born according to the flesh, whereas the son of the free woman was born through the promise.** The fundamental contrast is that of law and grace. Ishmael **was born according to the flesh;** he was **the son of the slave woman.** Ishmael's mother, Hagar, was a slave woman. When Sarah could not conceive she gave her slave girl Hagar to Abraham to bear him a son. The result of the union was Ishmael who was not born according to the promise by the special intervention of God, but in the normal way. On the other hand, Isaac **was born through the promise** and is **the son of the free woman.** Abraham was over one hundred years old (he was also old when Ishmael was born) and Sarah over ninety when Isaac was born. Isaac was born according to God's promise, by the intervention of God's grace. The promise of God alone enabled Abraham and Sarah to bring Isaac into the world. The contrasts – slavery/freedom, flesh/promise – are at the forefront of Paul's argument from the Abrahamic narrative against the Judaizers.

Paul sees this historical narrative as providing a considerable bulwark against the legalism presently attracting the Galatians. The significance of these contrasts is found in the fact that **these things are an analogy** (*allēgoroumena*).

Even though Baur's statement – that "nothing can be more preposterous than the endeavors of interpreters to vindicate the argument of the apostle as one objectively true" (cited by Meyer) – can summarize the view of most investigators of this passage, we should not be too quick to agree with him. We have observed over and over that Paul is the great redemptive-historical exegete and that it is perhaps the case that we are only beginning to appreciate that "organic relationship and dependence" (Murray) of themes that bind the Scripture into a unified whole.[1]

Perhaps interpreters of Paul have too quickly assumed that he is operating in this passage with exegetical sleight of hand, a mere reflection of rabbinic hermeneutics in opposition to his opponents.[2] When interpreting Paul it is always necessary to keep before us that he is committed to the truth that "all

---

[1] In an old but still very valuable work, *The Typology of Scripture*, I. 367, Patrick Fairbairn observes in words that contrast pointedly with those of Baur: "We affirm that the apostle's comment proceeds on the sound principle, that the things which took place in Abraham's house in regard to a seed of promise and blessing were all ordered specially and peculiarly to exhibit at the very outset the truth, that such a seed must be begotten from above, and that all not thus begotten, though encompassed, it might be, with the solemnities and privileges of the covenant, were born after the flesh – Ishmaelites in spirit, and strangers to the promise. The apostle merely reads out the spiritual lessons that lay enfolded in the history of Abraham's family as significant of things to come..."

[2] For a thorough exposition of the view that Paul's hermeneutic is rabbinic, see Steven Di Mattei, "Paul's Allegory of the Two Covenants (Gal 4.21-31) in Light of First-Century Hellenistic Rhetoric and Jewish Hermeneutics," *NTS* 52 (2006): 102-23.

Scripture is God-breathed" (2 Tim. 3:16). We must never forget that "his primary interest is in explicating the history of redemption... The formal side (Paul the theologian) and the material side (redemptive-historical interest) may never be divorced." Indeed, "our theology should be concerned not only with the material he provides but also with the *way* in which he himself treats it. Scripture must determine not only the content but also the *method* of our theology."[3]

Since this is the case, it is possible that we have simply failed to grasp the depth of Paul's understanding and intense insight into redemptive history, and that what has most often been assumed about this passage – that it is the least successful of Paul's arguments in Galatians and an almost unworthy approach – is in fact quite the opposite. What we have here is a profound, deep and penetrating understanding of the nature of Scripture as a unified whole, and a revelation of Paul's rich understanding of God's redemptive plan. After all, Paul's "almost exclusive concern is in expounding, explicating, interpreting, 'exegeting' the history of redemption as it has reached its climax in the death and resurrection of Christ."[4] We should not forget that Paul begins his argument with **for it is written**, which is almost certainly an endorsement of his method and not simply a reference to his source.[5]

Even though Paul uses the term "allegory" to summarize what he sees in the Torah, he does not have in mind the sort of thing done later by Dante or Bunyan, or even by Philo in his own day. By "allegory" Paul seems to mean **analogy** and is using the typological method. Paul clearly affirms the historicity of the events (4:22, 29) and in no way plays fast and loose with the factuality of the Genesis narrative. Rather,

---

[3] Richard B. Gaffin, Jr: "Paul As Theologian,"*WTJ* XXX (1968): 228.

[4] Gaffin, 225.

[5] Guthrie: "There is special point in the use of this authoritative formula after the apostle has appealed to them to listen. It also sheds light upon his allegorical approach to the interpretation of Scripture. It is evident that Paul regarded this method as carrying its full authority. The present phrase could, of course, be understood as no more than a reference to the contents of the law, but the apostle is more concerned about the significance than the facts of this story of Abraham's household."

he speaks of συστοιχεῖ (from *sunstoicheō*, "correspondence",
lit. "stand in the same line" *BDAG*) between the mountain in
Arabia and the present Jerusalem.[6] "Correspondence" seems
to define what Paul means by "allegory" and this, in turn, is
nearer to the concept of typology.

While Paul's method may be difficult to penetrate, calling
us to renewed efforts in plumbing the depth of his hermeneutic, his meaning is quite clear. Moving now to the mothers of
the sons he says **the women represent two covenants**. That
is, they represent two religions, two sharply contrasting approaches to the essential question of salvation. Paul's intent is
to contrast freedom versus slavery. Law or Gospel – there is
no third option! Paul, therefore, contrasts the covenant made
with Abraham with that of Sinai. He, therefore, identifies
Hagar with **Mount Sinai engendering slavery.** Sinai stands
for the law. Stated more fully, **now Hagar corresponds to Sinai, a mountain in Arabia. She stands for the present Jerusalem, with her slave children.**

As a slave mother Hagar's son was a child of a slave. The
only child she could bear would be a slave. A slave woman
could not give birth to a free child. So the law cannot produce
children but slaves. Just as the Mosaic economy of itself
was not able to bring freedom from the bondage of sin, so
she represents the bondage of the Judaizers' false gospel.
Moreover, she represents the present legal bondage of the

---

[6] M. Silva notes, in G. K. Beale and D. A. Carson, ed. (2007), *Commentary
on the New Testament Use of the Old Testament*, Baker Academic, 808: "Thus
if it turns out that Paul is pointing out a correspondence between two
historical realities, we may with good reason regard his reading of Genesis
as 'typological' rather than 'allegorical'. The central theological truth with
which he is concerned is the contrast between Spirit and flesh: God works
according to the former, while sinners depend on the latter. This contrast has
manifested itself in a notable way at various points throughout (redemptive)
history. It did during the patriarchal period, and it does now at the fullness
of time (4:4)."

See also F. F. Bruce (1975) "'Abraham Had Two Sons' – A Study in
Pauline Hermeneutics", *New Testament Studies: Essays in Honor of Ray
Summers*, Baylor, 83: "What Paul refers to here as allegory is not allegory in
the Philonic sense, but what we frequently call typology: a narrative from
Old Testament history is interpreted in terms of the new covenant."

contemporary Judaizing viewpoint found in Jerusalem. In a word, Hagar represents the bondage of the law.[7]

In contrast to Hagar stands Sarah. **But the Jerusalem above is free, and she is our mother.** Just as Hagar represents the present, earthly Jerusalem with its religion of law, because of God's promise Sarah represents the gratuitous nature of the gospel, the freedom of God's promise, **the Jerusalem above** which is **free** and – continuing the mother image of Sarah – **is our mother.** "By this other Jerusalem Paul means not merely the assembly of those who have left the earthly struggle to enter heaven: he means also the central point from which believers are gathered, nourished and governed, and the manner in which all this takes place. That is *above*, for Christ is there, and there is the citizenship of believers (Phil. 3:20). It is their spiritual gathering place" (Heb. 12:22) (Ridderbos). Those who belong to Christ belong to this Jerusalem, this realm of grace, and know the freedom that comes through Christ's redemption from the bondage of the law.

Paul next quotes Isaiah 54:1 from the Greek version of the Old Testament (LXX). **For it is written:**

"Be glad, O barren woman who has not given birth, break forth in joy and cry out, she who has experienced no birth pangs; because the children of the deserted woman are more than of the one who is married."

Isaiah addressed the Jews in exile, comparing their judgment to the barren woman forsaken by her husband, and their future restoration to that of a fruitful mother. The connection

---

[7] Literally "Hagar is Mount Sinai in Arabia". Paul makes the connection as close as possible. Bruce, *ibid*.: "The identification of Hagar with Sinai may have been helped along by the existence of the word *hagar* ('crag'), which has a similar sound to Hagar, and could have been used by some Arabian mountain which in Paul's time was equated with Sinai. But the identification simply indicates that Hagar is interpreted of the law, which holds men and women in bondage. When Paul speaks of 'the present Jerusalem,' he means not the literal city but the whole legal constitution of Judaism, which then had its world-centre in Jerusalem. Law means bondage; the community which is under the law is 'in slavery with her children' (Gal. 4:25). Similarly, 'the Jerusalem above,' which is the mother-city of free souls, is not located in the realms above the sky: it is the community of the new covenant."

with Paul's concern for the Galatians who are tempted to go to the law for salvation is seen by considering the breadth of context in which this passage is imbedded (Isa. 51:1-2: "Listen to me, you who pursue righteousness and who seek the LORD: Look to the rock from which you were cut and to the quarry from which you were hewn; look to Abraham, your father, and to Sarah, who gave you birth.") Paul, evidently, expects the context of Isaiah 54 to be familiar to his readers and that they will understand the connection between God's miracle of grace in making the barren Sarah fruitful and the gospel of grace that he preaches.[8] De Boer rightly sees this to be in continuity with Paul's eschatology. He sees the Isaiah text as "brought by Paul into the service of his christologically determined apocalyptic eschatology: the promise contained in Isaiah 54:1 has come to pass, as his application of the text to the Galatians in the next verse bears out: 'You, brethren, are children of promise like Isaac' (4:28)." He concludes that "the theological importance of the barrenness of Sarah and thus of the Jerusalem above, in my view, is that their offspring are born as a result of God's faithfulness to his promise" (cf. Gen. 21:1-2, LXX)."[9] It is to

---

[8] Silva, *Commentary on the New Testament Use of the Old Testament*, 809, observes: "Since Isaiah 54:1 follows immediately upon the 'song' of the Suffering Servant (no doubt alluded to in Gal. 2:20-21; 3:1,13), Paul evidently expected the Galatians to see the connection between faith in the crucified Christ and incorporation into the numerous people who have the new Jerusalem as their mother. It is true that a direct correspondence between Sarah/Hagar and the sterile/married woman of Isaiah 54:1 does not work, but as various commentators have pointed out, Paul seems to refrain from actually mentioning Sarah and a forsaken, cursed Jerusalem had previously been established by Isaiah; this background gives Paul the canonical authority to quote Isa. 54:1 within the context of the Galatians narrative."

He adds: "The point of the quotation, however, is to stress the link that believers enjoy not so much with Sarah precisely, but with the new, redeemed Jerusalem. If that free and heavenly city is the Galatians' true mother, how absurd to regress and become enslaved to a slavish Jerusalem abandoned by God!"

See also Karen H. Jobes, "Jerusalem, Our Mother: Metalepsis And Intertextuality In Galatians 4:21-31," *WTJ* 55 (1993): 299-320. Jobes observes, 313: "Paul's use of the quotation of Isaiah 54:1 is therefore quite apt when it is viewed within the nexus of Genesis 21 and Isaiah's transformation of the barrenness theme."

the miracle of God's gracious intervention and its promise of fruitfulness to which Paul exultantly turns.

Paul is now ready to apply the **analogy** to the Galatians. Believers in Christ are like Isaac: **Now you, brothers, like Isaac, are children of the promise.** Believers are not children of God according to the flesh but according to the promise of God's grace. We are like **the son born according to the Spirit.** But this very fact means that believers in Christ can expect the same expression of persecution that Isaac knew from Ishmael: **just as then the son born according to the flesh persecuted the son born according to the Spirit, so it is now.** Paul seems to have Genesis 21:9 in mind in which Ishmael mocked Isaac. Evidently, the Judaizing attempt to destroy the gospel of grace preached by Paul corresponds to the persecuting spirit of Ishmael. "A legalistic religion cannot be other than a persecuting religion, for it knows that it cannot endure unless its regulations are kept in the letter" (Duncan).

On the other hand, if the enemies of grace will persecute believers, we also are to live in expectancy of the inheritance of grace! **But what does the Scripture say? "Cast out the slave woman and her son. For the son of the slave woman will not inherit with the son of the free woman."** Even though he was mocked by his brother Ishmael, Isaac was the son of promise who received the inheritance (Gen. 17:18-21; 21:10-13). Sarah had asked her husband to cast out Hagar and Ishmael (Gen. 21:10) and the LORD had approved this request (Gen. 21:12). Since believers are, like Isaac, children of grace, how can we submit ourselves to a principle of law that leads to slavery? Stott observes: "Since it is 'the Scripture' which said 'Cast out the slave and her son', we find the law itself rejecting the law. This verse of Scripture, which the Jews interpreted as God's rejection of the Gentiles, Paul boldly reverses and applies to the exclusion of unbelieving Jews from the inheritance. As J. B. Lightfoot comments, "the Apostle thus confidently sounds the death-knell of Judaism."'

---

[9] Martinus De Boer, "Paul's Quotation of Isaiah 54:1 in Galatians 4.27," *NTS* 50.3 (2004): 378.

Paul then concludes his entire argument: **Consequently, brothers, we are not children of the slave woman but of the free woman.** The first person should be noted. Paul includes himself in the triumph of grace in the gospel. There are two kinds of people in the world: those who, like Ishmael, rely on law and are children of slavery; and those like Isaac – the products of grace who are children of freedom. Paul's argument calls the Galatians to be careful not to sacrifice the gospel of grace for a false gospel that enslaves its adherents.

14.
Christian Liberty
(5:1-15)

Translation

It is for freedom that Christ set us free; stand firm then and
do not again be entangled in slavery's yoke. Look, I Paul say
to you that if you allow yourselves to be circumcised Christ
will be of no use to you. I declare once more to every man
who allows himself to be circumcised that you are obligated
to keep the law in exhaustive detail. You are cut off from
Christ – all you who are seeking justification through the law
– you are fallen from grace. But we, in the Spirit by faith, await
eagerly the hope of righteousness. For in Christ Jesus neither
circumcision nor uncircumcision counts for anything, but
faith working through love.

You were running well. Who cut in on you, leading you
to disobey the truth? That persuasion is not from the one
who calls you. 'A little leaven leavens the whole lump.' I am
convinced concerning you in the Lord that you will not
think any other thing. The one troubling you shall bear his
condemnation, whoever he may be. But I brothers, if I yet
preach circumcision, why am I still persecuted? Then the
scandal of the cross would be abolished. I wish those agitating
you would emasculate themselves!

You were called for freedom, brothers. Only do not let
your freedom become an occasion for the flesh, but through

love serve one another. For the whole law is fulfilled in one command: 'You shall love your neighbor as yourself.' But if you bite and devour one another, watch out that you do not consume one another.

Summary

Paul now enlarges upon the theme of Christian liberty in a section beginning the ethical portion of the epistle. The indicative, 'it is for freedom that Christ set us free,' calls for a corresponding imperative, the preservation of that liberty. The Christian must 'stand firm' and never again yield to the slavery of the law's demands. All attempts to make believers subservient to the law's curse must be resisted!

Accepting legal prescriptions such as circumcision declares Christ's work to be of no avail. Paul presses the radical antithesis of law and gospel by insisting that the person who 'allows himself to be circumcised' is obligated to keep the whole law. Those taking this route cut themselves adrift from Christ.

In contrast to the implications of the Judaizing viewpoint, Paul points to the certainty of justification in Christ, a certainty that will stand in the Day of Judgment. The Spirit bestows through faith the 'hope of righteousness' for which believers 'await eagerly'. Paul looks confidently to the future in which believers 'shall be openly acknowledged and acquitted' (*Westminster Shorter Catechism, 38*). The gospel removes the heart's sense of dread.

For those in Christ, neither circumcision nor uncircumcision has any meaning but 'faith working through love'. Real vital faith works through love and is the pivotal issue rather than circumcision.

Paul reflects upon a time when the Galatians believed his gospel consistently but things have now changed. Having started well they have allowed themselves to be derailed. This is contrary to their calling and they should be warned: 'A little leaven leavens the whole lump.' Paul, however, is confident 'in the Lord' that they will return to their starting point. The Judaizing party, however, faces condemnation for their false teaching.

Evidently, the Judaizers accused Paul of preaching circumcision. But if that were the case, why would Paul be persecuted? Paul does not avoid the necessary scandal of the cross, but embraces it. He is so concerned over those who agitate the Galatians that he wishes the knife would slip!

Freedom can also be abused. It can become an occasion for the flesh. The antidote for this temptation is loving service to one another which is consistent with our calling to freedom. To this the law testifies: 'the whole law is fulfilled in one command: "You shall love your neighbor as yourself."' If this approach to freedom is set aside the Galatians may well annihilate themselves and each other.

Comment

Having concluded that believers **are not children of the slave woman but of the free woman**, Paul now enlarges upon the privilege of the liberty bought for us by Christ. The gospel is indispensable for ongoing Christian living and not just for its inception. It is determinative for the whole of the Christian's life. This section begins the ethical portion of the epistle, without transitional markers, simply taking up the theme of freedom with which the previous section concluded, but which is also the defining theme of Galatians as a whole. The epistle began with the declaration of the freedom purchased for us by Christ, **who gave Himself for our sins so that He might deliver us out of the present evil age** (1:4) and the whole argument of the epistle has unfolded what that means. Indeed, all of humanity outside of Christ is bound in death and dark night, living **in confinement under law** and the **basic elements of the world. But when the fullness of time came, God sent His Son, born of a woman, born under law, in order that He might redeem those under the law, so that we might receive adoption**.

It is the freedom purchased for us by Christ to which Paul now turns in this parenetic section of the epistle. He begins with the indicative, **It is for freedom that Christ set us free**; but immediately indicates that the indicative calls the believer to an imperative, the preservation of Christian liberty: **stand firm then and do not again be entangled in slavery's yoke.**

The Christian's calling and ethical task is the preservation of the liberty purchased by Christ by not coming again under the law's demands, and thus practically denying the freedom to which believers are called. "Freedom" (*eleutheria*) is a dative of purpose. "Freedom" is the purpose for which Christ came and gave His life! Believers are therefore called to **stand firm** (an imperative) and resist all attempts to make them subservient to the curse of the law. Cousar notes that "yoke of slavery" may reference a rabbinic expression, "yoke of the *torah*," applied to Jewish proselytes, "but understood by Paul as a wearisome burden (cf. Jesus' play on this expression in Matthew 11:29-30)." See also Acts 15:10.

If the Galatian Christians allow themselves to be circumcised, which includes the entire works-righteousness demands of the Judaizing party, they submit themselves **again** (v.1) to the bondage of the law's burdensome requirements that deny the grace of God in Christ. **Stand firm then and do not again be entangled in slavery's yoke.** Remember that earlier, in Galatians 4:3-10, Paul had identified trust in law-keeping with pagan idolatry through his use of the term *stoicheia*. The Judaizers' attempt to bring the believers of Galatia under circumcision is a clear example of one way that they are tempted to deny the liberty of Christ's atonement. **Look, I Paul say to you that if you allow yourselves to be circumcised Christ will be of no use to you.** Accepting Jewish legal prescriptions, such as the circumcision pressed upon them by the Judaizing party, means that they are declaring Christ's work to be of no avail. The reason Paul says acceptance of circumcision means that **Christ will be of no use to you** is because the claim that the law is necessary for salvation and the claim that Christ is the Redeemer are incompatible. One may not be a believer in salvation by a legal system and a believer in Christ at the same time! **For if righteousness is through law, then Christ died for nothing** (2:21). The antithesis is intense, complete and radical: the law *or* Christ, legal prescriptions *or* atonement, circumcision *or* grace. The view of the Judaizers and the gospel of Paul represent two opposing and hostile views of redemption. Both cannot be true and any attempt to mingle them is deadly.

Paul continues to place before the Galatian Christians this radical antithesis of law and grace by instructing them in the implications of the legal system of the Judaizers. **I declare once more to every man who allows himself to be circumcised that you are obligated to keep the law in exhaustive detail.** As Paul has already indicated in 3:10, the law's appetite is voracious and relentless. Acceptance of the Torah as the way of salvation obligates its followers **to keep the law in exhaustive detail.** "Probably the pseudo-apostles had sought at least to conceal or to weaken this true and – since no one is able wholly to keep the law – yet so fearful consequence of accepting circumcision, as if faith in Christ and acceptance of circumcision might be compatible with one another" (Meyer). The Galatians had failed to grasp the logic involved in the call to submit to circumcision. To come under this yoke was not an innocent addition to Paul's gospel of grace but a wholesale abandonment of grace. Circumcision and Jewish calendrical observances demand a different view of the matter of how one is saved. To follow the way of Torah for justification means to abandon salvation by grace.

Therefore, Paul adds: **You are cut off from Christ – all you who are seeking justification through the law – you are fallen from grace.** Again, this is a statement underscoring the completely antithetical relation of the two systems of law and of grace in justification. Paul has said that those seeking justification by law make Christ useless to them (v. 2) and now says "by implication, then 'Christ' is no longer a savior and 'grace' is no longer grace. As a result, such people do not merely change 'denominations', but become real converts to non-Christian Judaism" (Betz). The issue is how a sinner is declared righteous in God's sight. To accept the way of law represented by circumcision means to be estranged from Christ and all His benefits.

In contrast to the implications of his opponents' view, Paul points to the certainty of justification in Christ, a certainty that will stand in the judgment in the Last Day. **But we, in the Spirit by faith, await eagerly the hope of righteousness.** The pronoun **we** stands in the emphatic position stressing the contrast with the Judaizing viewpoint. It is also arresting since Paul, once committed to the way of salvation by Torah and circumcision, now includes himself with those who live by grace. Paul is no stranger to the siren call of works-righteousness; he understands the attraction from the inside out, but has been freed by God's Spirit. What is obtained **in the Spirit by faith** stands in contrast to **seeking justification through the law** in the preceding verse, which produces not certainty but uncertainty, not hope but despair.

What the **Spirit** bestows is received **by faith** – again a contrast to works of the law. What the Spirit bestows by faith is **the hope of righteousness** which believers **await eagerly**. **Hope** looks to the future and, as he says elsewhere, implies the certainty of faith since hope never disappoints (Rom. 5:5). Paul looks confidently to the Day of Judgment in which believers "shall be openly acknowledged and acquitted" (*Westminster Shorter Catechism, 38*). He is contrasting the certainty that comes to believers through faith in the Christ who died for their sins and removed their guilt, with the uncertainty that must surely arise when one attempts to earn merit through obedience to the law. Law brings uncertainty because we cannot meet its requirements; the gospel brings certainty because Jesus met the requirements for sinners and secures for time and eternity those who trust in Him.

Paul's reference to a future aspect of justification does not in the least detract from the full, free, and decisive justification in the present any more than Paul's insistence on a future aspect of adoption in Romans 8 detracts from its present reality (8:12-27). "We have peace with God" (Rom. 5:1), that is, the objective peace represented in our present, full justification. It is also true that justification participates in the already/not yet structure of his theology. As Richard Gaffin has put it, "in terms of the principle of 2 Corinthians 5:7, I am justified 'by faith,' but not (yet) 'by sight.'"[1] It is a radical thing to be a

---

[1] Richard Gaffin (2006), *By Faith, Not By Sight*, Paternoster, 92. The entire chapter should be consulted for a full discussion of this matter. A. A. Hodge, *The Confession of Faith, 392* provides this comment: "The saints will not be acquitted in the day of judgment on the ground of their own good deeds,

Christian, called to such a future! Paul knows that living in the certain hope of the reality of this promise determines how believers live in the present.

It is not superfluous to remark that in every age and at all times when the gospel is believed it produces assurance of faith in view of the coming judgment. Even in those times in which grace has been most obscured, theologians, when at their best, have recognized that the sinner can face the judgment only on the basis of the merit of Christ alone. A particularly gripping example of this is found in directions for the visitation of the sick, usually attributed to Anselm:

> Dost thou believe that thou canst not be saved but by the death of Christ? Go to, then, and while thy soul abideth in thee, put all thy confidence in this death alone – place thy trust in no other thing – connect thyself wholly with this death – cast thyself wholly on this death – wrap thyself wholly in this death. And if God would judge thee, say, "Lord! I place the death of our Lord Jesus Christ between me and Thy judgment, otherwise I will not contend, or enter into judgment, with Thee." And if He shall say unto thee that thou art a sinner, say unto Him, "I place the death of our Lord Jesus Christ between me and my sins." If He shall say unto thee that thou hast deserved damnation, say "Lord! I put the death of our Lord Jesus Christ between Thee and all my sins, I offer His merits for my own, which I should have but have not." If He say He is angry with thee, say, "Lord! I place the death of our Lord Jesus Christ between me and Thy anger."[2]

Of course, the Lord will never accuse one of His children. But when the believer looks death and judgment in the face he may *feel* accused by the inflexible law of God. The Lord, in love, has sent His own Son to die for the sins of His people and each believer finds hope and consolation, certainty and confidence in His merit alone! Paul's doctrine of justification removes the anxious worry that dominates in works-

---

but because their names are found written in the...book of God's electing love, and on the ground of their participation in the righteousness of Christ. Their good deeds will be publicly cited as the evidences of their union with Christ."

[2] Cited by James Orr, *The Progress of Dogma*, 228.

righteousness systems. Each believer rests in the promise of God in Christ. Justification is God's achievement, His judicial declaration. The aspirations found in Anselm's directions, as the subsequent history of dogma shows, could only be grounded in an understanding of justification by means of the imputed righteousness of Christ, just as Anselm's view of atonement has its ultimate fruition in this doctrine at the time of the Reformation.

For in Christ Jesus neither circumcision nor uncircumcision counts for anything, but faith working through love. Having mentioned the believer's future hope, Paul now mentions faith and love, a well-known triad in Paul. For those in union with Christ, neither circumcision nor uncircumcision means anything, that is, circumcision is not constitutive of the Christian life, nor can it bring about union with Christ and justification; rather, what matters are the qualities that result from that union, namely, **faith working through love.** This is the first occurrence of **love** in Galatians. Where faith is real and vital it will operate through love. "That is to say the believer loves, not because he or she has found people worthy of being loved, but because she or he has become a loving person. As Christians, we love because of what we have become when we believe, not because of the attractiveness of the people we meet" (Morris).

By **faith working through love** Paul does not mean that love is a precondition of justification. Paul's entire argument has made plain that there are no preconditions. But it is clearly taught by Paul that the declaration of righteousness on the basis of Christ's work calls forth an active, working faith. The Reformation expression is applicable here: the believer is justified by grace through faith alone; but that faith is not alone.

Cousar reminds us of Furnish's observation that the participle in verse 6 may be taken as a middle ("working," RSV) or a passive ("inspired," NEB margin); 'it may refer to love as the expression of faith or to God's love as the inspiration for faith. Furnish suggests that the two are complementary and further comments: "It has become evident that for Paul faith's obedience is an obedience in love, but an obedience which has the *character* of love because of its ground in God's own love by which the sinner has been claimed and thus reconciled to God. The Christian is summoned to love in a double sense: to be *loved* and to be *loving*. Within the precincts of Pauline theology these two are inseparable.'

There was a time when the Galatians believed Paul's gospel without alloy and were consistent with their profession, a time when they would not have been tempted to desert from their commitment to the truth. But now, things have changed. **You were running well. Who cut in on you, leading you to disobey the truth?** Having gotten off to a great start in the race, leaning forward toward the goal with resolve, they have now been hindered from staying the course. **Who cut in on you** expresses astonishment that they would permit themselves to be led **to disobey the truth** of the gospel. **That persuasion is not from the one who calls you.** That is, this persuasion in favor of the false gospel of the Judaizers contrasts with the persuasion that comes from the God who calls by grace. "Listening to the new voice is not merely an exchange of it for the divine one; it is to become apostate from the voice of God" (Ridderbos).

The addition of what is generally thought to be a proverb, **"A little leaven leavens the whole lump"** serves as a warning against the pervasive influence of error. As Ridderbos says, "small causes, big results". The false principle of works-righteousness in the matter of justification in God's sight, which denies the full efficacy of the atonement, cannot but have pervasive and devastating influence once it is allowed to enter the heart! The proverb also reminds us that there is a relationship between false doctrine and false living.[3] Paul applies this maxim also in 1 Corinthians 5:6 to the dangers of

---

[3] Guthrie: "The insidious permeation of wrong doctrines and wrong practices has all too often not been realized until too late to avoid the corruption of whole communities. In recent times the rooting out of the offending 'leaven' has been made infinitely more difficult because of the contemporary notion that anything savouring of heresy-hunting must be avoided at all costs. The apostle was no heresy-hunter, but he had an acute perception of the disastrous consequences of unchecked wrong."

compromise with sin and failing to exercise church discipline. The metaphor points back to the Mosaic Law's demand that Israelites remove leaven from their houses before observing Passover.

Despite their defection, however, Paul is persuaded of God's continued work in their lives through the gospel he preached. **I am convinced concerning you in the Lord that you will not think any other thing.** Paul's confidence is not in them but **in the Lord.** Due to the power of the gospel Paul still entertains the hope that the Galatians will not follow the Judaizing, false gospel of works. Obviously, the Galatians have not gone over lock, stock and barrel to the Judaizing position, and Paul aims at recovering them from whatever degree of defection has occurred.

With this aim in mind Paul also indicates his opponents. **The one troubling you shall bear his condemnation, whoever he may be.** When Paul speaks of **the one troubling you** he may be indicating that there is a ringleader behind the party troubling the Galatians. It is possible, however, that this is simply a way of referring to the Judaizing party and their influence. His point is that with which he began the epistle: those preaching a false gospel will be subject to condemnation (1:8, 9).

The connection between his reference to his opponents and his next statement is not plain. **But I brothers, if I yet preach circumcision, why am I still persecuted?** The question, of course, would have been clear to his readers. I have retained the "I" in the emphatic position (Greek) to underscore what appears to be Paul's astonishment or perhaps his desire to contrast himself with the Judaizers. Evidently, for whatever reason, the Judaizers had claimed that Paul preached circumcision. Perhaps the Judaizers had pointed to such circumstances as the circumcision of Timothy (Acts 16:3) or another similar instance in which Paul was willing to accept circumcision when the issue was not salvation by works of the law, and then twisted his purpose and claimed that Paul actually preached circumcision or minimized their differences.

At any rate, Paul makes plain that he does not **preach circumcision** and is **still persecuted.** In 6:12 Paul indicates that the Judaizers, on the other hand, preach circumcision in order to avoid the offense of the cross leading to persecution. If the "Christianity" of the Judaizers can appear to be nothing more than a variant of Judaism, then those adhering to its message could avoid persecution. But Paul will have none of it for **then the scandal of the cross would be abolished.** Salvation by a crucified Jew, a gospel of grace apart from works, was in Paul's day, and will always be, a **scandal**, a stumbling block to the world (1 Cor. 1:17-25). The church must take heed never to compromise the plain statement of salvation by grace alone, through faith alone, through the work of Christ alone, in order to appear more acceptable to the world. When the church does compromise the gospel she dishonors her Lord, keeps from needy sinners the one message needed for their salvation and is in danger of ceasing to be the church. We must take warning from the proverb, a little leaven pervades the whole lump of dough!

No wonder then, Paul adds the sardonic comment: **I wish those agitating you would emasculate themselves!** The comment has been subjected to many interpretations and some have attempted to ameliorate Paul's meaning.[4] But the purpose seems quite clear. Paul is so zealous for his converts and their salvation that he wishes the Judaizers would let the knife

---

[4] Duncan thinks that Gentile converts would have connected Paul's comment to heathen religion, especially Cybele. Ridderbos agrees saying that Paul has in mind "sacral castration which was practiced in some pagan religions and cults...undergone in a condition of raving madness." He adds: "such a mutilation of the gospel stands for Paul on one and the same level as the most despicable pagan practices, by means of which men tried to assure themselves of the favor of the gods."

Cousar is among those noting a possible connection with Deuteronomy 23:1 where castration is a cause for excommunication. "Paul may be expressing his disgust in a way that has pointed meaning for the advocates of circumcision. Instead of ensuring inclusion in the people of God, let them carry their message further and be totally excluded!"

Ramsay, on the other hand, *Historical Commentary*, 437, 438, completely distances himself from the prevalent interpretation and denies that Paul has castration in mind arguing, rather, that he means that the proper punishment for the offender is to be cut off from the fellowship "and the wish is expressed that he would cut himself off."

slip.[5] Note that in Philippians 3:2 Paul describes circumcision as mutilation. Though such vehement expression should be rare, evinced only in the most desperate of situations, should we wonder whether we have even a modicum of love for the gospel and zeal for God's glory compared with Paul?

Not only must freedom be preserved, but it can also be abused. Based upon a reminder of the indicative, **You were called for freedom, brothers**, Paul now turns his attention to the imperative: **Only do not let your freedom become an occasion for the flesh, but through love serve one another.** The freedom purchased for us by Christ can **become an occasion for the flesh.** Freedom is easily abused. Hence the *abuse* of freedom (a word occurring in various forms in Galatians eleven times) can become another way of failing to *preserve* freedom. By flesh here Paul means the sphere of corruption, that which works contrary to the Spirit (3:3; 4:23, 29; 5:16, 17, 19, 24; 6:8, 12-13). The term "flesh" distinguishes the motive of the heart characterized by self-love and concupiscence from the motives determined by the Holy Spirit. Whatever concrete situations Paul may or may not have in mind, the point is clear: those who are free can be tempted to use freedom for selfish ends. They must not look to the law for overcoming the flesh (3:2 ff.), but to the love that comes through the gospel and which brings with it newer and higher motives, called in a famous sermon by Thomas Chalmers, "the expulsive power of a new affection". Clearly Paul is focused on the motivation of the heart.

The antidote to that temptation is **through love to serve one another.** Literally, serve as "bond-servants" or "slaves" to one another. The paradox of grace! True freedom is expressed in hearts that serve, love and that are, in the Spirit, willing to be slaves of one another. This means that neither brother nor sister will treat the other as their slave, but each will seek the interest of the other. This gospel view of freedom

---

[5] The false gospel of these mutilators brings to mind a comment of B. B. Warfield, "Systematic Theology and The Preacher," *Selected Shorter Writings,* 2: 287: "A mutilated gospel produces mutilated lives, and mutilated lives are positive evils."

is the antithesis of the world's view of freedom in which the "inalienable right" of the personal pursuit of happiness is seen as the end of existence!

Grace calls believers to a manner of life. For Paul, theology inevitably brings with it ethical implications. Theology and ethics are interwoven and inseparable. Christian ethics finds its fulcrum in the freedom purchased by Christ. The gospel of grace is not only applicable at the point of the believer's entrance into the church, but is applicable to all Christian living. We never mature beyond the cross; we only learn more of its depths and how to apply its grace to life. The same gospel by which we initially come to faith in Christ is the same gospel by which we continue to grow in grace.

The calling to freedom (**you were called for freedom**), a calling that comes from God by grace, brings with it a responsibility to live it out in Christian community; hence, **you were called to freedom, *brothers.*** And, in the community of faith, freedom in Christ expresses itself appropriately when it is exercised in the context of love and service to one another. This is the way in which freedom is demonstrated, the manner of life to which grace calls us. Otherwise, the believer's exercise of freedom simply becomes another form of bondage, a denial of the freedom purchased for him by the One who loved and served *him*!

One demonstrates that he is free in Christ when he can serve others rather than seek to be served, and love people after the pattern of Christ's love to him. The believer is lord of all in Christ. Therefore he may serve others without ultimately giving up one thing since the believer possesses all things in Christ. Believers are now free to love. The Galatians' interest in the law should lead them to understand this: **For the whole law is fulfilled in one command: "You shall love your neighbor as yourself"** (Lev. 19:18; Matt. 22:37-40). Paul unpacks this in more depth in Romans 13:8-10 concluding that "love does no wrong to a neighbor; therefore love is the fulfilling of the law" (ESV). **But if you bite and devour one another, watch out that you do not consume one another. But**, that is, if you choose to abuse liberty and to live for self rather than serve in Christ-centered love, the result may well be that like animals who **bite and devour one another**, you may well **consume one another.** In sum: "He who loves his fellow-man has fulfilled the law" (Rom. 13:8, NIV). "Thus *love puts the law in proper perspective.* It frees people from misuse through the law and frees the law from misuse by people" (Cousar).[6]

We do not know precisely the situation that Paul addresses. Perhaps some claimed that possession of the Spirit validates libertine living, a constant danger in the pagan culture in which the Galatians lived out their faith. Paul, on the other hand, shows that possession of the eschatological Spirit promotes careful living and constant concern for others. Paul then sees Christian freedom in the context of loving service and commitment to the church. Self-protection, seeking for the fulfillment of one's personal interests at the expense of others, denounces rather than exercises freedom. Promoting peace, overcoming strife, showing gentleness, patience and love manifests a heart from sin set free and reveals the operation of the Lord's gracious call. Since freedom is a grace freely given, liberty in Christ is shown by grace freely poured out in the lives of others. Even the works of believers are now, because of the cross, expressions of grace!

---

[6] Cousar's comments are outstanding: "Love is not just one virtue among a list of virtues, but the sum and substance of what it means to be a Christian. In dying with Christ and in the subsequent new life, persons discover that they are recipients of God's love, and faith essentially means surrendering to this love (2:20; Rom. 5:5, 8). Only out of such surrender does the fulfillment of Leviticus 19:18 become a reality."

"As sinners are placed 'in Christ,' they are remade by love so that they no longer are characterized by self-interest. 'For the love of Christ controls us, because we are convinced that one has died for all; therefore all have died. And he died for all, that those who live might live no longer for themselves but for him who for their sake died and was raised' (2 Cor. 5:14-15)."

15.
The Spirit and the Flesh
(5:16-26)

Translation

So I say, live in the Spirit and there is no possibility that you will yield to the desires of the flesh. For what the flesh desires is against the Spirit, and the Spirit is against the flesh; for these things oppose one another so that you do not do the things you wish to do. But if the Spirit is leading you, you are not under law.

The works of the flesh are clear: such works as sexual sin, uncleanness, indecency, idolatry, sorcery, quarrels, rivalry, jealousy, fits of rage, selfish ambition, dissensions, factions, envying, drinking bouts, revels, and things like these. I warn you, as I did before, that those practicing such things shall not inherit the kingdom of God.

By contrast the fruit of the Spirit is love, joy, peace, patience, kindness, goodness, faithfulness, gentleness, and self-control. Against such things there is no law. But those who are Christ's have crucified the flesh with its passions and lusts. Since we live in the Spirit, let us follow in the Spirit. Let us not be conceited, provoking and envying one another.

Summary

Paul now calls upon the Galatians to live according to the eschatological Spirit. Believers are to "live in the Spirit" with the promise that in so doing they "will not yield to the desires of the flesh". There must be a conscious effort to follow the Spirit's lead since Spirit and flesh are opposed to each other. The believer is not impotent in this battle against the flesh. Those led by the Spirit are not "under law". The source and impetus of obedience is not law but the Holy Spirit.

Paul lists examples of fleshly deeds. This list is not exhaustive but selective, stressing relational conflict. The deeds of the flesh and the promise of the inheritance of God's kingdom are incompatible.

Paul denominates as "fruit" (singular) the deeds of the Spirit because they are produced from one source, the Holy Spirit, and because the virtues in the list work out "love" which heads the list. "Against such things there is no law." Law may prescribe but it cannot enable.

When Christ died, believers shared in the cross, which ended their relationship to the flesh. This redemptive-historical reality must be applied to their lives. Therefore, "since we live in the Spirit, let us follow in the Spirit." Let us be consistent with the newness of life imparted to us by the Spirit, living within His sphere, following His lead.

Paul began and ends with exhortation. "Let us not be conceited, provoking and envying one another." To follow the Spirit means living a life of love.

Comment

Having warned the church in Galatia against destructive biting and devouring of each other he now calls upon the believers to be who they are in Christ and to love one another by living according to the eschatological Spirit. Paul's teaching on this essential relationship between theology and ethics will be used in the Spirit's hand to raise awareness not only of their obligations to one another but also of the Spirit's assistance. **So I say, live in the Spirit and there is no possibility that you will yield to the desires of the flesh.** I have chosen to translate "flesh" very literally since it is a term used in a variety of ways in the New Testament (and by Paul) and since, also, the term as used here cannot be easily translated by one phrase. Flesh (*sarx*) here is "practically the synonym of sin" (Vos, *Pauline Eschatology*, 298). The

Spirit (*pneuma*) is its antithesis. Even this, however, needs unpacking and more precise definition.

Paul, of course, uses the term *sarx* in a variety of ways in his epistles. In some instances it means man's corporeal nature (e.g., 2 Cor. 4:10,11; Gal. 4:13, 14; 1 Cor. 15:39). *Sarx* also refers to the complete person, body and soul, a virtual synonym for "human being" (e.g. Rom. 3:20; 1 Cor. 1:29; Gal. 2:16). *Sarx* can also refer to racial solidarity (e.g. "Israel", Rom. 11:14). But *sarx* most often in Paul's writings has the specialized meaning of "the present sphere of existence determined and conditioned by sin and death", "an environment" or, more precisely, can be considered as the functional equivalent to *aeon*, or world order (Eph. 6:5, Philem. 16; 1 Cor. 1:18–3:21), bringing along with it an ethically deprecatory connotation (Rom. 8:6-8). Spirit and flesh represent two spheres of existence, comprehending two distinctly diverse and antithetical, ethically qualified world orders: Spirit referring to the age to come and its overlapping with the present age; flesh referring to the present, evil age (Gal. 1:4) from which the believer has been delivered by Christ's atonement and resurrection from the dead. What Paul has in mind is the massive transition that is the consequence of the resurrection of Jesus from the dead! He means two opposing ages, the age to come and the present evil age; two opposing kingdoms: darkness and light; two different and opposing ethical environments; two completely different spheres of existence. Paul means the difference between living under law as a means of approaching God and living under grace. Flesh means all that sinners outside of Christ trust in to save themselves.

Cousar rightly says that *sarx* means "this historical, natural and earthly sphere from which people deceive themselves into thinking they can derive ultimate meaning. As such, it is the inveterate enemy of the Spirit, who comes as the power of God's new age and who leads ultimately to eternal life." Therefore, the translation of *sarx* as "sinful nature" (NIV) is misleading because it gives the impression that "each individual is divided into two natures, a higher or spiritual side and a lower or fleshly side, which vie for control." This is not what Paul means; instead he is referring to "two realities on which individuals can base their existence, two directions toward which they can move" or, perhaps better, two mutually exclusive spheres of existence or environments that constitute exclusive ages or world orders. And, as R. Jewett says, cited by Bruce, "the flesh is Paul's term for everything aside from God in which one places his final trust." The believer is not composed of two natures but of one nature, once fallen and now renewed, but still imperfect. Hence the believer's life – renewed but imperfect – becomes the battleground for consistency with that renewed nature.

Believers are called upon to **live in the Spirit** (literally, "walk by the Spirit," an imperative meaning to live in such a way that their life is Spirit directed), that is, to submit to His leadership and function under His sway so that they will not **yield to the desires of the flesh**, an example of which has just been given in the possibility of devouring one another in the Christian community. This latter clause is an emphatic negative with a future reference. In other words, it is not merely a command, but it is a command with a promise. The one living by the Spirit's direction will not live according to the flesh. The offensive weapon against the enemy, the flesh, is living by the Holy Spirit. To **live in the Spirit**, therefore, means to live in view of, and under the sway of, the coming age that has entered their lives through Christ's resurrection.

However, since believers, though delivered from this present evil age (1:4), still exist in the overlap of the ages (see 2:20) and are not yet fully sanctified, the contest between this present evil age and all that characterizes it (the flesh) and the age to come and all that characterizes it (the Spirit) continues in their lives. **For what the flesh desires is against the Spirit, and the Spirit is against the flesh; for these things oppose one another so that you do not do the things you wish to do.** There must be, then, a conscious awareness and effort to follow the Spirit's lead and not be misled by the flesh. To follow the flesh is inconsistent for Christians because it is a realm from which they have been delivered and to which they no longer belong! "But the believer is not the helpless battleground of two opposing forces. If he yields to the flesh, he is enslaved by it, but if he obeys the prompting of the Spirit, he is liberated and can make a positive and willing response to the command 'Walk by the Spirit' and similar moral imperatives, 'doing the will of God from the heart' (as it is put in Eph. 6:6)" (Bruce). There is also encouragement in Paul's statement of the struggle: **so that you do not do the things you wish to do**. This indicates that on a fundamental level the believer's will has been changed so that the Spirit may now lead him.

Paul stresses the antithetical relationship of the Spirit and of the flesh and their opposition within the Christian life. Flesh and Spirit are radically opposed to each other. The opposition exists precisely because of the presence of the eschatological Spirit and would not be present otherwise. To express this another way, the opposition of Spirit and flesh, and the Christian's struggle due to this antithesis, is normal Christian living on this side of the eschaton. Indeed, the struggle keeps the believer's goal beyond his grasp, so that **you do not do the things you wish to do**. The believer struggles against the flesh and does not fully attain his goal; yet he is not impotent against temptation and sin due to the presence of the life-giving Spirit in his life (cf. Rom. 7:15-20).

This is why Paul adds, **but if the Spirit is leading you, you are not under law**. To be under the law is to be under the curse (3:10) and to be under the sway of the law, to be impotent against sin in one's life. The law points out sin but it cannot empower believers in order to overcome sin. Only the Holy Spirit can fulfill that function. Therefore, Paul emphasizes that those led by God's Spirit are **not under law**, that is, are no longer impotent and ill equipped to deal with sin. "To be 'led by the Spirit' is to walk by the Spirit – to have the power to rebut the desire of the flesh, to be increasingly conformed to the likeness of Christ (2 Cor. 3:18), to cease to be under law" (Bruce).[1]

---

[1] Bruce: "It is not surprising that, in the one other reference to the leading of the Spirit to be found in his letters, Paul says that 'all who are led by the Spirit of God are sons of God' (Rom. 8:14). So in Gal. 4:4f. the redemption effected by Christ for those previously 'under law' meant their receiving 'adoption as sons' (...as in Rom. 8:23). If to be 'under law' is to be a slave, to

What constitutes fleshly deeds? How are they recognized? Paul says that they are obvious. In pointing out the works of the flesh and of the Spirit Paul is contrasting not only the deeds but also the results of following the one or the other. **The works of the flesh are clear: such works as sexual sin, uncleanness, indecency, idolatry, sorcery, quarrels, rivalry, jealousy, fits of rage, selfish ambition, dissensions, factions, envying, drinking bouts, revels, and things like these.**[2]

Porneia, "sexual sin", means fornication, involvement with *pornai* (harlots), but also sexual sin generally (1 Thess. 4:3; 1 Cor. 6:18). *Akatharsia*, "uncleanness" or "impurity", is often linked with sexual sin (e.g. 2 Cor. 12:21; Col. 3:5; Eph. 5:3 and here). Ramsay notes (*Historical Commentary,* 448) that "vice was not regarded as wrong in pagan society: it was regarded as necessary – the only evil lying in excess. But in the old religion it was inculcated as a duty..." *Aselgeia*, "indecency" or "self-abandonment" (*BDAG*) (Eph. 4:19; 1 Pet. 4:3; Jude 4; 2 Pet. 2:2; Rom. 13:13). Ramsay sees this as referring to those things publicly indecent and points to the Phrygian religious practice of public self-mutilation. *Eidōlolatria* means "idolatry", "the worship of idols". *Pharmakeia* is sometimes connected with drugs and means "sorcery" (Rev. 9:21; 18:23). Bruce says that "sorcery was a serious offence in Roman law: it was dealt with by a standing court, the *quaestio perpetua de sicariis et ueneficis* (in which no very sharp distinction was made between the *ueneficus* as sorcerer and as poisoner)."

Echthrai means 'quarrels', hostilities between people, while *eris* means 'strife' or 'rivalry'. Bruce defines it as 'quarrel-someness', adding, 'Paul is specially concerned to keep ἔρις out of his churches (cf. 1 Cor. 1:11; 3:3); it is the antithesis

---

be led by the Spirit is to be a freeborn son or daughter, to enjoy 'the glorious liberty of the children of God' (Rom. 8:21) – the liberty for which, as Paul has just told the Galatians, they have been 'called' (v 13)."

[2] Ramsay, *Historical Commentary,* 447 ff., notes that "in the list of fifteen faults, there are three groups, corresponding to three different kinds of influence likely to affect recent South Galatian converts from paganism. Such converts were liable to be led astray by habits and ways of thought to which they had been brought up, owing to (1) the national religion, (2) their position in a municipality, (3) the customs of society in Hellenistic cities."

of the "peace" which is the fruit of the Spirit (v. 22).' *Zēlos* means 'zeal' and can be a word with positive meaning but in this context it means the vice of selfishness, 'jealousy' (note how Paul relates the word to *eris* in Romans 13:13, 1 Corinthians 3:3, and 2 Corinthians 12:20). *Thumoi* means 'fits of rage'. *Eritheia* refers to 'a mercenary spirit, selfish ambition' (Bruce). *Dichostasiai* means 'dissensions' and *aireseis* conveys a similar idea, 'factions' (1 Cor. 11:19) and *phthonoi* points to "a grudging spirit that cannot bear to contemplate someone else's prosperity" (Bruce).

Ramsay points out that one possible source of tension and division in the South Galatian churches might have stemmed from the fact that in Antioch and Lystra there existed a division between the Roman or Latin citizens of the Colonia and the native dwellers. Surely the churches had both Roman and non-Roman members. Moreover, even though no significant Roman element dwelt in Iconium and Derbe there were differences involved in the native Greek and Jewish elements. These elements might well combine to tempt segments of the church membership to rivalry and they needed to learn to apply the gospel of grace to these potential or real divisions. Moreover, there were urban rivalries that characterized Graeco-Asiatic city life and classing the churches of the Province of Galatia together was in itself an appeal to unity. Beyond the societal divisions, striving to establish a record of righteousness through law-keeping makes a person view others as competitors in the race for God's approval. It makes sinners hypercritical of others as a way of placating their own uneasy consciences or to make themselves look more righteous by comparison to others. This is the source of conflict!

Methai means "drunkenness" but often refers to the dissipation that comes with it (Luke 21:34; Rom. 13:13). And finally, *kōmoi* related to drunkenness in Romans 13:13 but means "revelries" and perhaps in some instances, "orgies". William Ramsay (*Historical Commentary*, 453) tells us that, among the Greeks, "Komos, the Revel, was made a god, and his rites were carried on quite systematically, and yet with all the ingenuity and inventiveness of the Greek mind, which lent perpetual novelty and variety to the revellings. The Komos was the most striking feature of Greek social life." Ramsay suggests the probability that those adopting Greek manners and civilization adopted also the Komos.

We should not think that this list is in any way exhaustive. Rather, the vices named are contextual, relating to the pagan setting from which the Galatian Christians were converted. "Moral" sins, that is, actions that men think are "good", might also fill the list in certain settings, since the motive for doing them is legal rather than evangelical. These things belong to that order of existence described in the preceding passage as indulging the flesh, and serving self rather than one another. They are contrary to love.

Cousar points out that "of the fifteen items listed as 'works of the flesh,' eight have to do with conflicts of one sort or another." He adds, "flesh defines the realm in which people think they can make their own mark in life and in so doing set themselves in opposition to God." Against the chaotic works of the flesh Paul raises a serious alarm: **I warn you, as I did before, that those practicing such things shall not inherit the kingdom of God.** "There is a fundamental incompatibility between life determined by the flesh and life in the reign of God" (Cousar). This "fundamental incompatibility" is plainly because these things are contrary to the presence and leading of the Holy Spirit who is the installment and guarantee of the coming age (Rom. 8:23; 2 Cor. 1:22; Eph. 1:14). These things indicate that a person is living under law and point to a heart that continues to function without Christ as Redeemer. All sin is a failure to trust Christ alone and puts self-salvation in His place.

But if the deeds of the flesh against which Paul must warn the church are obvious, so too are the deeds of the Spirit, which he commends. **By contrast the fruit of the Spirit is love, joy, peace, patience, kindness, goodness, faithfulness, gentleness, and self-control. Against such things there is no law.**

Agapē, "love", was already referenced in verse 6 as the fulfillment of the law (Rom. 5:5; 8:37; 2 Cor. 5:14). *Chara* means "joy" (note its connection with "love" in Romans 5:11). *Eirēnē*, "peace" is based on the objective peace made possible through the cross of Christ (Rom. 5:1) and characterizing Christian community (1 Cor. 14:33; Eph. 4:3). *Makrothumia* means "patience". Bruce says that if the English language possessed the adjective "long-tempered" as the counter of "short-tempered" this would well sum up the word's meaning. *Chrēstotēs*, "kindness", like patience and love, is a "communicable attribute" of God (1 Cor. 13:4; and as an attribute of God, Rom 2:4). *Agathōsunē* means "goodness", including "generosity". *Pistis* may mean "faith" or "trust" but also "faithfulness" which makes more sense in a list such as this (1 Cor. 12:9; Rom. 12:3, 6). *Prautēs* means "gentleness" (characteristic of Jesus himself, Matt. 11:29), while *egkrateia*, "self-control," "has something in common with πραΰτης [*prautēs*] but denotes control of more sensual passions than anger" (Bruce).

These deeds and virtues are expressions of Christian freedom, expressions of love to God and neighbor. Also, it is essential to note that they are the fruit of the Holy Spirit. In contrast to **works of the flesh** (plural) the resulting work of the Spirit in our lives is to produce **fruit** (singular). This is because the work of the Spirit is one and because all of the virtues are the working out of **love** that begins the list. Paul is still concerned to point out that love fulfills the law. **Joy, peace, patience** and the other virtues in the list are the ways in which **love** is manifested in the Christian life.[3]

---

[3] Cousar observes: "If there are those in the Galatian congregations who have been carried away by their ecstatic experiences of the Spirit and have become the occasion for controversy, this list calls them back to earth and to the fundamental activity of God in human lives. It contains beyond the gift of love, a striking number of terms which have about them the mark of restraint and steadiness over against exuberance and self-assertion."

Luther, *Works*, 31, 300, says that the Christian's manner of life is the result of the alien righteousness of Christ: "This righteousness is the product of the righteousness of the first type, actually its fruit and consequence..." He cites Galatians 5:22 and adds: "Therefore it hates itself and loves its neighbor; it does not seek its own good, but that of another, and in this its whole way of living consists. For in that it hates itself and does not seek its own, it crucifies the flesh. Because it seeks the good of another, it works love. Thus in each sphere it does God's will, living soberly with self, justly with neighbor, devoutly toward God."

Living by the Spirit, expressing freedom by love, is not a new but equally burdensome yoke of slavery, a replacement of one form of drudgery for another. The Spirit produces these graces. Augustine's prayer comes to mind: command what You will and give what You command. The Spirit produces within the believer the life that He commands. The Spirit is the Spirit of the new age bringing with Him the enabling of the age to come (3:1-5; 4:6).

Against such things there is no law states again the thought of verse 18 – **but if the Spirit is leading you, you are not under law** – and serves as an encouragement to believers that the Spirit is operative in their lives and enables the dominance of this fruit over against the deeds that characterize the flesh. But also, as Bruce puts it, Paul "means that when these qualities are in view we are in a sphere with which law has nothing to do. Law may prescribe certain forms of conduct and prohibit others, but love, joy, peace and the rest cannot be legally enforced. 'A vine does not produce grapes by Act of Parliament; they are the fruit of the vine's own life; so the conduct which conforms to the standard of the Kingdom is not produced by any demand, not even God's, but it is the fruit of that divine nature which God gives as the result of what he has done in and by Christ' (S. H. Hooke, 'What is Christianity?' in *The Siege Perilous* [London, 1956], 264)." We should not conclude, however, that there is no place for the so-called third use of the law. Paul is not addressing that question but is addressing the matter of power or impetus in obedience.[4]

Lists of virtues, such as the fruit in this passage, were common in Paul's day, especially among Stoics. But those catalogues were duties and not products of the Spirit's life. Paul's ethic is entirely different. It is an ethic of the Holy Spirit! It is not through a detailed analysis of the fruit of the Spirit, a constant introspective, psychological analysis of ourselves, that we grow in the fruit of the Spirit. It is by walking in the Spirit that the Spirit produces His fruit. This is an important

---

[4] See C. E. B. Cranfield, "Has the Old Testament Law a Place in the Christian Life?: A Response to Professor Westerholm," in *On Romans*, 109-24.

pastoral observation that should be dwelt upon. The tendency of many Christians to focus inappropriately upon themselves rather than upon Christ is a genuine hindrance to growth in grace. Healthy self-examination is called for but not a self-focus that loses its attentiveness to Christ alone through whose Spirit we are sanctified.

Believers can be confident of the Spirit's work because it is the fruit of Christ's atonement. **But those who are Christ's have crucified the flesh with its passions and lusts**. When Christ died for the Galatian believers they shared in that cross (probably indicated by the aorist tense of "crucified"). Just as in 2:19 Paul has said that the cross brought to an end his relationship to law, as a means of justification and securing life, so here the cross has ended his relationship to the flesh. In 6:14 he will affirm that by that same cross of Christ he, Paul, has been crucified to the world, and the world to him. In the grand redemptive-historical and epochal event of the cross, in which the Galatians also shared through Christ their representative and substitute, the dominion of sin was abolished and that of Christ established! This was applied to their hearts in the Spirit's transition of them from wrath to grace. This redemptive-historical reality must always be applied to their life choices and practice.

Therefore, **since we live in the Spirit, let us follow in the Spirit**. Let us work out the relationship between the indicative and the imperative. Let us be consistent with the newness of life imparted to us by the Spirit, living within His sphere, following His lead. Let us not deny the freedom with which we have been set free in Christ. To **follow in the Spirit** means that the battle between the two realms of "flesh" and "Spirit", along with the choices involved for the Christian, is not resolved by pulling ourselves up by our own bootstraps, by simply gritting our teeth and trying harder. If living a fleshly existence means works-righteousness, or living for human approval, always living for the demands of the world or the lust of the heart, to **follow the Spirit** means the opposite. We do not enter the battle in our own strength, nor fight it to win God's favor or the world's. "Rather, Christians are called to

entrust themselves to the Spirit, to God's activity, and simply
to follow his guidance. It is not a reluctant Spirit who has to be
persuaded or persistently begged to make available to us God's
new world. The Spirit is, as it were, eager to function with
power in the church and in individuals to produce his 'fruit'
and only needs to be allowed the opportunity" (Cousar).

How, then, should believers apply this reality to their
daily struggle with sin? Paul's answer is that they belong to
the realm of the Spirit and this defines them. To live as if this
were not the case is beneath their dignity as Christians. Live
as a member of God's new environment! As Paul says in Romans 6:11, 12, "In the same way, count yourselves dead to sin
but alive to God in Christ Jesus. Therefore do not let sin reign
in your mortal body so that you obey its evil desires" (NIV). "In
the death of Christ sin suffered the definitive loss of its right to
rule."[5] And, on that basis, every Christian is now active in the
fight against sin, evil, and the flesh. Grace calls them to active
submission to the Holy Spirit who uses His own appointed
means – the Word of God preached and read, the sacraments,
worship, prayer, the fellowship of God's people – to aid His
people in the struggle. Having died to sin, we must kill sin.

This entire section of Galatians along with chapter 6 is
particularly applicable to relationships. Paul began with an
exhortation and ends with an exhortation that applies to
relationships in the church. Exhortation is an instrument in
the hand of the Spirit to spur believers on in their Christian
vocation. **Let us not be conceited, provoking and envying
one another**. To **follow in the Spirit** means not vaunting our
wills and desires over others, as well as caring for those who
struggle (6:1ff.). We must remember that in the fruit of the
Spirit love leads the list and all other virtues work out the
meaning of love in relationships. Whatever is contrary to love
is contrary to the right exercise of Christian freedom. On the
other hand, a Christian can see that he is following the Spirit
when his life is determined by love. It is that concrete.

---

[5] Anders Nygren, *Romans*, 243.

16.
Let Us Not Be Conceited
(6:1-10)

Translation
Brothers, if anyone is overtaken in a transgression, you who live by the Spirit must restore such a person in a spirit of gentleness, keeping a close eye on yourself, so that you are not also tempted. Bear one another's burdens, and in this way you will fulfill the law of Christ. For, if anyone thinks that he is somebody when he is not, he deceives himself. Each one should put his own work to the test, and then he shall have reason to boast in himself and will not compare himself to another. For each person shall bear his own burden.

Those who are taught the Word must share in all good things with him who teaches the Word.

Do not be deceived: God is not mocked, for whatever a man sows, this he will also reap. Because he who sows in the flesh will himself of the flesh reap corruption, but he who sows in the Spirit, of the Spirit will reap life everlasting. Let us not grow weary in doing good, for in due time we will reap if we do not grow faint. So then, while we have time, let us work to do good to all, most of all to those of the household of faith.

Summary
Having in the prior section concluded with an exhortation, "let us not be conceited, provoking and envying one another," Paul now illustrates how this gracious attitude reveals itself in

the Christian community. When a fellow Christian falls into sin, those "who live by the Spirit" should gently restore him, while being careful not to fall into temptation themselves. Bearing burdens fulfills the "law of Christ".

In helping a brother, a believer can become haughty and so should examine his own life and avoid making his brother the standard for comparison. For "each person shall bear his own burden" in the Day of Judgment. No other believer can stand for us, only Christ.

Paul adds a second example of following the Spirit by humble service. "Those who are taught the Word must share in all good things with him who teaches the Word." This should not be seen as an isolated admonition, but as another example of how to live a Spirit-led life.

Paul next encourages the church to persevere in well-doing in view of the Judgment. "God is not mocked," says Paul, and those who sow to the flesh will reap corruption while those who sow to the Spirit will reap everlasting life. Therefore, "let us not grow weary in doing good, for in due time we will reap if we do not grow faint." Meanwhile, during this "time" between Christ's ascension and return believers must be busy with caring, loving deeds, especially in the "household of faith".

Paul has not switched from a gospel of justification by grace to one of acceptance through works. The Judgment will be the day of open acquittal and the believer's works will be seen as "the essential and manifest criterion" (Gaffin) of true faith, but not the basis of their acceptance. Christ alone is the basis of the believer's acceptance with God.

Comment

In the prior section Paul concluded with an exhortation, **let us not be conceited, provoking and envying one another.** Following the Spirit means living with grace and showing love to one another in the church. Paul now gives a more concrete example of how "love fulfills the law" and what it means to follow in the Spirit as we interact in community. He begins with the case of a fellow Christian who has fallen into sin.

Brothers, if anyone is overtaken in a transgression, you who live by the Spirit must restore such a person in a spirit

of gentleness. The term **overtaken** seems to imply that the one who has fallen was surprised by the occasion of transgression in his life. What is the church to do when this happens? Paul addresses the church as the *pneumatikoi*, the "Spirituals", those who are possessed of and **who live by the Spirit**. It is possible that there were those boasting of being "spiritual", in which case Paul presents a case to demonstrate what being spiritual truly means! Paul has already argued in 5:16-26 that all believers live by the Spirit. Rather than addressing an elite subdivision of the church, the apostle is calling all who believe in Jesus, and who therefore have His Spirit, to a pattern of behavior that befits their new identity.

In view of the life described in 5:16-26 the church is lovingly to help the brother and **must restore such a person in a spirit of gentleness**. There is no attention given to the attitude of the one overtaken in transgression, but simply a call to care and help him in his need. The goal is not punishment but gentle restoration. "The restoration…is to be completely devoid of stigma" (Martyn). And it is important to note that the church must not simply let such things slip by! This contradicts the love we are called to display as we follow the Spirit. To allow a fellow believer to sin and turn the other way does not demonstrate love. A **spirit of gentleness** can refer to the Holy Spirit or to the human spirit. In either case the source of **gentleness** is the Holy Spirit (5:23). A case could be made for an upper-case **"S"** translating a **Spirit of gentleness**. Cousar notes that Bultmann (*Theology of the NT,* I. 337) says that the phrase is a Semitic way of saying "the gentle Spirit". In either case Paul points to the gentle attitude of the Christians attempting the restoration as the result of the Spirit's work (5:23). The modern church would do well to heed both the admonition to show care and concern by taking active steps to restore those who fall into serious transgression as well as the call to reflect the fatherly character of God in the process.

At the same time, the believer (Paul has changed to the singular) who helps must do so **keeping a close eye on yourself, so that you are not also tempted**. The operative principle is mutual caring for one another in the church. But when such love is shown, the involvement of caring members of the church can be so deep that they too may forget their weakness and be tempted to sin. Involvement requires much wisdom and not everyone will be prepared in the same way. Indeed, wise leadership may find it necessary to remove some well-intended helper from a circumstance when they see that the burden is beyond his capability of bearing. This also is mutual burden-bearing in the church.

Bear one another's burdens, and in this way you will fulfill the law of Christ. Restoring a fallen brother is hard, exhausting and demanding. Paul sees the sinner's need as a burden and one that the church is called to help bear. But bear it we must as we follow the Spirit in loving relationships. The burdens of others within the church are our own by virtue of our union with one another in our union with Christ. **The law of Christ** is striking. Ridderbos observes: "Not that in such a statement Christ is being set up over against Moses as a new lawgiver. The claim of the law which was once given continues in effect (cf. 5:14), but this accrues to the believers from Christ. He stands between the law and believers. He guarantees its fulfillment in believers by the Holy Spirit. The new element is not the content of the law, although Christ's coming and His work modified it, but in the root of obedience, namely, Christ. And above all the bearing of another's burden harmonizes in every respect with what Christ by word and deed taught His own. In this real love becomes manifest, the fulfillment of the whole law (cf. 5:14)."

Helping one another and especially the gentle restoration of fallen sinners in the church is the opposite of being **conceited, provoking and envying one another** (5:26). But it sometimes happens when helping a brother through the quagmire of his fall into sin that those helping can feel superior and become haughty. Such an arrogant attitude is contrary to living by the Spirit's leading and contrary to love. This is what Paul means by saying **if anyone thinks that he is somebody when he is not, he deceives himself**. Each person is called to examine his own life. **Each one should put his own work to the test, and then he shall have reason to boast in himself and will not compare himself to another**. The fallen brother is not the standard for comparison. Each one must "prove" his own work. "If we are concentrating on ironing out the imperfections in what we are doing, we are unlikely to be critical of what other people are accomplishing. Paul is not, of course, advocating that Christians should be habitually boastful; he is saying that they should so live that their lives will give evidence of praiseworthy qualities" (Morris).

In view of this Paul says, **for each person shall bear his own burden**. Paul is not contradicting his previous exhortation to **bear one another's burdens** (v. 2). It seems that Paul has the judgment in mind, a time in which no one can look to the failings of another to justify himself, as we sometimes do when we become arrogant in view of others' faults, but each must stand in the merit of Christ alone. Looking to one's own heart and seeing one's need of Christ on the great Day is the antidote to self-delusion. Who looking at the needs of his own heart will boast at the expense of someone else? Rather, this sober assessment produces humility. Caring for those who are struggling with sin must always be carried on with such an attitude in the church.

Paul gives another example of following the Spirit in humble service to each other: **Those who are taught the Word must share in all good things with him who teaches the Word**. Often this is seen as an isolated exhortation, somewhat dangling and disconnected from his argument. But there is no need for this. Rather, it is best to see this as another example of following the Spirit in humble service to each other. By **all good things** Paul seems to mean the material needs of the pastor, as the parallel in 1 Corinthians 9:4-14 suggests.[1]

---

[1] Note also Philippians 4:10; 1 Thessalonians 2:6, 9; 1 Timothy 5:17, 18. Ramsay, *Historical Commentary*, 457: "Paul, who was never content simply to convert, but was equally watchful to organise and to build up, by subsequent care and watching, his young Churches, could not safely neglect to provide for their permanent guidance when he was absent, and the frequency of his references to the subject attests the importance that he attached to it." The entire discussion is illuminating in which Ramsay adds (459): "One of the objects that Paul had most at heart was to train his converts in voluntary liberality, as distinguished from payments levied on ritual." Indeed, "there is no bond so strong to hold men together as the common performance of the same duties and actions."

Paul, then, offers another illustration of loving behavior in the church. That he takes this as an illustration affords a glimpse into the value Paul places upon the means of grace.

Having furnished these concrete examples of loving one another in the church Paul encourages believers to persevere in well-doing, and he does so by emphasizing an eschatological focus, a view of the Judgment Day which explains the prevalence of the future tense. **Do not be deceived: God is not mocked, for whatever a man sows, this will he also reap. Because he who sows in the flesh will himself of the flesh reap corruption, but he who sows in the Spirit, of the Spirit will reap life everlasting.** Those who help the fallen and share with the minister of the Word, sow in the Spirit and will reap eternal life, whereas those who do not do these things sow to the flesh and are counted as mockers of God. Paul has not fallen into a salvation by works but does justice to the transformative work of the Spirit in the believer's life. Reaping is a frequent figure for the judgment in Scripture and this seems to be in Paul's mind as he presses upon the church their calling to continue in loving service to one another. It is an encouraging, if awesome, thought that the believer moves on toward the day in which he will reap eternal life.

Knowing that the judgment is coming Paul continues, **Let us not grow weary in doing good, for in due time we will reap if we do not grow faint.** It is clear that though the thought of the judgment is always serious, yet it is not intended as a threat to true believers but as an encouragement, an incentive to keep pressing toward the goal. Paul therefore concludes, **So then, while we have time, let us work to do good to all, most of all to those of the household of faith.** The NIV rendering, "Therefore, as we have opportunity, let us do good to all people," misses Paul's eschatological reference intended by the word "time" (*kairos*). The "time" Paul has in mind anticipates the **time we will reap** (v.9), the Day of Judgment. So **while we have time** means that during this period between Christ's ascension and return the church is to be busy with loving concern and caring deeds. Verse 10 is about the season for sowing and planting, the time we have now to do good, in anticipation that the seeds sown now in love will increase the final harvest. Doing good for others knows no limits,[2] but Christians are called to give special attention to caring for the people of God, believers who form one monumental **household of faith**. Perhaps Paul has the specific issues in the Galatian churches in mind and is keen to see believers zealously demonstrate love to one another.

By stressing that Christians must live in view of the coming judgment Paul has not forsaken his commitment to justification by grace through faith that forms the basis of his epistle! The judgment in which believers participate is no isolated theme in Paul's writings (1 Cor. 3:12, 13; 4:5; 2 Cor. 5:10; 1 Thess. 4:6; Rom. 14:10). But Paul never utilizes this serious theme as a threat, as if to bring the certainty of faith into question. Richard Gaffin has summarized Paul's view of the relationship between the Christian's faith, works and the judgment well: "For Christians, future judgment according to works does not operate according to a different principle than their already having been justified by faith. The difference is that the final judgment will be the open manifestation of that present justification, their being 'openly acquitted' as we have seen. And in that future judgment their obedience, their works, are not the ground or basis. Nor are they (co-)instrumental, a coordinate instrument for appropriating divine approbation as they supplement faith. Rather, they are the essential and manifest criterion of that faith, the integral 'fruits and evidences of a true and lively faith', appropriating the language of the *Westminster Confession of Faith* 16:2" (*By Faith, Not by Sight*, 98).[3] It is precisely as the Christian anticipates that Day with confidence that he will press on with vigor in Christ's service knowing that "God did not appoint us to suffer wrath but to receive salvation through our Lord Jesus Christ" (1 Thess. 5:9).

---

[2] Dennis Johnson has suggested to me in personal correspondence that this is the point of the parable of the good Samaritan: to challenge the natural human proclivity implicit in the question, "Who is my neighbor?" to try to circumscribe as narrowly as possible the "boundaries" of neighborliness, limiting to "reasonable" dimensions our obligations to love others as we so naturally love ourselves (Luke 10:25-37).

[3] See also Ridderbos, *Paul*, 178-81.

17.
A New Creation
(6:11-18)

Translation

See with what big letters I am writing to you in my own hand! Those wishing to make a good showing in the flesh are trying to force you to be circumcised, only so that they may not be persecuted for the cross of Christ. For not even those who are circumcised keep the law, but they wish you to be circumcised so that they might boast in your flesh. May I never boast except in the cross of our Lord Jesus Christ, through which the world is crucified to me and I to the world. For neither circumcision nor uncircumcision is anything, but a new creation. And to all those who will keep in line with this rule, peace and mercy be upon them, that is, upon the Israel of God.

From now on let no one trouble me, for I bear in my body the marks of Jesus.

The grace of our Lord Jesus Christ be with your spirit, brothers. Amen.

Summary

Paul's conclusion is no mere formality. Critical themes from his epistle are expounded. Evidently, Paul wrote the ending of the letter to authenticate its contents and perhaps to stress the themes that tie it together. Taking the pen from the amanuensis Paul wrote with "large letters".

His conclusion contains a final barrage against the Judaizers who attempted to force circumcision on the Galatians in order to avoid persecution for Christ's cross. The Judaizers were not consistent with their own position. "For not even those who are circumcised keep the law, but they wish you to be circumcised so that they might boast in your flesh." The Judaizers had been circumcised but they could not bear the law's burden. They were not concerned with the gospel but with boasting in the flesh, that is, with manipulating the Galatians to become their converts.

Paul responds, "May I never boast except in the cross of our Lord Jesus Christ, through which the world is crucified to me and I to the world." Paul will never glory in circumcision but only in his crucified Savior.

Indeed, everything is different since Christ came. The "new creation" has come and is what matters, not circumcision or uncircumcision. And it is by this standard of evaluation that the Christian is to judge everything. Upon those living by this standard, those constituting the new Israel of the new age, Paul invokes peace and mercy.

Concluding his argument Paul wishes the discussion to come to an end, desiring the Galatians to have done with the Judaizers and to heed his argument. "From now on let no one trouble me, for I bear in my body the marks of Jesus." Paul knows one Lord only, and he bears his marks of ownership through persecution. The Judaizers might live to avoid the offense of the cross, but Paul, living by the gospel, is willing to bear its reproach.

Paul's benediction draws together the themes of grace and mercy in Christ, a benediction pronounced upon Paul's brothers! "The grace of our Lord Jesus Christ be with your spirit, brothers." Amen.

Comment

Paul's concluding remarks are not to be carelessly read. They contain much of great importance for understanding his epistle and theology. Many themes of Paul's letter to the Galatians are brought together in the conclusion.

It was Paul's habit to dictate to a secretary and to conclude his letter with a personalized message written in his own hand (2 Thess. 3:17). So at this point Paul takes the pen from his amanuensis and writes the ending himself. **See with what big letters I am writing to you in my own hand!** Literally Paul pens, "I wrote," which is an epistolary usage by which Paul is underlining the importance of his message. The verb is an epistolary aorist; when the letter was read, its writing would already have happened. Its purpose is to say to the reader: "Look here, mark this!" Paul must be stressing the importance of his letter as a whole as well as the ending or perhaps, as Morris suggests, authenticating the letter (cf. 2 Thess. 3:17). He writes in large letters, possibly for emphasis and not just because this is simply the way he wrote in distinction from professional scribes. The reference only makes sense if he mentions the detail for a purpose. Perhaps his writing was recognizable to the Galatians.

At any rate, the letters written so large contain a final salvo against the Judaizers. **Those wishing to make a good showing in the flesh are trying to force you to be circumcised, only so that they may not be persecuted for the cross of Christ.** Why did the Judaizers pursue their program so vigorously? Paul insists that they were attempting to avoid persecution – and this is the essential point – **for the cross of Christ.** They perhaps wish to **make a good showing in the flesh** to fellow Jews who would more likely accept them if their converts were circumcised. We do know that Paul's insistence that Gentiles were not required to undergo circumcision evoked libelous rumors against Paul that even Jewish Christians apparently believed – see Acts 21:20-26. They wished to be masters and not servants of God's people. Moreover, "a Christianity that could not, if need be, identify itself through circumcision as a part of Judaism did indeed renounce the legal protection that the Jewish religion enjoyed in the Roman Empire" (Lührmann).[1]

---

[1] Lührmann also says on 5:2: "Under Roman rule circumcision, as the sign of belonging to Judaism, was at the same time a guarantee of participation in certain privileges that the state granted to the synagogue. Thus a Christianity that renounced circumcision also renounced its claim to rights accorded Judaism. Not until later, after the Jewish insurrections, did the Roman emperor Hadrian prohibit circumcision."

This **good showing** was more important to the Judaizers than
the basic message of Christianity as summed up in **the cross
of Christ**. Therefore the Judaizers attempted to compel the
Galatians to be circumcised as an indispensable part of the
brand of "Christianity" that they preached. A Christianity
severed from the cross is no longer Christianity, and a
Christianity that trims its message in order to avoid offense
will not long remain true Christianity.

However, the Judaizers were not consistent with their own
position. **For not even those who are circumcised keep the
law, but they wish you to be circumcised so that they might
boast in your flesh.** The participle, **those who are circumcised**,
refers to the Judaizers as indicated by what follows: **but they
wish you to be circumcised so that they might boast in your
flesh.**[2] The Judaizers had been circumcised but they could not
bear the burden of the law, and yet they want the Galatians
to be circumcised and submit to the yoke of the law that they
cannot themselves keep! See Acts 15:10.

Paul also singles out a second motive for the Judaizing
program, **so that they might boast in your flesh**, meaning in
their circumcision. They were not concerned with the gospel
and its application to the hearts of their hearers but were
preoccupied with boasting in the flesh, perhaps counting
converts.

But Paul will have none of it. He will boast only in the
gospel! **May I never boast except in the cross of our Lord
Jesus Christ, through which the world is crucified to me
and I to the world.** Paul will never glory in circumcision but
only in the cross. This is true and genuine boasting. Whether
we translate "through which" which makes the cross the
antecedent and seems more likely, or "through whom" which
makes Christ the antecedent, the idea is the same: Paul glories
only in the crucified Savior.[3] Through the cross Paul died to

---

[2] Or, as Bruce says it should be "taken as a middle with causative
significance."

[3] Bruce: "But the nobler object of Paul's present boasting was, by all
ordinary standards of his day, the most ignoble of all objects – a matter
of unrelieved shame, not of boasting. It is difficult, after sixteen centuries
and more during which the cross has been a sacred symbol, to realize

this present evil age (*kosmos* is the functional equivalent of *aiōn* in 1:4) and the present evil age was dead to him (cf. 2:20). Those things in which he once boasted no longer matter to him (Phil. 3:4-6). "His acceptance of the crucified Christ was not simply an interesting episode: it was a death to a whole way of life and a rising to a new mode of existence" (Morris).[4]

Paul now stresses that a new world order has arrived in Christ. **For neither circumcision nor uncircumcision is anything, but a new creation.** That is, in the new creation order that has dawned upon us in the coming of Christ circumcision or uncircumcision is not even a question. Neither has a place in God's new order, his plan of redemption. Whether one is circumcised or uncircumcised is of no importance whatsoever (cf. 3:28). What matters is **a new creation.** Paul's thought is paralleled in 2 Corinthians 5:17 and context, in which he makes it clear that the new creation is the result of Christ's atonement and resurrection. So here also, the cross of Christ makes the circumcision question null and void since God has intruded the age to come. The Christian belongs to this **new creation** (2 Cor. 5:17) in which the law as a means to salvation is irrelevant.

---

the unspeakable horror and loathing which the very mention or thought of the cross provoked in Paul's day. The word *crux* was unmentionable in polite Roman society…even when one was being condemned to death by crucifixion the sentence used an archaic formula which served as a sort of euphemism: *arbori infelici suspendito,* 'hang him on the unlucky tree'."

[4] After commenting on verse 14, Richard Gaffin in "The Usefulness of The Cross," *WTJ* XLI (1979), 244, adds: "Risking a generalization that has all manner of significant exceptions, it does seem fair to say that the churches of the Reformation have shown a much better grasp of the 'for us' of Christ's cross and the gospel than they have of the 'with him' of that gospel, particularly *suffering* with him. The question we must continue to put to ourselves is this – and certainly we will hardly be so blind as to suppose that for the church in today's world this is anything less than a most searching and urgent question: do we really understand the exclusive efficacy of Christ's death, if we do not also grasp its inclusive aspect? For the New Testament the efficacy of the Atonement has not been applied where it does not issue in 'the fellowship of his sufferings' and 'conformity to his death.' Really, we should say that the fellowship of Christ's sufferings is an inseparable benefit of the Atonement." He adds: "There are few truths which the church down through its history has been more inclined to evade; there are few truths which the church can less afford to evade."

It is by this new standard – that of the new age – that Christians are to evaluate life and all things. Hence Paul's first of two blessings, **and to all those who will keep in line with this rule, peace and mercy be upon them, that is, upon the Israel of God** stresses the new standard of evaluation, the rule (*kanōn*) by which the believer measures all things. This new standard of evaluation is radical and thoroughly pervasive (cf. 2 Cor. 5:16)! Surely, Paul excludes nothing from this new standard of measurement! He points to the ongoing application of this standard to life by using a future tense: **to all those who will keep in line with this rule....** Invoking **peace and mercy be upon them, that is, upon the Israel of God** (cf. Pss. 125:5; 128:6). Paul is not blessing two distinct groups, first those who boast in the cross, and then a separate group, "the Israel of God" – as if this Israel could boast anything other than the cross and expect God's peace and mercy. Dispensationalists may speak of two peoples of God, national Israel and the church; but Paul unequivocally has affirmed that those who belong to Christ are "Abraham's seed" and that those whose only link to Abraham is "according to the flesh" are slaves, not heirs. Paul is recognizing that the Christian life is based completely upon the work of Christ through whom we have peace with God that comes to us by sovereign mercy. Those persons saved by this mercy and who are at peace with God he further designates **the Israel of God** (the *kai* is epexegetic). The entire church, Jew and Gentile, is now God's Israel.

Paul has now concluded his argument. He has poured himself into reasoning with the Galatians and has done all he could by means of this letter to rescue them from the works-righteousness of the Judaizing faction. **From now on let no one trouble me, for I bear in my body the marks of Jesus.** That is, "let no one continue this argument, but heed what I say." The Judaizers may be living to avoid persecution but Paul accepts the cross and the suffering that comes with it: **for I bear in my body the marks of Jesus** (*stigmata tou Iēsou*). A *stigma* was a brand placed upon a slave (*BDAG*). Paul has one Lord and Master, Jesus Christ. Paul bears his marks of ownership, evidently the wounds and injuries suffered in the service of gospel preaching (4:13, 5:11; 2 Cor. 4:7-10; 11:23-27). Ramsay comments: "The marks are those cut deep on Paul's body by the lictor's rods at Pisidian Antioch and the stones of Lystra, the scars that mark him as a slave of Jesus."[5] Paul's thought here is far removed from medieval legends about saints bearing "the stigmata" as miraculous signs of extraordinary piety. Paul's "stigmata" were inflicted in the process of spreading the gospel of grace. The comment can only have deep and significant meaning if it brings back memories to the readers and speaks to them of incidents of which they are indeed aware.

Paul's (second) benediction (see 6:16) is in keeping with the passionate theme of his letter and is intended to press the gospel of grace upon the hearts of his readers. **The grace of our Lord Jesus Christ be with your spirit, brothers. Amen.** The gospel which imparts benediction to the spirit is all of **grace**, has its source in **our Lord Jesus Christ**, and binds Paul to the Galatians as **brothers**. Paul is concerned to address the Galatians as **brothers**, believers who need to heed the gracious word of the cross. To this he adds: **Amen.** And so must all who are justified by grace alone, through faith alone, on the sole basis of the work of Christ alone. SOLI DEO GLORIA!

---

[5] *Historical Commentary*, 472. Ramsay continues (472, 473): "This custom to mark slaves by scars – produced by cuts, prevented from closing as they healed, so as to leave broad wounds – is familiar even yet to the observant traveller, though since slavery was brought to an end in Turkey cases are now few, and will after a few years have ceased to exist. The same custom existed in the country from ancient times. It was practiced on the temple slaves from time immemorial; and the Galatian slave owners practiced it on their slaves, as Artemidorus mentions, having adopted it from their predecessors in the land."

Bibliography

Barr, J., "Abba Isn't Daddy". *JTS* 39:28-47, (1988).

Barth, Markus, *Justification*. Trans. A. M. Woodruff III. Eugene, Oregon: Wipf and Stock (2006).

Bauer, W., *A Greek-English Lexicon of the New Testament and Early Christian Literature (BDAG)*, trans. and adapted by W. F. Arndt and F. W. Gingrich, third edition ed. by Kurt Aland and Barbara Aland, with Victor Reichmann (2000).

Behm, Johannes, ἀνατίθημι *TDNT*, I. 353-356. Trans. Geoffrey W. Bromiley. Grand Rapids: Eerdmans (1978).

Berger, Adolf; Nichols, Barry; Treggiari, Anne T., "Adoption". *OCD*. Oxford: Oxford University Press (1996).

Berkouwer, G. C., *Faith and Sanctification*. Grand Rapids: Eerdmans (1952).

Berkouwer, G. C., *Faith and Justification*. Grand Rapids: Eerdmans (1954).

Betram, Georg, ἔργον *TDNT*, II. 635-655. Trans. Geoffrey W. Bromiley. Grand Rapids: Eerdmans (1978).

Betz, Hans Dieter, *Galatians*. Philadelphia: Fortress Press (1979).

Bridges, Charles, *The Christian Ministry*. Edinburgh: Banner of Truth (rpt. 1976).

Bruce, F. F., "'Abraham Had Two Sons' – A Study in Pauline Hermeneutics" in *New Testament Studies: Essays in Honor of Ray Summers,* Baylor University Press, 71-84 (1975).

Bruce, F. F., *The Epistle to the Galatians*. Grand Rapids: Eerdmans (1982).

Bultmann, Rudolf, *TDNT*. Transl. Kendrick Grobel. New York: Charles Scribner's Sons (1955).

Bultmann, Rudolf, πείθω *TDNT*, VI.1-11. Trans. Geoffrey W. Bromiley. Grand Rapids: Eerdmans (1979).

Bultmann, Rudolf, πιστεύω *TDNT*, VI.174-228. Trans. Geoffrey W. Bromiley. Grand Rapids: Eerdmans (1979).

Burton, Ernest De Witt , *A Critical and Exegetical Commentary on The Epistle to the Galatians*. Edinburgh: T. and T. Clark (1959).

Busch, Eberhard, *Karl Barth, His Life From Letters and Autobiographical Texts*. Philadelphia: Fortress Press (1976).

Büchsel, Friedrich, ἀγοράζω *TDNT*, I. 124-28. Trans. Geoffrey W. Bromiley. Grand Rapids: Eerdmans (1978).

Calder, W. M., "Adoption and Inheritance in Galatia". *JTS* 31:372-74 (1930).

Calvin, John , *Galatians, Ephesians, Philippians and Colossians*. Vol. 11. Trans. T. H. L. Parker. Grand Rapids: Eerdmans. Original of Galatians, 1548 (1979).

Campbell, K. M., "Covenant or Testament? Heb. 9: 16, 17 Reconsidered". *EQ* 44: 107-11 (1972).

Clowney, Edmund P., "The Biblical Doctrine of Justification by Faith" in *Right With God: Justification in The Bible and The World*. Ed. D. A. Carson. Grand Rapids: Baker (1992).

Cole, R. Alan, *Galatians*. Grand Rapids: Eerdmans (1989).

Cousar, Charles B., *Galatians*. Louisville: John Knox Press (1982).

Cranfield, C. E. B., "St. Paul And The Law". *SJT* 17: 43-68 (1964).

Cranfield, C. E. B., *A Critical and Exegetical Commentary on The Epistle to the Romans*, I. Edinburgh: T. and T. Clark (1975).

Cranfield, C. E. B., "Has the Old Testament Law a Place in the Christian Life?: A Response to Professor Westerholm" in *On Romans*, Edinburgh: T. and T. Clark (1998).

Cranfield, C. E. B., "'The Works of the Law' in the Epistle to the Romans" in *On Romans*. Edinburgh: T. and T. Clark (1998).

De Boer, Martinus C., "Paul's Quotation of Isaiah 54:1 in Galatians 4.27". *NTS* 50.3: 370-89 (2004).

De Boer, Martinus C., "The Meaning of τὰ στοιχεῖα τοῦ κόσμου in Galatians". *NTS* 53.2: 204-24 (2007).

Delling, Gerhard, στοιχεῖον *TDNT,* VII. 670-87. Trans. Geoffrey W. Bromiley. Grand Rapids: Eerdmans (1979).

Denney, James, *Studies in Theology*. London: Hodder and Stoughton (1904).

Di Mattei, Steven, "Paul's Allegory of the Two Covenants (Gal. 4:21-31) in Light of First-Century Hellenistic Rhetoric and Jewish Hermeneutics". *NTS* 52: 102-23 (2006).

Duncan, George S., *The Epistle of Paul To The Galatians*. London: Hodder and Stoughton (1947).

Dunn, J. G. D., "The New Perspective on Paul". *BJRL* 65: 95-122 (1982-83).

Dunn, J. G. D., "The Incident at Antioch". *JSNT* 18:3-57 (1983).

Dunn, J. G. D., *The Epistle To The Galatians*. Peabody, Mass.: Hendrickson Publishers (1993).

Eadie, John, *A Commentary on the Greek Text of the Epistle of Paul to The Galatians*. Edinburgh: T. and T. Clark (1869).

Ellicott, Charles J., *St Paul's Epistle To The Galatians*. London: Longmans, Green, Reader, and Dyer (1867).

Fairbairn, Patrick, *The Typology of Scripture*. Grand Rapids: Guardian Press. Original 1900 (1975).

Fung, Ronald Y. K., *The Epistle To The Galatians*. Grand Rapids: Eerdmans (1988).

Furnish, Victor Paul, *Theology and Ethics in Paul*. Nashville:Abingdon Press (1968).

Gaffin, Richard B., "Paul as Theologian". *Westminster Theological Journal*. XXX: 204-32 (1968).

Gaffin, Richard B., "The Usefulness of The Cross". *WTJ* XLI: 228-46 (1979).

Gaffin, Richard B., *By Faith, Not By Sight*. London: Paternoster (2006).

Glover, T. R., *Paul of Tarsus*. New York: Richard R. Smith (1930).

Greijdanus, Seakle, *De Brief Van Den Apostel Paulus Aan De Gemeenten in Galatië*. Amsterdam: H. A. Van Bottenburg (1936).

Guthrie, Donald, *New Testament Introduction*. Downers Grove, Illinois: Inter-Varsity Press (1970).

Guthrie, Donald, *Galatians*. London: Oliphants (1974).

Hauck, Friedrich, κοινός *TDNT,* III. 789-809. Trans. Geoffrey W. Bromiley. Grand Rapids: Eerdmans (1979).

Hay, David M., "Paul's Indifference to Authority". *JBL* 88:36-44 (1969).

Hendriksen, William, *Galatians and Ephesians*. Grand Rapids: Baker Book House (1979).

Hodge, A. A., *The Confession of Faith*. Edinburgh: Banner of Truth. Original 1869 (1983).

Jeremias, Joachim, *The Central Message of The New Testament*. New York: Charles Scribner's Sons (1965).

Jeremias, Joachim, *The Prayers of Jesus*. Philadelphia: Fortress Press (1979).

Jobes, Karen H., "Jerusalem, Our Mother: Metalepsis And Intertextuality in Galatians 4:21-31." *WTJ* 55:299-320 (1993).

Johnson, Dennis E., *The Message of Acts in the History of Redemption*. Phillipsburg, New Jersey: Presbyterian and Reformed Publishing (1997).

Johnson, S. Lewis, "Role Distinctions in the Church" in *Recovering Biblical Manhood and Womanhood*. Wheaton: Crossway (1993).

Kim, Seyoon, *Paul and The New Perspective*. Grand Rapids: Eerdmans (2002).

Kirk, K. E., *The Epistle To The Romans*. Oxford: Oxford University Press (1937).

Kittel, Gerhard, δόξα *TDNT*, II. 233-55. Trans. Geoffrey W. Bromiley. Grand Rapids: Eerdmans (1978).

Ladd, George Eldon, *A Theology of the New Testament*. Grand Rapids: Eerdmans (1974).

Lasor, W. S., "Arabia". *ISBE* I. 220-26 (1979).

Lategan, Bernard, "Is Paul Defending His Apostleship in Galatians?" *NTS* 34:411-30 (1988).

Letham, Robert, *The Holy Trinity*. Phillipsburg, New Jersey: Presbyterian and Reformed Publishing (2004).

Lightfoot, Joseph Barber, *The Epistle of St. Paul To The Galatians*. Grand Rapids: Zondervan. Original 1865 (1966).

Lohse, Eduard, *A Commentary on the Epistles to the Colossians and Philemon*. Trans. William R. Poehlmann and Robert J. Karris. Philadelphia: Fortress Press (1971).

Longenecker, R. N., "The Pedagogical Nature of the Law in Galatians." *JETS* 25:53-61 (1982).

Longenecker, R. N., *Galatians*. Dallas: Word Books (1990).

Lührmann, Dieter, *Galatians: A Continental Commentary*. Trans. O. C. Dean, Jr. Minneapolis: Fortress Press (1992).

Lull, D. J., "'The Law Was Our Pedagogue': A Study in Galatians." *JBL* 105: 481-98 (1986).

Luther, Martin, "Two Kinds of Righteousness" in *Luther's Works*, 31:297-301. Philadelphia: Fortress Press (1957).

Luther, Martin, *Lectures on Galatians, 1535* in *Works* vol. 26. Saint Louis: Concordia Publishing House (1963).

Lyall, Francis, "Roman Law in The Writings of Paul – Adoption". *JBL* 88: 458-66 (1969).

Machen, J. Gresham, *The Origin of Paul's Religion*. Grand Rapids: Eerdmans (1970).

Machen, J. Gresham, *Machen's Notes On Galatians*. Ed. John H. Skilton. Philadelphia: Presbyterian and Reformed Publishing (1973).

Macleod, John, *Scottish Theology In Relation To Church History since the Reformation*. Edinburgh: The Banner of Truth Trust (1974).

Martyn, J. Louis, *Galatians*. New York: Doubleday (1997).

Matera, Frank J., *Galatians*. Collegeville, Minnesota: The Liturgical Press (2007).

Meyer, Heinrich August Wilhelm, *Critical and Exegetical Hand-Book To The Epistle To The Galatians*. Trans. G. H. Venables. New York: Funk and Wagnalls (1884).

Michel, Otto, συγκλείω *TDNT*, VII. 744-47. Trans. Geoffrey W. Bromiley. Grand Rapids: Eerdmans (1979).

Morris, Leon, *Galatians: Paul's Charter of Christian Freedom*. Downers Grove, Illinois: Inter Varsity Press (1996).

Moule, C. F. D., "Adoption". *IDB*. New York: Abingdon Press (1962).

Moule, C. F. D., *The Origin of Christology*. Cambridge: Cambridge University Press (1977).

Moule, Handley, C. G., *Charles Simeon*. London: Inter Varsity Press. Original 1892 (1948).

Moulton, J. H. and Milligan, G. (1997), *Vocabulary of The Greek New Testament*. Original publication 1930.

Murphy-O'Connor, Jerome, *Paul The Letter Writer*. Collegeville, Minnesota: The Liturgical Press (1995).

Murray, John, "The Unity of the Old and New Testaments," in *Collected Writings of John Murray*, I (Vol. I). Edinburgh: Banner of Truth Trust (1976).

Neill, Stephen, *Paul To The Galatians*. London: Lutterworth Press (1957).

Neill, Stephen, *The Interpretation of The New Testament*. Oxford: Oxford University Press (1988).

Oepke, Albrecht, δύω *TDNT*, II. 318-21. Trans. Geoffrey W. Bromiley. Grand Rapids: Eerdmans (1978).

Orr, James, *The Progress of Dogma*. Grand Rapids: Eerdmans. Original 1901 (1952).

Owen, John, *The Works of John Owen*, II. Edinburgh: Banner of Truth Trust (rpt. 1980).

Preisker, Herbert, ὄρθρος *TDNT*, V. 449-451, Trans. Geoffrey W. Bromiley. Grand Rapids: Eerdmans (1979).

Ramsay, W. M., *A Historical Commentary on St. Paul's Epistle to the Galatians*. London: Hodder and Stoughton (1900).

Ramsay, W. M., *St. Paul The Traveller and the Roman Citizen*. New York: G. P. Putnam's Sons (1905).

Ridderbos, Herman, *Paul: An Outline of His Theology*. Trans. John Richard De Witt. Philadelphia: Eerdmans (1975).

Ridderbos, Herman, *The Epistle of Paul To The Churches of Galatia*. Trans. Henry Zylstra. Grand Rapids: Eerdmans (1984).

Robertson, A. T., *Word Studies in The New Testament*, IV. *The Epistles of Paul*. Grand Rapids: Baker (1931; n.d. for reprint).

Robertson, A. T., *The Minister and His Greek New Testament*. Grand Rapids: Baker (1977).

Rossell, William H., "New Testament Adoption – Graeco-Roman or Semitic?" *JBL* 71:233-34 (1952).

Schlier, Heinrich, ἐκπτύω *TDNT*, II. 448-49. Trans. Geoffrey W. Bromiley. Grand Rapids: Eerdmans (1978).

Schnelle, Udo, *Apostle Paul His Life and Theology*. Trans. M. Eugene Boring. Grand Rapids: Baker Academic (2003).

Schreiner, Thomas R., "Is Perfect Obedience To the Law Possible? A Re-examination of Galatians 3:10". JETS 27/2: 151-160 (1984).

Schreiner, Thomas R., "Works of Law In Paul". *NT* 3:217-244 (1991).

Schrenk, Gottlob, εὐδοκία *TDNT*, II. 738-751. Trans. Geoffrey W. Bromiley. Grand Rapids: Eerdmans (1978).

Silva, Moisés, Galatians in *New Bible Commentary* eds. G. J. Wenham, J. A. Motyer, D. A. Carson, R. T. France. Downers Grove, Illinois: Inter-Varsity Press (1994).

Silva, Moisés, *Interpreting Galatians*. Grand Rapids: Baker Academic (2001).

Silva, Moisés, "Faith Versus Works of Law in Galatians," in *Justification And Variegated Nomism*, 2. 217-248 (2004).

Silva, Moisés, Galatians in *Commentary on the New Testament Use of the Old Testament*. eds. G. K. Beale, D. A. Carson. Grand Rapids: Baker Academic: 785-812 (2007).

Stott, John R. W., *The Message of Galatians*. Downers Grove, Illinois: Inter-Varsity Press (1986).

Turner, Nigel, *Syntax.* Vol. 3 of *A Grammar of New Testament Greek,* by James Hope Moulton. Edinburgh: T. & T. Clark (1963).

Verseput, D. J., "Paul's Gentile Mission and The Jewish Christian Community". *NTS* 39:36-55 (1993).

Vos, Geerhardus, *The Pauline Eschatology.* Grand Rapids: Baker. First published 1930 (1979).

Vos, Geerhardus, "The Alleged Legalism in Paul's Doctrine of Justification" in *Redemptive History and Biblical Interpretation.* Ed. Richard B. Gaffin, Jr. Phillipsburg, New Jersey: Presbyterian and Reformed Publishing (2001).

Warfield, Benjamin B., "It Says:" "Scripture Says:" "God Says" in *Inspiration and Authority of The Bible.* Philadelphia: Presbyterian and Reformed Publishing (1970).

Warfield, Benjamin B., "The Indispensableness of Systematic Theology To The Preacher" in *Selected Shorter Writings of Benjamin B. Warfield,* 2: 280-288. Nutley, New Jersey: Presbyterian and Reformed Publishing (1973).

Warfield, Benjamin B., *The Plan of Salvation.* Avinger, Texas: Simpson Publishing. Original 1915 (1989).

Westerholm, Stephen, *Perspectives Old and New on Paul: The "Lutheran" Paul and His Critics.* Grand Rapids: Eerdmans (2004).

Witherington, B., "Rite and Rights of Women - Galatians 3:28," *NTS* 27:593-604 (1980-81).

Wright, N. T., *The Climax of the Covenant.* Edinburgh: T. & T. Clark (1991).

Wright, N. T., *Paul.* Philadelphia: Fortress Press (2005).

Zerwick, Maximillian, *Biblical Greek Illustrated by Examples.* Rome: Editrice Pontificio Istituto Biblico–Roma (2001).

Scripture Index

231

Subject Index